EMINENT HISTORIANS

Scholar, author, former editor and minister, Arun Shourie is one of the most prominent voices in our country's public life and discourse.

Also by Arun Shourie with HarperCollins India

Does He Know a Mother's Heart:
How Suffering Refutes Religions

The World of Fatwas:
Or the Shariah in Action

Worshipping False Gods:
Ambedkar, and the Facts Which Have Been Erased

Falling over Backwards:
An Essay Against Reservations and Against Judicial Populism

Self-Deception:
India's China Policies – Origins, Premises, Lessons

EMINENT HISTORIANS

Their technology, their line, their fraud

ARUN SHOURIE

HarperCollins *Publishers* India

First published by Rupa Books in 1998
This edition published in India in 2014 by
HarperCollins *Publishers* India

P-ISBN: 978-93-5136-591-4
E-ISBN: 978-93-5136-592-1

8 10 9 7

HarperCollins *Publishers*
A-75, Sector 57, Noida, Uttar Pradesh 201301, India
1 London Bridge Street, London, SE1 9GF, United Kingdom
Hazelton Lanes, 55 Avenue Road, Suite 2900, Toronto, Ontario M5R 3L2
and 1995 Markham Road, Scarborough, Ontario M1B 5M8, Canada
25 Ryde Road, Pymble, Sydney, NSW 2073, Australia
195 Broadway, New York, NY 10007, USA

Typeset in 11.5/13.5 Adobe Garamond
by Jojy Philip, New Delhi 110 015

Printed and bound in India by
Replika Press Pvt. Ltd.

For
Anita
Everything

Contents

Introduction

In June–July 1998, progressives kicked up quite a racket. The government has packed the Indian Council of Historical Research with pro–Ram Mandir historians, they shouted. It has surreptitiously altered the aims and objectives of the Council, they shouted.

As is their wont, they had sparked the commotion by giving wind to a concoction.

As is their wont too, they were charging others with *planning* to do in *some undefined future* what they had themselves been actually doing for decades – that is, write history to a purpose.

The commotion led me to look into their record – to look at what they had made of an institution like the Indian Council of Historical Research, and to read the textbooks they had authored.

Small scandals turned up too. So accustomed have we become to crores being raked off that the amounts mentioned in this narrative will seem less than the pilfering of pickpockets. That is so in part because our standards have become so lax. And in part because the real crime of these eminences does not lie in the loss they have inflicted in terms of money. It lies in the condition to which they have reduced institutions. It lies in their dereliction – because of which projects that were important for our country have languished. It lies even more in the use to which they have put those institutions.

They have used them to have a comfortable time, of course. They have used them to puff up each other's reputations, of course. But the worst of it is that they have used their control of these institutions to pervert public discourse, and thereby derail public policy.

They have made India out to have been an empty land, filled by successive invaders. They have made present-day India, and Hinduism even more so, out to be a zoo – an agglomeration of assorted, disparate specimens. No such thing as 'India', just a geographical expression, just a construct of the British; no such than as Hinduism, just a word used by Arabs to describe the assortment they encountered, just an invention of the communalists to impose a uniformity – that has been their stance. For this they have blackened the Hindu period of our history, and, as we shall see, strained to whitewash the Islamic period. They have denounced ancient India's social system as the epitomy of oppression, and made totalitarian ideologies out to be egalitarian and just.

They have belittled our ancient culture and exaggerated syncretistic elements which survived and made them out to have been an entire 'culture', the 'composite culture' as they call it. Which culture isn't? And all the while they have taken care to hide the central facts about these common elements in the life of our people: that they had survived in spite of the most strenuous efforts spread over a thousand years of Islamic rulers and the ulema to erase them, that they had survived in spite of the sustained efforts during the last one hundred and fifty years of the missionaries and British rulers to make us forget and shed these elements, that the elements had survived their efforts to instead inflame each section to see its 'identity' and essence in factors which, if internalized, would set it apart. Most of all, these intellectuals and the like have completely diverted public view from the activities in our own day of organizations like the Tabhligi jamaat and the Church which are exerting every nerve, and deploying uncounted resources to get their adherents to discard every practice and belief which they share with their Hindu neighbours.

These intellectuals and their patrons have worked a diabolic inversion: the inclusive religion, the pluralist spiritual search of our people and land, they have projected as intolerant, narrow-minded, obscurantist; and the exclusivist, totalitarian, revelatory religions and ideologies – Islam, Christianity, Marxism-Leninism – they have made out to be the epitomes of tolerance, open-mindedness, democracy, secularism!

This has been their real crime. It has also been a bit of a feat. For they have been just a few: during the Ayodhya controversy, for instance, every other week a press statement would appear in favour of the stand of the Babri Masjid Action Committee – one week over the names of 'eminent historians', the next over the signatures of 'distinguished social scientists', and the week after that in the name of 'leading intellectuals'! But they would always be the same lot. Always the same small lot: six in one statement, eight in the next; their high was forty-two once. But what commotion they have been able to create, and what mischief.

They have been able to do so because of what they were advancing – for instance, the Marxist 'thesis' they were parroting in their textbooks – was in accord with the temper of the times. Because their kinds were in critical positions in professions like journalism and universities. And because the rulers reckoned that to garner votes it would be politic to dress up in progressive plumes; patronizing persons who had taken out a copyright, so to say, on the progressive hue was accordingly useful.

Most of all, they were able to work their mischief because of the control they came to acquire over institutions.

Times have changed: the committed progressive of yesterday is the unthinking conservative today.

The needs of the rulers have changed: who can fool the masses today by nationalizing banks and parading certificates from progressives?

The theory in which progressives preened about had been shown decades ago to be without basis. At that time no one listened. But today no one invokes it! For it has floundered on the one test the progressives had said alone mattered: the test of practice. Whatever the theoretical imperfections, whatever the empirical evidence, the one thing that counts is that it has worked in practice – in the Soviet Union, in eastern Europe, in China: that was their argument. And as only those facts about these countries were facts which they certified, the argument could scarcely be countered. Today that very argument works to the opposite effect: whatever the logical coherence you claim for it, whatever scraps of empirical evidence you adduce in its favour, the one thing that counts is that it has failed in practice!

So, the fashions are changing, the patronage of rulers is evaporating, their holy books have been repudiated in their Meccas.

All that remains is their hold over governmental institutions. The remedy is twofold. First, enable a multitude of other institutions to come up: for this, a few changes in laws, some marginal incentives for setting up and running foundations, and faith in others – that persons outside the state also are eager to do good by the country – are all we need. Second, loosen the hold over existing institutions of eminences of the kind surveyed here: for this all that is needed is to document what they have made of these institutions.

The Historians

1

A characteristic concoction

'Rational vs National,' screamed the headline of the new pall-bearer of secularism, the magazine *Outlook*. 'Fresh evidence available with *Outlook* reveals that not only has the ICHR [the Indian Council of Historical Research] been packed with "sympathizers,"' the story announced, 'but a new statement of objectives or resolution [sic] has been added, changing certain key words from the original Memorandum of Association of 1972, legitimized by an Act of Parliament. While the original Memorandum of Association states that ICHR's aims would be to give "rational" direction to historical research and foster "an objective and scientific writing of history," the new resolution, which will be included in the *Gazette of India*, states that ICHR now seeks to give a "national" direction to an "objective and national presentation of history." So, "rational" has been changed to "national", and "scientific" too has been changed to "national" ...'

'Tampering with history,' proclaimed the old pall-bearer, *The Hindu*. 'Apprehensions of this kind [that the fabled "Sangh parivar" is out to rewrite history] have been substantiated by a related decision. The resolution by the Ministry of Human Resources Development – nodal Ministry under which the ICHR comes – that details the new nominations carries with it an amendment to the Memorandum of Association by which the ICHR was set up; while the institution was set up "to foster objective and scientific writing of history such as will inculcate an informed appreciation of the country's national and cultural heritage," the new government's mandate is that the ICHR will give a "national direction" to an "objective and national presentation and interpretation of history." This amendment is certainly not just a matter of semantics. Instead, one can clearly see in this an intention on the part of the BJP-led government to rewrite history....'

The next issue of the CPI(M) mouthpiece, *Peoples Democracy*, reproduced this editorial! And carried with it an article by one of the ringleaders, K.N. Panikkar. 'Saffronisation of historical research,' proclaimed the heading. Panikkar repeated the charge of the word 'rational' having been replaced by 'national'. He added another: the Memorandum of Association of the ICHR mentions five objectives, he said, but the resolution put out by the saffron brigade mentions only two.

Thus, the charge rested on three bits of 'evidence', that the Memorandum of Association of the ICHR had been changed; second, that a word – 'rational' – in the resolution announcing the new members of the ICHR had been surreptitiously replaced by another word – 'national'; third, that while the original Memorandum of Association had specified five objectives for the ICHR, the new resolution cut out three of these.

Having been educated by *The Hindu* that the 'nodal ministry' for the matter was the Ministry of Human Resources Development, I rang up the secretary of that ministry. Has the Memorandum of Association of the ICHR been changed? I asked. No, he said. It has not been changed, he said.

And then about the resolution announcing the new members. The allegation, you will recall, was that the aim which in the Memorandum of Association is, 'to give a national direction to an objective and RATIONAL presentation and interpretation of history...', had been altered in the resolution to read, 'to give a national direction to an objective and NATIONAL presentation and interpretation of history....'

I have before me the statement of the Ministry of Human Resources Development [No. F. 30-28/86-U3] dated 6 October 1987, that is of *eleven years ago.* It gives the text of the resolution of the Government of India announcing the new members – announcing, among other things, that Irfan Habib is being appointed as chairman with retrospective effect from 9 September 1986. The corresponding expression in it is, 'to give a national direction to an objective and NATIONAL presentation and interpretation of history....'

I have before me the statement of the Ministry of Human Resources Development [No. F. 30-13/89-U3] dated 15 May 1991. It gives the text of the resolution of the government of India announcing the new members – announcing, among other things, that Irfan Habib is being reappointed as chairman with retrospective effect from 12 March 1990. The corresponding expression in it is, 'to give a national direction to an objective and NATIONAL presentation and interpretation of history...'

To test my hypothesis yet again, I looked for and obtained the immediately preceding statement of the ministry. It bore the number F. 30-3/94-U.3, and was dated 8 September 1994. Like the others, it furnished the text of the resolution of the Government of India announcing the new members – announcing, among other things, that Ravinder Kumar, another 'historian' of the same hue, was being appointed as chairman with retrospective effect from 8 September 1990. The corresponding expression in it was, 'to give a national direction to an objective and NATIONAL presentation and interpretation of history...'

That is how far I was able to get on my own. I requested the secretary of the ministry: could he please request someone to look up resolutions of the earlier years, and see whether they contained anything different? Could he help me trace when this 'alteration' got made?

The secretary was able to trace resolutions going back up

to 1978 – that is, *twenty years.* Each of them carried the very same words!

The research of the secretary and his colleagues established that – to reproduce the word the secretary used – the whole mystery had arisen from a 'typographical error': some typist banging away on his typewriter some twenty-odd years ago typed 'rational' as 'national'. As each typist, when asked to type out the subsequent resolution, copied the preceding one, that word continued to be typed as 'national' year after year. The leftists inferred no conspiracy. But, lo and behold, now that a BJP government was in power, inferring conspiracies – to use their favourite phrase – was a historical necessity. It was objective history! It was progressive methodology! I half-expected them to put on their Sherlock Holmes caps again, and establish that the governments of Mrs Indira Gandhi, of Rajiv Gandhi, of V.P. Singh, of Narasimha Rao had all been in league with the RSS, and therefore parties to this grave conspiracy!

I then rang up Vinod Mehta, the editor of *Outlook* and president of the Editors Guild of India. 'But the reporter says she has the text and everything,' he said. I narrated what I had found. He promised to check and get back to me. When we talked again he said he had sent me the text of the resolution. But that was the current one. My point had been that the 'change' on which *Outlook* had built its story had existed in all resolutions for at least twenty years. He said he would get back to me. He never did. Nor did senior journalists of two other publications that had built their stories on the fabrication, and who, after I requested them to ascertain the basis of their accounts, had promised to get back to me.

Exactly the same thing held for that fabrication of K.N. Panikkar: about five objectives having become two. In every single one of the resolutions – including the 1994 resolution under which Panikkar had himself been nominated to the ICHR, a resolution he can find printed at page 342 of *The Gazette of India*, 22 October 1994 – exactly the same sentences had been used: only those objectives had been mentioned as were mentioned in the resolution issued in 1998! And another thing: if an RSS publication publishes even an interview with me, that is further proof of my being communal; but so tough are the hymen of these progressives that, even when they contribute signed articles to publications of the Communist Party, their virginity remains intact!

Such forgeries, such allegations are the standard technology of this school. Fabricating conspiracy theories is their well-practised weapon. And they have a network: stories containing the same 'facts' about the ICHR had figured prominently in paper after paper. In *The Asian Age* on 6 June: 'ICHR revamp has RSS tilt'. In *The Indian Express* on 8 June: 'Historians cry foul as HRD Ministry paints ICHR saffron'. In the *Hindustan Times* on 9 June: 'Historians see saffron in ICHR appointments'. In *The Hindu* editorial of June 12: 'Tampering with history'. In *Outlook* of 22 June which was on the stands on 15 June. The frontmen having spoken, the ventriloquist had stepped forth – the *Peoples Democracy* of 21 June: 'Saffronisation of historical research'.

The associated charge, repeated in *Outlook* and all the other publications, was that historians who had now been nominated to the ICHR were ones who supported the proposition that there had been a Ram temple at Ayodhya before it was replaced by the Babri mosque. Assume that the charge was entirely correct. What about the members who had not been renominated? They were the intellectual guides and propagandists of the Babri Masjid Action Committee. They represented it at the meetings Mr Chandrashekhar's government had convened for settling the matter by evidence. That was an outstanding initiative of Mr Chandrashekhar: for such contentious issues ought to be dissolved in the acid of evidence. These leftist 'historians' had attended the initial meetings. They had put together for and on behalf of the Committee 'documents'. It had been a miscellaneous pile. And it had become immediately evident that this pile was no counter to the mass of archaeological, historical and literary evidence which the VHP had furnished, that in fact the 'documents' these guides of the Babri Committee had piled up further substantiated the VHP's case. These 'historians', having undertaken to attend the meeting to consider the evidence presented by the two sides, just did not show up!

It was this withdrawal which aborted the initiative that the government had undertaken of bringing the two sides together, of introducing evidence and discourse into the issue. Nothing but nothing paved the way for the demolition as did this running away by these 'historians'. It was the last nail: no one could be persuaded thereafter that evidence or reason would be allowed anywhere near the issue.

Not only were these 'historians' the advisers of the Babri Masjid Action Committee, its advocates in the negotiations, they simultaneously issued all sorts of statements supporting the Babri Masjid Action Committee's case – which was the 'case' they had themselves prepared! A well-practised technique, if I may say so: they are from a school in which members have made each other famous by applauding each other's books and 'theses'!

And these very 'historians' are cited as witnesses in the pleadings filed by the Sunni Waqf Board in the courts which are considering the Ayodhya matter!

Witness number 63: R.S. Sharma;
Witness number 64: Suraj Bhan;
Witness number 65: D.N. Jha;
Witness number 66: Romila Thapar;
Witness number 67: Athar Ali (since deceased); …
Witness number 70: Irfan Habib;
Witness number 71: Shireen Moosvi, also from Aligarh Muslim University;
Witness number 72: B.N. Pandey (since deceased); …

Witness number	*74*:	R.L. Shukla; …
Witness number	*82*:	Sushil Srivastava; …
Witness number	*95*:	K.M. Shrimali;
Witness number	*96*:	Suveera Jayaswal; …
Witness number	*99*:	Satish Chandra; …
Witness number	*101*:	Sumit Sarkar;
Witness number	*102*:	Gyanendra Pandey; …

Their deceitful role in Ayodhya – which in the end harmed their clients more than anyone else – was just symptomatic. For fifty years this bunch has been suppressing facts and inventing lies. How concerned they pretend to be today about that objective of the ICHR – to promote objective and rational research into events of our past! How does this concern square with the guidelines issued by their West Bengal government in 1989 which *Outlook* itself had quoted – 'Muslim rule should never attract any criticism. Destruction of temples by Muslim rulers and invaders should not be mentioned?' But incorporating their wholesale fabrications of the destruction of Buddhist viharas, about the non-existent 'Aryan invasion', that is mandatory – to question them is to be communal, chauvinist! The capture of institutions like the ICHR has been bad enough, but in the end it has been a device. The major crime of these 'historians' has been this partisanship: *suppresso veri, suggesto falsi.*

But these are not just partisan 'historians'. They are nepotists of the first order. I had documented several years ago the doings of some of them in regard to the appointments in the Aligarh Muslim University. Their doings in the ICHR were true to pattern. How is it that over twenty-five years persons from their school alone had been nominated to the ICHR? How come that Romila Thapar had been on the Council four times? Irfan Habib five times? Satish Chandra four times? S. Gopal three times?… The same pattern held for the post of chairman.

But we are getting ahead of the story: what was their answer when their fabrication – 'rational changed to national' – was nailed? As, unlike Shourie, who, a resident of Delhi, is a BJP MP from UP, I am not a member of parliament, wrote their spokesman, Panikkar, 'I have no means to ascertain from the ministry' whether what Shourie has written is true!

A much favoured device: when caught peddling a lie, insinuate that the other man is privileged! And that, as you are from the toiling masses, you cannot ascertain whether the facts he has stated are true. Therefore, what you stated must stand as fact. QED!

2

Eminent entrepreneurs!

'This is an old charge which keeps surfacing now and then,' wrote one of those 'eminent historians', K.N. Panikkar, in response to an article of mine – the charge that close to two crores had been spent on the 'Towards Freedom' project of the Indian Council of Historical Research, and little had been achieved. 'About a year back *Times of India* carried a front page story on this. The historians had then clarified through a public statement published in several newspapers, that they have not drawn any money from the ICHR and that they worked for five years purely in an honorary capacity. When he [that is, me] gets the information from the ministry, if he does, that the editors have not taken any money, I would normally expect Shourie to tender a public apology. But given the intellectual honesty and cultural level reflected in his article, I do not think it would be forthcoming. The alternative of suing for defamation the likes of Shourie is below one's dignity. But I do expect at least the ministry to make a public statement on the factual position.'

Strong stuff, and definitive, one would think. It turns out that on 17 July 1998, in answer to a question tabled in the Rajya Sabha, the ministry stated that only one part of the project had been completed and published since the original volume of Dr P.N. Chopra. This was the volume – in three parts – by Dr Partha Sarthi Gupta covering 1943–44. In answer to another question, the ministry reported that 'After publication of the volume he was paid an honorarium of Rs 25,000/- in September 1997.'

Dr Partha Sarthi Gupta, in other words, was the one editor who had completed the work which he had undertaken. For that he had been paid Rs 25,000. The others had not completed the work they had undertaken, they had therefore not been paid the Rs 25,000 which were to be paid to them only when their volumes were completed and published. That is how our friend was proclaiming that they had been toiling as social workers – we have been working in an honorary capacity, we have not taken a penny!

Their not having collected the money because they had not completed the work apart, how much store should we set by their claim – in this case the claim that they had been toiling away as social workers?

Each of these persons had availed of staff and other facilities throughout these years – ostensibly for producing volumes under the Towards Freedom Project. Substantial sums of public funds had been spent on this staff and these facilities. Should these not be put to their account?

How many staff members and research assistants were used by these scholars? I inquired. What amounts were spent on them? What is the status of the volumes the scholars were to produce? I inquired. The answers of the ICHR for the period 1988–89 to 1997–98:

Scholar	*Research staff used**	*Amount spent*
Sumit Sarkar	1 + 5	Rs 4,56,617
K.N. Panikkar	1 + 6	Rs 4,84,973
Gyanendra Pandey	1 + 5	Rs 3,15,522
Bipan Chandra	1 + 8	Rs 1,19,691
Mushirul Hasan	1 + 11	Rs 7,36,159
Partha S. Gupta	1 + 5	Rs 4,47,625
Bimal Prasad	2 + 6	Rs 4,70,567

Scholar	*Research staff used**	*Amount spent*
Ravinder Kumar	1 + 6	Rs 4,30,826
Basudev Chatterjee	12	Rs 16,88,426

** The first number indicates regular staff on the pay roll of the ICHR, and the second number indicates the strength of research staff engaged on consolidated salary.*

These were expenditures directly against their names, and on their recommendations. In addition, of course, were the Rs 37,15,207 spent during the editorship of P.N. Chopra, the Rs 7,87,484 spent during the first period of the editorship of S. Gopal. And as these sums totalled Rs 97,23,097 only, there was an additional crore which had been spent on the project – that too could have been spent on the directions of these eminent scholars only. But 'honorary', you must believe.

An afterword is in order to this sorry tale of the Towards Freedom Project. As far as history writing is concerned, few things could have been more important than to bring alive for subsequent generations what our leaders felt and did in the long struggle to wrest freedom for the country. And just see how these eminences have handled this responsibility: a project which was to have been completed in five years in a few lakh has been dragged for twenty-seven years, a crore and seventy-odd lakh have been gobbled up in its name – and the volumes are still said to be on their way. This is gross dereliction – independent of what the volumes will contain, and what they would have left out.

The tale contains an institutional warning also: for this is not the first time that the project to write the history of the freedom movement has been hijacked, and eventually derailed. In the Introduction and Appendix to his three-volume *History of the Freedom Movement in India*,[1] Dr R.C. Majumdar recorded

[1] R.C. Majumdar, *History of the Freedom Movement in India*, 1962, Second revised edition, Firma K.L. Mukhopadhyay, Calcutta, 1971.

what happened to the original project – how at his instance the Indian Historical Records Commission passed a resolution in February 1948 that a history of the country's struggle for freedom ought to be prepared; how the education ministry headed by Maulana Azad sat over the matter till Dr Rajendra Prasad, the then president of the country, nudged it ahead; how an Editorial Board was set up; how Majumdar was appointed director for the project; how the first volume was prepared; how it met with the approval of the Editorial Board; how the government, having stated in one breath that the volumes were well on their way to getting ready, alleged in the next that there had been some differences in the Board about the content of the first volume which had been circulated; how suddenly the Board was dissolved; and the project handed over to a previous secretary of the education ministry; how some of the members become turncoats.

The result? Mediocre volumes which no one reads, volumes which further what was then the official line...

By contrast the British produced their version through the *Transfer of Power* documents: we never wanted to stay, we wanted to leave as soon as possible, we laboured to prevent the partition of the country, we transferred power, freedom had not to be wrested from our hands.... There was the Indian side to the events. This was available at the time in the recollections of those who had led the movement against the British – for many of them were still alive; it was available in their private papers. The Towards Freedom Project was to garner this record. As control over institutions passed to the Leftists, the entire project was yoked to advancing their Line and Theses.

The moral is plain: do not rely on governments, do not rely on governmental institutions for national tasks; individuals, small groups dedicated to the country – they alone can do them for the country.

The Towards Freedom Project wasn't the only one on which large amounts had been spent and which had not been completed. There was an 'Economic History of India Project'. Rupees *nineteen lakh and fifty-five thousand* had been spent on it. Nothing had been published as a result. Though, the ministry told the Rajya Sabha, 'according to the information furnished by the ICHR', two volumes of the project – on railways and agriculture – were 'ready for the press'.

In response to an unstarred question (number 3466) the ministry also told the Rajya Sabha that 'Professor Bipan Chandra was sanctioned a sum of Rs 75,000/- during 1987–88 for the assignment entitled "A History of the Indian National Congress". A sum of Rs 57,500/- [*fifty seven thousand five hundred*] has been released to him till 23.6.1989. The remaining balance of Rs 17,500/- is yet to be released because a formal manuscript in this regard is yet to be received.' A glimpse into how one must view the claim to have been 'doing all this in a strictly honorary capacity'. It is as if Bipan Chandra were to go about saying, 'See, I have not even taken the Rs 17,500/- which the ICHR still owes me.' And do not miss that effort from the ICHR to help to the extent possible – 'The remaining balance of Rs 17,500/- is yet to be released *because a formal manuscript in this regard is yet to be received.*'

I, therefore, wrote to the ministry, 'Does this mean that some *informal* manuscript has been received? Or that *no* manuscript has been received? If the latter is the case, how is it that nine years having passed, the scholar having taken Rs 57,500/- for a project and not having submitted the manuscript, no action has been taken?'

After a few reminders, the ministry eventually wrote to say, '... it has been confirmed by ICHR that no manuscript – *either formally or informally* – has been received so far.' As regards the action taken, the ministry said, information is being obtained from the ICHR.

Later I learnt that the Rs 75,000/- which had been allotted to this 'eminent historian' for this project – 'The Oral History Project' – had been but a part, a small part of the total take. Bipan

Chandra was given in addition rupees *two lakh* by the ICSSR and rupees *four lakh* through the Jawaharlal Nehru University. Neither institution received any manuscript in return.

Actually this matter had become an issue when time came for this 'eminent historian' to retire from the JNU. The university, naturally, could not do without his eminence. A proposal was, therefore, put up to engage him again after retirement. The then registrar of the university pointed out that, according to the university's rules, the retirement dues, etc., could not be settled, and a contract to engage Bipan Chandra again could not be entered into till the accounts for the *four lakh* had been submitted, and that Bipan Chandra had studiously neglected to furnish the accounts. No accounts came. The then vice chancellor papered over the matter.

As nothing but nothing had turned up in the ICHR in return for its grant, the second part of my query remained: what action had the ICHR taken in the matter? Eventually I was told, 'No action has been initiated on this as Dr Bipan Chandra is stated to be still working on the project.' That was the position *nine years* after his eminence had collected the money!

From documents which have been furnished in response to my queries, it turns out that this is the pattern. The ICHR commenced a *National Movement Project* – to which I shall come in a moment – to document our freedom struggle from the mid-1850s. Bipan Chandra took Rs 12,000/- to produce the volume covering 1885–86. Result? *Nothing has been heard of it since.* He took another Rs 12,000/- for the volume covering 1932–34. Outcome? *'Not submitted,'* says the ICHR. Being eminent, Bipan Chandra is naturally in the circle of friends among whom the *Towards Freedom Project* was parcelled. To assist him to shoulder his onerous load in this regard, the ICHR has employed over the years one 'regular' staff member plus eight staff members 'on consolidated salary'. Result? '*Volume not submitted.*'

But, to be fair, this pattern is not confined to this eminent historian alone. It has been the pattern for the entire institution manned and controlled by these 'eminent historians'.

V.N. Gadgil, the Congress member, asked a written question in the Rajya Sabha about the projects which had been undertaken by the ICHR, and what had happened to them. In its reply (to Unstarred Question number *3476 on 17 July 1998)* the Ministry of Human Resources Development stated, 'According to the information furnished by the ICHR, three major projects – namely, "Towards Freedom", "Dictionary of Inscriptions", and the "Economic History of India" – started between 1976 and 1992 have been continued during the last five years. These are in different stages of completion…'

The rat was there for everyone to see: Gadgil, after all, had not asked about 'major projects', nor had he said anything about projects 'started between 1972 and 1992'. Therefore, I asked, 'But what about the project for documenting the National Freedom Movement from 1857 to 1937? How many volumes were to be produced under it? To whom was each volume assigned? How much was paid to each scholar? How much has been spent on each volume? How many volumes have been produced under this project?'

The ministry replied, '… the Indian Council of Historical Research have stated that *no project was commissioned by them to document the National Movement between 1857 and 1937.*' What a foolish evasion! All I had to do was to draw the attention of the ministry to successive annual reports of the ICHR which had been presented to Parliament over two decades: report after report had listed this as one of the major projects which the ICHR had initiated! Please look at the account commencing from page 26 of the *Annual Report* for 1972–1973, I wrote; please look at the account commencing from page 16 of the *Annual Report* for 1973–1974, I wrote…

The result? Eventually, the ministry conceded that such a project had indeed been undertaken. *Nineteen volumes* were to have been produced. The volumes were assigned to different scholars – our eminences as usual led the rest! Rs 12,000 were doled out for each volume. The result? Here, in the words of the ICHR, is a list of the period to be covered by the volume, the scholar to whom it was assigned, the money the scholar collected, and the result:

1. *Before 1857:* K. Rajayan: Rs 12,000; *Submitted but not traceable.*
2. *1857–1885:* S.R. Mehrotra: Rs 12,000; *Not submitted.*
3. *1885–1886:* Bipan Chandra: Rs 12,000; *Not submitted.*
4. *1896–98: Not assigned.*
5. *1899–1902:* B.R. Grover: Rs 12,000; *Submitted and published.*
6. *1902–1903: Not assigned.*
7. *1903–1905: Not assigned.*
8. *1905–1907:* Sumit Sarkar: Rs 12,000; *Not submitted.*
9. *1907–1909:* Sumit Sarkar: Rs 12,000; *Not submitted.*
10. *1910–1915:* M.N. Das: Rs 12,000; *Not submitted.*
11. *1915–1919:* T.K. Ravindran: Rs 12,000; *Not submitted.*
12. *1919–1920:* V.N. Dutta: Rs 12,000; *Submitted and published.*
13. *1920–1922:* Sita Ram Singh: Rs 12,000, *Submitted, under production.*
14. *1922–1924:* Sreekumaran Nair: Rs 12,000; *Submitted and published.*
15. *1924–1926:* Amba Prasad: Rs 12,000; *Not submitted.*
16. *1927–1929:* Bimal Prasad: Rs 12,000; *Not submitted.*
17. *1930–1931:* Bimal Prasad: Rs 12,000; *Not submitted.*
18. *1932–1934:* Bipan Chandra: Rs 12,000; *Not submitted.*
19. *1934–1937:* Gopal Krishna: Rs 12,000; *Not submitted.*

As you read the amounts, do remember that they were paid out in the mid-1970s, when they amounted to much, much more than they do in these days of scams.

In a communication Dr S.R. Mehrotra points out that in his case he did not receive a penny, that the entire amount was paid directly to a colleague who was assisting him. His communication sheds light on the way the Council was brought to seed under the eminents. Dr Mehrotra writes that he had initially been assigned the task of collecting documents relating to a brief two-three-year period. Later this was extended to cover a period of thirty years. His colleague and he completed the collection, and had their manuscript ready almost twenty years ago. He pointed out to the ICHR that he had been asked to cover a period ten to fifteen times longer than that assigned to other scholars, that the typescript of the documents consequently extended over 3,000 pages. He said that for these reasons, the Council may publish the work in two or three parts instead of limiting it to just one volume.

'Years passed,' he writes with a sheaf of correspondence to prove his point, 'but, despite several reminders, the ICHR could not decide this simple issue.' As a result the typescript has languished for twenty years. The project itself was forgotten till questions were asked about it now. And recall that the project was no less than documenting the country's struggle for freedom. What a comment on the sense of responsibility with which the eminences have conducted the affairs of the Council!

And what about the project to document the Praja Mandal Movement, the freedom movement in the princely states? I inquired. The requisite details are being collected by the ICHR, the ministry wrote.

After a reminder, the ministry wrote, 'The ICHR had taken [sic] such a project. *No further information is readily available.*' 'Surely, you would not like to leave the matter at that,' I had to write. 'Was a large sum of public money not spent on the project? Who had been assigned the project? What has resulted from the large expenditure of public money?' Eventually, the ICHR furnished the details. These conformed to the norm, so to say: the project was assigned to one of the key point men of the 'eminent historians' in the Council, R.C. Shukla. Staff was assigned. Materials are reported to have been collected between 1976 and 1982. A sum of rupees *four lakh and thirty-five thousand* was spent. The net outcome? 'No *publication has come out on PMM [the Praja Mandal Movements], to the best knowledge of the Council,'* wrote the Council.

What about the project to document 'Peasant Movements'? I inquired. *Fourteen volumes* were to be produced, the ICHR wrote. Six of these were assigned among three scholars at Rs 12,000/- per volume. *One* of these has been published. Two are listed as '*Not Submitted*'. And three as *'Submitted but not traceable'*.

What about the 'Economic Data and Statistics Project,' which was listed with such fanfare in the Annual Reports till some years ago? I asked. Six volumes were to be produced under it, the ICHR wrote. The authors, the subjects they were to cover in the volume assigned to them, the money which was paid to them, and the outcome, in the words of the ICHR, are as follows:

B.B. Chaudhuri: 'Agriculture, Rent and Revenue'; Rs 12,000; *Not submitted.*

S. Bhattacharya: 'Financial and Currency Policies'; Rs 12,000; *Not submitted.*

Surendra Gopal: 'Trade (inland and foreign) in the 17th and 18th Centuries'; Rs 12,000; *Not submitted.*

Nilmoni Mukherjee: 'Trade (inland and foreign) in 19th and 20th Centuries'; Rs 12,000; *Not submitted.*

A.K. Bagchi: 'Indian Industries (1860–1939)'; Rs 12,000; *Not submitted.*

V.B. Singh: 'Labour, Prices, and Wages (1914–45)'; Rs 12,000; *Submitted but not traceable.*

In a word, as against six volumes which were to have been published, *not one has been published.* The money having been disbursed, the project just disappeared from the radar screen!

Only to be succeeded by an even more ambitious project around the same theme, the 'Project on Documentation on Economic History.' What about this one? I asked. After all, it had been listed by the ICHR itself as one of the major projects the Council had undertaken. The project was commenced in 1992, said the ICHR. *Seventeen volumes* were to be produced *between 1992 and 1997.* The total cost was to have been Rs 25 lakh. As of today, the ICHR disclosed, *no volume* has been published. And a cool rupees *nineteen-and-a-half lakh* have already been spent.

What about the 'Medieval Sources Project'? I asked. After some search, the ICHR supplied the following list of the scholars to whom the work was assigned, the subject each was to cover, the money sanctioned, and the result:

Satish Chandra & Co.: Hindi translation of 'Early Sources of Akbar's Reign'; *Not completed,* money not indicated.

Irfan Habib: *Akhbarat-e-Aurangzeb:* Rs 27,000; *Not completed.*

Moonis Raza: 'Atlas of the Mughal Empire': Rs 22,400; *Not completed.*

Anis Faruqi: *Tashir-ul-Aqwani:* Rs 9,000; *Not completed.*

Satish Chandra: 'Documents on Social and Economic History': Rs 23,000; *Not completed.*

P. Saran: *Tarikh-i-Akbari:* Rs 18,500; *Submitted but not traceable.*

But on that last entry, more in a moment.

What about the much-touted 'Translation Project'? I inquired. It began in April 1972, the ICHR says, when the National Book Trust proposal for translating the volumes in the Bharatiya Vidya Bhavan Series on the history and culture of India was received in the ICHR. A committee consisting of the usual eminences – S. Gopal, Tapan Raychaudhuri, Satish Chandra, Romila Thapar – was constituted. This committee resolved that the Bharatiya Vidya Bhavan volumes – which in fact are the very best and most outstanding of works produced in the last fifty years – 'are not suitable for translation into Indian languages', and that this proposal should not be pursued any further. The committee suggested that alternative titles be selected for translation.

And, lo and behold!, the largest number of titles which the eminent historians selected were of the eminences themselves, and of those who advocated their line! R.S. Sharma, a former chairman of the ICHR: five titles; S. Gopal: three titles; Romila Thapar: three titles; Bipan Chandra: two titles; Irfan Habib: two titles; his father, Mohammed Habib: two titles; Satish Chandra: one title...; Works of E.M.S. Namboodiripad, translated; work of that British controller of the Indian communists during the 1940s, Rajani Palme Dutt, translated.... But nothing of Lokmanya Tilak, nothing of Sir Jadunath Sarkar, nothing of R.C. Majumdar...

What amount has been spent on this project?, I inquired, how much royalty was paid to the authors? I inquired. The ICHR has incurred an expenditure of rupees *forty-one lakh and eighty-nine thousand,* the ministry said, and added, 'Authors of the books selected for translation were *not* paid royalties.'

Having got to know their ways by now, I persisted. Had I used the wrong word? I inquired. Had they got payment under some head other than 'royalties'? The ICHR eventually disclosed that in fact authors were paid 'a lump sum for translation rights': Rs 1,000 per language per volume if the book was more than 200 pages, and Rs 500 per language per volume if the book was less than 200 pages. Hence, R.S. Sharma got a total of Rs 47,000 for his books; Bipan Chandra, Rs 14,000; Irfan Habib, Rs 11,000; Romila Thapar, Rs 12,000....

As is well known, among historians, the National Fellowship of the ICHR is an honour. It also fetches the scholar a substantial amount for continuing his work. The scholar selected for the National Fellowship used to be given Rs 4,000 a month as fellowship, plus Rs 1,000 a month for secretarial assistance. In addition he was provided a contingency grant of Rs 10,000 a year for each of the three years. The amounts are much higher now: the basic fellowship fetches Rs 8,500 a month for the scholar. The terms and conditions associated with the fellowship place the greatest emphasis on the nature of the project the scholar is to pursue during his tenure as a national fellow. The project is to entail 'research of a fundamental or innovative character under the Fellowship', says the official publication of the ICHR. 'The project taken up by a National Fellow sould be specific, separate and distinct from any project previously undertaken,' say the rules governing the fellowship. The scholar was to furnish a report every six months, now he is to do so once a year, detailing the progress of the project. 'Acceptance of the National Fellowship carries with it a formal acceptance of the terms and conditions of the Award,' the rules specify. While indicating acceptance of the fellowship, they specify, the scholar must sign a special form indicating that he is accepting the terms and conditions attached to the fellowship.

In a word, there has to be a specific project which is different from anything which has been done before, it has to entail research of a fundamental and innovative nature. The project is to be completed, so much so that biannual, now annual reports about the progress towards completing it have to be submitted to the ICHR. And what has been happening? I asked the ICHR. Which scholars have been awarded National Fellowships by the Council? What projects had they agreed to complete during the fellowship? What has been the outcome of grants under this scheme?

Between 1985 and 1997, the ICHR states, twenty-two National Fellowships were awarded. Five of the scholars did not avail of them. Of the remaining *seventeen*, only *two* have submitted 'Manuscripts/Reports'. Two, the Council is confident, 'are about to submit' these. Far from completing the work they had undertaken, the remaining thirteen have not even submitted their project reports. Only one scholar is still working under this scheme. Recently the chairman of the ICHR wrote to the scholars who had availed of the fellowship requesting information about the work they had done under the scheme. Only two condescended to even reply.

The list of these distinguished scholars and the status of their projects is as follows:

Scholar	*Project*	*Years*	*Status of Project*
G.C. Pande	Not mentioned	May '85–Apr. '88	Not received
G.S. Talib	Not mentioned	Aug. '85–Feb. '86	Expired after release of second instalment
K.A. Nizami	Not mentioned	Jan. '86–Jan. '89	Received
Debala Mitra	History, art and architecture of Bodhgaya and its images	Nov. '85–Oct. '88	Not received
S. Gopal	Not mentioned	Not availed of	
A.R. Kulkarni	Socio-economic history of Indapur and Maratha Historiography	Mar. '87–Feb. '90	Additional grant sanctioned to complete work; report awaited
P.N. Chopra		Not availed of	

Scholar	*Project*	*Years*	*Status of Project*
R.S. Sharma	Making of caste and state systems in Madhya Pradesh (AD 400–800)	June '88–May '91	Not received
Satish Chandra	Character of the state and state system in India, particularly from the sixteenth to end of the eighteenth century	June '88–June '91	Not received
B.B. Lal	Project regarding archaeology of sites relating to the Ramayana	Aug. '88–July '91	Not received
Amalesh Tripathi	Nationalism in India, 1885–1947	Nov. '88–Oct. '91	Not received
M. Athar Ali	Structure of Mughal nobility in Aurangzeb's reign, 1659–1707	Jan. '90–Jan. '93	Report awaited; still availing of grant
J.S. Grewal	Sociocultural dimensions of Sufi poetry in Punjabi	Apr. '94–Mar. '97	Treated as current
A.Q. Rafiqui		Not availed of	
I. Mahadevan	Early Tamil paleography	Oct. '92–Sep. '95	Awaited

Scholar	*Project*	*Years*	*Status of Project*
Ashin Dasgupta	The Indian maritime merchant	Sep. '91–Aug. '94	Not received
Vishnu Mitra	Not mentioned	Expired before joining	
Nilmoni Mukherjee		Not availed of	

At the least the list speaks ill of the standard of managing the Council's affairs!

What other projects have been undertaken? I inquired, and to what result? The ICHR's list:

1. K.K. Dutta: 'Old Zamindari Records of Bihar': Rs 12,000; *Submitted two volumes but not traceable.*
2. B. Ramakrishna: 'Writings of Veerasalingam': Rs 12,000; *Not submitted.*
3. Bipan Chandra: 'Oral History Project': Rs 75,000 from ICHR, Rs 2,00,000 from ICSSR, and Rs 4,00,000 from JNU; *Not completed.*

And so, we are back to our friend.

3

How to do it!

In its reply to the Rajya Sabha question, the Ministry of Human Resources Development had listed three projects as 'major' ones – we have seen what happened to two of them. What about the third one, the one on *Inscriptions?* I asked. And learnt that it too could match the others in ambition – and in non-achievement too. In addition, the records relating to it give us a glimpse of the entrepreneurial techniques of the eminent.

This particular project was started in 1987. It was to produce a *Dictionary of Socio-Economic and Administrative Terms in Indian Inscriptions.* The *Dictionary* was to be in *nine* volumes – that is a key element in the technology; always propose many volumes! The project was to be completed in fifteen years – another key element: who knows who will be around fifteen years hence! Twenty lakh rupees were to be taken for the project – a third element: never be niggardly in demanding public funds!

Who were to be in charge? Our good friends. R.S. Sharma, a leading light of the Leftists, a former chairman of the ICHR, later a leading advisor to the Sunni Waqf Board in its efforts to wrest the Babri Masjid site – he graciously agreed to be the 'General Editor'. K.M. Shrimali, who was very voluble on behalf of the camp in the recent controversies, and K.V. Ramesh, with as much grace, agreed to be the 'Main Editors'. In addition an 'Advisory Board' of another eleven eminences was constituted to oversee the project – this is always a good device: thereby friends can meet at government expense, and responsibility of the main suspects is always scattered.

Work had scarcely begun, and the scope of the project was enlarged: Arabic, Persian and Urdu inscriptions too would be included. And soon this new part too was enlarged: farmans and the like in these languages would also be included, not just inscriptions. This too is always useful: enlarge the project every few months, the new items become the explanation for not having kept to the deadlines specified for the original proposal! And who would do this part of the project? Why, the most eminent of them all, 'Responsibility for compiling the Arabic, Persian and Urdu inscriptions was accepted by Professor Irfan Habib on the request of the ICHR,' the records state. How kind!

Everyone was to work in an 'honorary capacity' – but in the special sense in which these worthies use the term 'honorary'! Each of the two 'Main Editors', the 'Editorial Committee' of the project decided in its meeting on 20 September 1990, would be paid 'an honorarium' of Rs 5,000/- for every four months. The 'General Editor' too would be paid an honorarium of Rs 3,000/- for every four months. A very important rule that – never take money, take honoraria! The committee also decided, 'Professor Shrimali may be allowed to purchase relevant books in connection with the work of the project if the books are not supplied to him by the ICHR within a reasonable time' – a bit of honorariness which every scholar would lust after!

By 1994 there was a problem; there was little progress to record, though money was getting spent. The then chairman, Ravinder Kumar [very eminent, the head of the Nehru Museum and Library, etc.] convened a meeting of what the record christens the 'Consultative Committee'. The solution? The committee decided that a revised proposal be prepared! Another sure winner: months can be put to debating, drafting, redrafting, circulating, finalizing this; soon you can be arguing that the revised proposal contains elements which can be attended to only with an enhanced budget …

Better still – prepare not a 'revised proposal', prepare a '*draft* revised proposal'. And this is what was done. A 'draft revised proposal' was prepared, and, the record states, 'handed over to the Chairman [Ravinder Kumar] for necessary action and approval.'

Sunk without trace! 'It seems, that the draft proposal was not approved,' states the review note prepared by the chairman for the ICHR meeting on 31 August and 1 September 1998, 'and work was not taken up as per revised plan [sic].'

A spat is always useful, specially one involving principle, personal honour, self-respect. And, happily, one erupted. At a meeting of the Research Projects Committee, someone – perhaps Irfan Habib, I am not able to make out from the record – raised an objection: a committee 'in which there was very substantial membership of those who were to be beneficiaries of such a decision' should not have decided about payments to be made to the editors etc., he objected. Arguments ensued, tempers rose. But even as it decided that this shall be a 'firm policy for the future', the meeting decided that 'each Main Editor, on completion of a particular volume with which he has been associated, be paid an honorarium of Rs 25,000.'

It noted that this decision was strictly in accordance with precedent! 'The Committee was prompted to this decision,' the minutes record, 'in the knowledge that in the "Towards Freedom" project of the ICHR each volume Editor was to be paid Rs 25,000 for his contribution.' Unassailable logic: as editors were to get that amount under one project which was not getting anywhere, why not under another project which was not getting anywhere either?

That decided, through an innocuous sentence tagged on to the end of a paragraph, the minutes slipped in another opportunity: 'It may be noted,' the minutes noted, 'that *two or more* Main Editors may be associated with the completion of each volume of the Dictionary project.' From two 'Main Editors' for nine volumes, to 'two or more Main Editors' for each volume!

'As for the Chief Editor [a promotion that, he had till now been known as the "General Editor"!],' the minutes recorded, 'he should receive a sum of Rs 30,000 on the publication of each volume.'

R.S. Sharma, as befits his eminence as much as his Leftism, threw a fit – always a useful thing to do a few years into a project: you can then allow yourself to be persuaded, and, when questions are raised later about nothing having been done, you can always claim that you in any case had not wanted any part of the project. 'In view of the strictures passed on the "beneficiaries" of the Dictionary project in the RFC [Research Projects Committee] meeting,' he wrote to the Council, 'I would not like to continue as Chief Editor. I neither asked for any "benefice"/"benefit" in any meeting or outside nor did I receive any remuneration for the work that I did for the project. As far as I can remember none of the Main Editors asked for any benefit or remuneration in any meeting of the Editorial Committee.'

H.D. Deve Gowda, the then prime minster, and S.R. Bommai, the then minister for human resources development, selected the well-known art historian, Professor S. Settar to be the chairman of the ICHR. In a sense an outsider, he was duly alarmed at the state of such projects. He addressed letters to Sharma, Shrimali and Ramesh in March 1997 inquiring about the work they had done. Months went by, he could not nudge anyone concerned to get on with the work. He accordingly convened a meeting of R.S. Sharma and Irfan Habib on 29 September 1997. He was asked to contact Shrimali and Ramesh again.

Ramesh now deployed the next weapon: ask for more! Fools will always throw in good money after bad. He wrote back saying that for him to do the work, the Council should appoint three more scholars to assist him [so helpful was he that he specified the names of the three also!], that the Council should provide him with a computer assistant, and also with rented accommodation! The chairman wrote pointing out that already Rs 45,000 had been paid to Ramesh, that seven years had passed, and asked how much more time was required. Another year 'may be required' if the terms he had proposed were met, Ramesh answered!

In despair, Settar turned to Irfan Habib and Sharma again and 'appealed' to them to help out – another tactic: subalterns block the pass; the only way the fellow can hope to proceed is by beseeching, and thereby getting in the debt of the principals! Sharma recalled that he had already dissociated himself from the project – vide the 'beneficiaries' spat. In any event, the two met Settar, and agreed to submit – by now you would have guessed – a revised project each!

'The detailed note of the revised project promised by Professor Sharma has not been received so far,' the ICHR was informed at its meeting on 31 August–1 September 1998. 'Professor Irfan Habib has yet to send his detailed proposal which he promised to send on 10.3.98.'

As more and more queries were being made about the project, R.S. Sharma wrote to the chairman on 7 July 1998 that 'at present I and Shrimali are terribly busy with the editing of *Comprehensive History of India,* Vol. IV, pt. 2. I will consult Shrimali to find out whether he can spare some time for the project this year, though I am not hopeful. A meeting of Ramesh, Shrimali and other members of the editorial board should be helpful for completing the project as soon as possible.' Notice the tone: far from being the one who shares a major part of the responsibility for the state of affairs, the person is offering to do a favour, and, against his better judgement, contact Shrimali and see if something can be done to help the chairman out!

The result? By now eleven years have passed. Rupees *three lakh seventy-four thousand* have been spent. Nothing but nothing has been published. Thousands of 'cards' are said to have been compiled by specially hired 'compilers' – these 'cards' remain in the personal custody of Shrimali and Ramesh. And the chairman is under advice that, to get the project going, he has to convene a meeting of the very persons who have brought the project to this state – with the caveat, of course, that the conditions specified by one of them must first be met, and that the other – the TV star – is 'terribly busy' on some other project!

And, never forget, if the ICHR takes any step to bring them to account, if it takes any step to hand over the project to anyone else, it is doing so because these eminent historians are secular, and the Council is now set upon saffronizing history!

4

A fitting tribute

In his question V.N. Gadgil had asked the minister to state 'whether several hundred manuscripts are either missing from the Council's custody or are totally damaged; if so, what action the government has taken in the matter.' In its written reply to the Rajya Sabha the ministry stated, 'The ICHR has informed that a few manuscripts are reportedly either missing or have not been sent to the Press for certain reasons. The Council have intimated that it has initiated action to ascertain whether any manuscript has been lost or appropriated otherwise.'

Another rat: see how the case of manuscripts which were 'missing' had been clubbed with that of manuscripts which 'have not been sent to the Press for certain reasons.' And how the case of manuscripts which have been lost had been clubbed with that of manuscripts which have been 'appropriated otherwise'.

I, therefore, wrote to the ministry inquiring, 'How many manuscripts are covered by the phrase "a few manuscripts"?' Second, could information please be compiled separately for manuscripts which have been 'lost' and those which have 'not been sent to the Press for certain reasons'? Third, 'Since when has the ICHR "initiated action to ascertain whether any manuscript has been lost or appropriated otherwise?" What is the current status of this so-called action? In particular, is it a fact that the manuscript submitted by one of the most distinguished historians of medieval India, Dr P. Saran has been "missing"? Is it a fact that an inquiry has been instituted to ascertain whether this very manuscript has been purloined by a staff member of the ICHR itself and printed under his name?'

Late at night on 24 July 1998, I received, not one but two letters from the ministry. One stated that details in this regard were being collected. The second letter of the same day stated, 'As regards missing manuscripts, the Council has stated that to the best of their knowledge *no manuscript is missing.*' I naturally had to draw the attention of the ministry to the fact that this was at considerable variance with what they had implied in reply to Gadgil's question.

But much more curious was what they said about the specific manuscript to which I had drawn their attention – namely, that of Dr Parmatma Saran. The note accompanying one letter said, 'The Council has been requested to furnish details in this regard.' The note accompanying the second letter of the same day said, 'As regards Dr. Parmatma Saran's manuscript entitled "*Tarikh-i-Akbari*" (English translation) *it does not appear to have been received in the Council.* However, an extensive search is on to trace it in the archives.'

I pointed out to the ministry that this assertion was, to say the least, odd. How did it square with the fact that the Annual Report of the Council for 1976–77 on pages 10 and 11 had listed the 'English translation of Arif Qandhari's *Tarikh-i-Akbari* by Dr Parmatma Saran' as being among the volumes which '*have already been completed and received in the Council*'! How did what was being said now – that the manuscript '*does not appear to have been received in the Council*' – square with the fact that the Annual Report of the Council for 1977–78 had on page 9 listed '*Tarikh-i-Akbari of Arif Qandhari:* English translation by Dr. Parmatma Saran' as having '*been received in the Council*'?

The ICHR at last took a step closer to the truth. It wrote,

Yes, the Annual Reports confirm that the manuscript prepared by Dr Saran was indeed received in the Council. By now I had learnt a vital fact. Dr Saran had died. His son-in-law had written to the Council in 1995. He had pointed out that the Annual Reports of the Council had themselves stated that the manuscript had been received by the ICHR, and had added, 'As we understand, this project of my father-in-law was to be later published by the ICHR. We are not aware if this has indeed been done by the ICHR although nearly 20 years have elapsed since the translation was completed, *but we have been extremely disturbed to hear stories to the effect that not only has someone else published the translation as his own work, but that this has been done by a member of the staff of the ICHR...*'

The ICHR now acknowledged that an inquiry had been initiated in 1995. The heads of the Publications Section, of the Grants-in-Aid Section, and of the Medieval Unit had been asked what had happened to the manuscript. The Grants-in-Aid Section had confirmed that the manuscript had been received. The Publications Section had said the manuscript had never been forwarded to it. That left the section which was in a sense responsible for overseeing the project – the Medieval Unit. The deputy director in charge of this unit said that the manuscript was not traceable in his unit. Not satisfied with the reply, the then director had once again urged the deputy director, Medieval Unit, 'to do his best efforts [sic] to trace out the manuscript'.

But the friends, all entangled in those 'interlocking webs of mutual complicity', intervened. And the inquiry was killed.

Guess who obtained a PhD from Rajasthan University in 1992 by submitting 'an annotated English translation of Arif Qandhari's *Tarikh-i-Akbari*'. Guess who has published the book in his name. The very same deputy director in charge of the ICHR's Medieval Unit – Tasneem Ahmad!

The issue having been pursued, the chairman of the ICHR launched a massive search for the Saran manuscript.

And, guess what! The appropriator had thought that he had executed the perfect crime – that he had destroyed the manuscript of Dr Saran. But the thorough search initiated by the current chairman of the ICHR yielded sixty-two pages of the manuscript in another file – with corrections in the late Dr Saran's own hand! And wonder of wonders – *that manuscript written twenty years earlier was an exact verbatim prelude to the book published by Tasneem Ahmad as his own!*

A new committee was therefore constituted to compare the two and assess the chances that this miracle could have happened without the deputy director of the Council, Tasneem Ahmad, having stolen Dr Saran's work!

How fulsome they have been in commending each other – the patrons and subalterns!

The Foreword to the book first sets out the significance of Arif Qandhari's *Tarikh-i-Akbari:* it confirms what we know from Abul Fazl's *Akbar Nama,* says the eminent historian, it furnishes information we did not have earlier. He then recalls what has been done in regard to Qandhari's history by scholars already, 'The *Tarikh-i-Akbari* has been excellently edited and annotated by Muinuddin Nadvi, Azhar Ali Dehlawi and Imtiaz Ali Arshi.' And so, the need of the hour: 'What it [the *Tarikh-i-Akbari]* now needed was a full-scale English translation.' [No mention of the fact that the work had already been translated by Dr Saran – under the aegis of the ICHR itself!] This pressing need, at last fulfilled, proclaims the eminent historian: 'This has been provided by Dr. Tasneem Ahmad in a very competent manner, aiming at faithful accuracy and at a critical assessment of the information here received by comparing it with that offered by other sources.'

Not just that. This most eminent of historians writes:

> The publication of Dr. Tasneem Ahmad's translation is a notable contribution to the National celebration of the 450th Anniversary of Akbar's birth. I feel confident that it would

> reinforce the interest in Akbar's age widespread among those who have a care for the long process of the creation of a composite culture and a unity that together constitute what is India.

Not just the needs of history, therefore, those of secularism, of unity based on a composite culture too fulfilled! The dignitary writing the Foreword? Irfan Habib himself – who, among other things, has been chairman of the ICHR twice, and a member five times! And don't miss the description of India – just the composite culture and unity which it has taken a long process to create! The unity of course being nothing but a manifestation of, and totally dependent on, that composite culture! So, composite culture it is.

The compliments duly returned: 'The first and foremost [sic],' writes Tasneem Ahmad, 'I express my profound sense of gratitude, very personal regards and respects to Professor Irfan Habib, who *encouraged and guided me at every stage of the work.* In spite of his very pressing engagements and pre-occupation, he ungrudgingly spared his valuable time to *examine with care every intricate problem, arising out* [sic] *during the course of work.'*

The debt to another of these eminences not forgotten either: 'My debt to my revered teacher,' writes Tasneem Ahmad, 'Professor Satish Chandra is incalculable. He took *great pains in reading and correcting the work* and his *considered suggestions* have paid me rich dividend.'

'Examining with care every problem arising out during the course of work'? Taking 'great pains in reading and correcting the work'? Advancing 'considered suggestions' which 'pay rich dividend'? – when the entire manuscript has been lifted word for word from the work of Dr Parmatma Saran!

It isn't just a part of that composite culture that a subaltern should execute such genuflections towards his patrons. It is plain prudence. By thanking them for 'guidance at every stage', for 'corrections' and 'suggestions', the subaltern ensures that they too are culpable, and, therefore, to protect themselves, if for no other reason, they will shield him!

The plagiarized book is appropriately dedicated: 'To the memory of my revered *Ustad*,' writes Tasneem Ahmad, 'Professor S. Nurul Hasan'– a 'scholar' famous for his unwritten works, the factotum who initially coordinated the capture of academic institutions by the progressives. How fitting – that when it comes to dedicating something to such a person, the devotee should give as offering a stolen manuscript!

And what do we learn now?

'For some time an allegation has been made on one of the employees of the Council,' began a note prepared for the ICHR meeting held on 31 August and 1 September 1998, 'that a work entitled *Tarikh-i-Akbari,* translated by Professor Parmatma Saran under the scheme of the ICHR, was appropriated by the Deputy Director of a Medieval Unit [of the ICHR itself].' Because of the persistence of this allegation, and because of questions raised by members of Parliament, it goes on to say, the chairman constituted a fact-finding committee on 8 August 1998 to get to the bottom of the matter.

The committee consisted of Professor K.S. Lal, an authority on medieval India, Professor Harbans Mukhia of the Jawaharlal Nehru University and Dr T.R. Sareen, former director of the ICHR. It was asked to assess, inter alia, whether Dr Parmatma Saran's manuscript had been received in the Council [you will recall that in one of their letters to me the Ministry of Human Resources Development had said that it did not seem that the manuscript had ever been received), and to ascertain whether the manuscript had been 'in any form plagiarised by any body, within or outside the Council.'

The manuscript of sixty-two pages which had been recovered in the almirahs of the ICHR was turned over to the committee. Here are the committee's findings on the questions:

(1) On the strength of the published *Annual Report* of the ICHR for the year 1976–77 (p. 11), it is obvious that the translation of *Tarikh-i-Akbari* into English done by Professor Parmatma Saran was received in the Council. This is also confirmed by the report submitted by the Grants-in-Aid Unit of the Council dated 24.8.1995 when a preliminary enquiry was constituted to locate the manuscript. The fact[s] [are] that full payment of honorarium was made to the scholar (which in normal case is only done after the receipt of the completed manuscript), and the second project was granted to Professor P. Saran only after completion of the first project. This related to the translation of *Mirat-ul-Istlab,* which was assigned to Professor P. Saran in February, 1978. This also indirectly confirms the receipt of the earlier manuscript on *Tarikh-i-Akbari.* With this evidence, the Committee is led to believe that there is no reason to doubt the receipt of the manuscript *Tarikh-i-Akbari* by the Council.

(2) The Committee was provided with sixty-odd pages of type-script of the translation of *Tarikh-i-Akbari* done by Professor P. Saran. These pages were recovered from the file dealing with the translation assigned to Professor P. Saran. These pages were compared with that published by one of the members of the ICHR, Shri Tasneem Ahmad, and the Committee found overwhelming similarity between Professor P. Saran's translation and Shri Ahmad's book. The Committee felt that the similarity could not be accidental and the element of plagiarism cannot be ruled out.

How befitting: as tribute to the 450th anniversary of Akbar, to that 'composite culture and unity that together constitute India' – a plagiarised book!

And the finale: in his office at the ICHR Tasneem Ahmad has kept on display a photograph – it shows him presenting the book to the then president of India, Dr Shankar Dayal Sharma! The touch of a well-practised hand!

5

When cornered, cry 'Petty', 'Personal', 'Uncivilized'

By late June – early July 1998 the controversy which had begun by the 'rational' versus 'national' fabrication planted by these eminent historians had reached quite a pitch. Newspaper after newspaper had taken up the matter. The matter had also come up in Parliament. Manoj Raghuvanshi, who runs the popular programme *Aap ki Adalat, Aap ka Faisla,* on ZEE TV, invited one of these eminences, K.M. Shrimali, and me to discuss the matter.

With much righteousness Shrimali remarked that he was full of apprehensions because the sorts of persons who were now taking over the ICHR were persons who had been distorting history, and suppressing facts. 'For example?' asked Manoj Raghuvanshi.

Beef was eaten in ancient India, said Shrimali, and these people suppress this fact.

I have never understood this charge. Assume that beef was eaten 5,000 years ago, why should anyone want to suppress the fact? And how would the fact that beef was eaten then dilute the fact that today the Hindus hold the cow in reverence? Several tribes the world over were cannibals. Today they are not. Does that mean that their desisting from eating each other is less of a fact?

Customs change, beliefs change, rituals change. For public

policy the current belief is the one which has to be taken into account. The original Qibla towards which the Prophet asked his followers to bow was Jerusalem, not the Kaba at Mecca. Does that mean that the reverence which Muslims now have for the Kaba is a put-on? Or consider the matter the other way round: almost every single ritual connected with the haj is a carry-over from the pre-Islamic pagan period; does this fact make the rituals less significant? The point for public policy is that for thousands of years now Hindus have revered the cow; that in the passages asking Muslims to sacrifice animals to His glory, Allah in the Quran does not say they should sacrifice cows; that the most feverish efforts of the ulema in India to find some hadis in which the Prophet may have ordered Muslims to sacrifice cows have failed to yield anything; that, therefore, there is not the slightest difficulty in construing the beliefs of the two communities harmoniously: Muslims may sacrifice animals other than the cow and thereby heed what they regard as the command of Allah. The problem arises because 'Muslim divines' like Maulana Ahmad Riza Khan, Ali Mian, etc., insist that, precisely because Hindus revere the cow, it is the religious duty of Muslims to butcher the cow in India. But to revert to the TV programme.

And what is the evidence for that? asked Raghuvanshi.

There are hundreds of writings to that effect, Shrimali said loftily.

In which Veda, in which text, which verse in which text? asked Raghuvanshi.

I have not brought the books with me, said Shrimali, but the evidence is all over.

But name one text, name one verse, Raghuvanshi persisted.

Shrimali could not or did not name a single text, to say nothing of any verse or passage from it.

Someone from the audience interjected. Here are the four Vedas, he said, handing over the books, read us a single passage from any of them which supports what you are saying.

Raghuvanshi took the books from the person and took them over to Shrimali. Shrimali refused to look at them. Indeed, he recoiled.

Raghuvanshi then went to his table and began reading out passage after passage from the Vedas in which there were strongest possible commands to *not* eat beef.

At my request he asked Shrimali to read the verses himself.

Shrimali refused to do that. Instead, he became even more aggressive. So what if I cannot recall a text or recite a verse? he said. But you are an expert on ancient India, Raghuvanshi said. What has my not being able to recall a verse have to do with my being an expert? Shrimali answered.

Even if you produce scores of verses against eating beef, that will not prove that beef was not eaten, Shrimali now maintained. But when the Vedas lay down that the cow is *not* to be killed, how do you keep saying that there was no prohibition against eating beef? Raghuvanshi asked. That there was a prohibition does not mean that it was not eaten – that seemed to be Shrimali's new tack! Surely, the point was about the norm, about what was expected, enjoined: true, that our penal code prohibits murder does not mean that no murders take place; but the fact that some persons still murder does not mean that murders are approved as an industry!

I did not say the Vedas, he said, I said 'Vedic literature'.

All right. Name a single book from 'Vedic literature' which supports your position. He did not do so.

The exchange went on – with Raghuvanshi and the audience asking for a single passage, for the name of a single book, and Shrimali refusing – failing is the correct word – to furnish either.

The programme was broadcast in the third week of July. Clearly Shrimali had come out in poor light. He therefore started writing critiques of the programme in newspapers – or rather that he started writing the same critique in different newspapers.[1]

'Blatant editing of the programme,' he charged. 'Mr Raghuvanshi combined the role of both the prosecutor and the judge,' he wrote.

'I am less bothered about highly personalized and somewhat uncivilized attack on me in the context of the question on beef eating,' he said. Personalized attack? Uncivilized attack? Everyone was polite. All that the audience asked for, the only thing I asked for in the single interjection I made, the only thing that Raghuvanshi asked for a dozen times, was that Shrimali name a single book, a single passage in that single book which would substantiate what he was saying. How do those requests become a 'highly personalized attack'? How does asking for substantiation become an 'uncivilized attack'?

The substance apart, notice the umbrage that these people take. They traduce, they abuse, they denounce, they spit and run, but if you so much as ask them to substantiate what they are saying, they are deeply offended. A highly personalized attack, they scream. An uncivilized attack, they shriek.

That he could not cite the passage or name the book, Shrimali now made out, had no bearing on the point he was making. Writing in *The Hindu* he said:

> It is sought to be projected that there is no case for beef eating in ancient India just because I could not recite any *shloka* (verse). I was reminded of a telling passage in the *Chhandogya Upanishad* where brahmans reciting mantras are compared with many dogs who play amongst themselves by forming a circle by holding one another's tails. I am sure, if I had recited that passage, it would not have reached the public.

[1] The following statements of Shrimali are taken from *The Hindu*, 10 September 1998.

In a word: substantiating an assertion adds nothing. For, the assertion, as it is being made by so eminent an authority, is by that reason itself a fact! In any case, if the authority had substantiated the fact, the substantiation would have been deleted because those who were asking him to substantiate his assertion were biased and partisan!

And, of course, the disdain: in any case, what these blockheads were asking me to do was beneath an authority like me, for I am The Historian! These fools do not even have the capability of understanding the nuances of my argument! To put the point in Shrimali's words:

> The entire segment failed to grapple with the main question of the methodology of historical enquiry. My focus on how a historian is expected to explain contradictory evidences on any historical problem has been deliberately eliminated. *Mantrocharana* (recitation of a *mantra)* is not history writing. Neither the host, nor perhaps anyone in the monolithic audience, and not even Mr Shourie had the capability of understanding such nuances of historical writing.

The discussion had moved on to Aurangzeb. Was Aurangzeb a religious bigot or not? Raghuvanshi had asked. Shrimali would not give a clear answer even though Raghuvanshi kept repeating the question. Shrimali recalled the fact we shall soon encounter at some length – that Aurangzeb's court had many Hindu nobles! But so were there many Indians among the persons the British honoured with titles! And both for the same reason. How does the fact wipe away the destruction of temples, for instance, by Aurangzeb?

When Manoj asked me the same question, I remarked that at least Aurangzeb had entertained no doubt about the fact that his primary impulse was the religious one. And that he faithfully implemented an essential element of his religion, Islam, that is to destroy the places of worship of other religions.

When Raghuvanshi asked me for evidence on that point, I read out some of the passages from the *Akhbarat* of the court of Aurangzeb himself. The programme broadcast one or two of these passages.

Shrimali's comment on the exchange?

> More glaring partisanship displayed by the host is evident in the complete blacking out of my detailed exposition of the other side of alleged religious bigotry of Aurangzeb. On this issue too, Manoj has not only deliberately omitted factual information given by me on the basis of contemporary sources but also my emphasis on the role of a historian in writing about such issues. [All this about those Hindu nobles.] In contrast, Shourie's readings of long passages from questionable sources was retained.

'Questionable sources?' But the passages were from the contemporary bulletins of the court of the very person who was under discussion. They were from histories and accounts written at that very time, in many cases written on the very day the news reached the emperor and his court.

But that is standard technique – the reader of his comment will not be able to go back to the programme and verify the fact for himself. It is unlikely that he would have sufficient background to be able to assess the veracity of a source. So, when an eminent historian says that the sources were 'questionable', they must have been questionable!

The staff of the ICHR brings me yet another example of the way these eminent historians respond when cornered. At the prompting of these very persons, the World Archaeology Conference decided that there would be special sessions on the destruction of the mosque at Ayodhya during the WAC Inter-Congress in Croatia on the Destruction and Conservation of Cultural Properties.

One of these eminent historians approached the organizers and offered to do a paper on the question. On 3 November

1997 the person in charge in the UK wrote to the historian that they were pleased to accept his offer, that he should send the full text of his paper by 31 January so that it could be included alongwith the other papers which were to be distributed to the participants. He also wrote to the historian that if the latter needed help with the cost of his airfare he should contact 'X' at university 'Y' and the person would see what money was available for the purpose.

Our historian sent the paper. On 9 February 1998 he applied to the ICHR for financial assistance to cover the airfare to and from the venue of the session, the registration fee of $300, as well as 'such incidental daily expenses as are permissible under the rules'.

Given the clout of such persons, the request was cleared within three days and he was sanctioned 'a partial travel grant of Rs 20,000/-'. He was duly informed on 13 February 1998 of this decision. In the letter informing him of the decision of the Council, he was requested to ensure that the funds would be utilized after duly adjusting the funds he might receive from other sources, including 'self-funding'.

Within a few days the Council learnt that, in fact, the World Archaeology Congress was liable to meet expenses – including airfare – of the participants who had been asked to present papers.

On 23 February 1998 the eminent historian wrote again to the ICHR saying, 'There is a possibility that I may be granted some funds either by the University of Delhi or the hosts to pay the airfare. I hope that in such a situation the Council will have no objection to transfer the sanctioned amount to meet other expenses, if necessary.'

No correspondence transpired thereafter. The historian was given Rs 18,000 as advance.

On 22 April 1998 the organizers sent a fax to our eminence, informing him that they had sent the air ticket and that it could be picked up at the Scandinavian Airlines desk at the

New Delhi airport. Did he have a place to stay in London, or would he want them to organize something? they inquired.

The Conference came and went. Our friend returned to Delhi. As others had also attended the Conference, by now the Council knew exactly what expenses had been met in the case of participants by the organizers. The atmosphere too had changed: a new government was in place; the Council itself had been reconstituted – the old eminences had been replaced.

It was only on 23 July 1998 – eight months after he originally received the offer from the organizers about the airfare – that this distinguished historian informed the Council that 'Since the amount sanctioned was very inadequate, I had to look for other sources to meet my travel expenses. I was able to get full travel grant (both ways) from the hosts. In view of this, I shall be grateful if the amount sanctioned by the Council is transferred to meet my daily expenses.'

There was much discussion, and many notings on the file within the ICHR. The officers concerned pointed out that the amount had been sanctioned only for travel, that under the rules the amount could not be used for any purpose other than the purpose for which the sanction had been granted by the Research Projects Committee, etc. There is a delicate point, the chairman recorded on the file, in that the Council may not have given a per diem allowance to other scholars. In any case, it was decided, 'let the scholar furnish an account of the expenses he had incurred and also intimate the grants which he had received from other sources.'

Accordingly, the officer concerned wrote to our distinguished eminence on 14 August 1998, requesting him to furnish details on the two points.

Below my dignity! Petty! screamed our eminence. The University Grants Commission 'pays certain allowance for such expenses at an approved rate', wrote the historian to the Council, 'and one is not expected to submit vouchers for petty expenses. Asking for such details is, therefore, uncalled for. I find it quite petty.'

'I am, therefore, withdrawing my request and refunding the amount which had been given to me as advance,' he wrote.

Should I give the name of the historian?

But wouldn't that also be petty? Would that also not be 'a personal attack', 'an uncivilised attack'?

In any case, the operational rules are clear.

Remember your dignity is so high that you are not to be bound by rules that apply to mere mortals.

Second rule: Cornered, take offence. Recall how in the case of the *Inscriptions* project, R.S. Sharma had slipped out of the net by taking umbrage: as the term 'beneficiaries' has been used to describe the editors, I shall have nothing to do with the project! The same device to deflect accountants: '....uncalled for. I find it quite petty'!

The third rule is an even more potent weapon, and, therefore, as we shall see, even more frequently used.

6

'....after selling himself in the flesh market'

'This is an old charge which keeps surfacing now and then,' wrote one of these historians, K.N. Panikkar in *The Asian Age*[1] in response to an article in which I had nailed the 'rational' vs 'national' forgery they had circulated. He said that *The Times of India* too had put out a front-page story about the Towards Freedom Project the previous year. And the historians had clarified the facts through a public statement...'

We have seen more of the facts since. But what he said – 'This is an old charge...' – is something to bear in mind – there is never a right time to ask a question about them. If events are still fresh, their response always is: 'But where are the facts?' If you happen to have enumerated and substantiated the twenty facts about which evidence is in, their response is: 'But he has not taken into account item 21; this selective focus on just a handful of facts shows that he is working to a purpose.' When sufficient time has elapsed, and you have garnered and presented evidencc about *all* the facts, their response is: 'But this is an old charge. That he is raking it up now shows how the forces of reaction are panic-stricken at the growing consolidation of forces of secularism and democracy.'

And there is never a right person to question them either.

[1] *The Asian Age,* 7 July 1998, p. 13.

If the critic happens to have been one of them at some time in the past, and speaks from inside knowledge, they denounce him: 'His writing itself shows that he has crossed the barricade.' If he has not, they shout: 'A habitual Left-baiter, notorious for having been at the World Bank, a self-confessed apologist for the forces of reaction....'

And each time they set forth a spate of angry words! 'If he believes, as he apparently does, that the fame of historians like S. Gopal, R.S. Sharma, Romila Thapar and Irfan Habib who are held in high academic esteem, both nationally and internationally, are [sic] based on cheap manipulation,' wrote Panikkar, 'there must be something congenitally wrong with his mind. Otherwise it is possible that he is reflecting his own personal experience as to how a "fellow" like him who writes communal mythology has come to be regarded a distinguished journalist.'

'Finally, about hymen and virginity about which Shourie, as a good Hindu, is rightly concerned,' Panikkar continued. 'In the public eye his hymen has not remained intact, not because where he writes or to whom he gives interviews and articles, only because what he writes. Needless to say that the RSS publications carry his interviews and articles only because they are rabidly communal. He cannot hope to remain a virgin after selling himself in the flesh market. Being a BJP member of Parliament and an ideologue of Hindu communalism, Shourie should get his hymen tested, if he is still under misconception about his virginity.'

That is scholarly response. Indeed, in their circles it passes for 'devastating refutation'! But one must go the extra mile: proclaim your belief in double standards – yes, I do what he does, but I do so because I believe in *The Cause!*

'As for me, unlike him, I do not hunt with the hound and run with the hare,' Panikkar continued, though it wasn't clear what the colloquism was in aid of. 'I contribute signed articles to the publications of the Communist Party, because I believe in the ideals it stands for – democracy, secularism and socialism. By doing so, if my hymen is broken, I do not lament it, as Shourie does.'

All this as an answer to the facts about the working of the ICHR to which I had drawn attention!

Of course, there was one devastating fact which Panikkar reserved for the end. 'Incidentally, for the sake of record,' he concluded in a sort of crescendo to his peroration, 'the name of this man' whom Shourie describes as a "ring leader" is not K.N. Panicker, but K.N. Panikkar. If not his facts, he should at least get the spelling right.'

It just so happened that as his name had been spelled differently in the newspapers, I had taken the spelling from the 22 October 1994 issue of *The Gazette of India* which had announced his appointment to the ICHR!

An old charge.... Strong words.... Guilt-by-association.... In a word, shout, scream, throw a label, paste a motive – and thereby frighten.

How familiar.

'The criticism that communists decide their policy not in the interests of their own country but in the interests of the Soviet Union is neither new nor original,' thundered the Communist Party of India at Gandhiji and the Congress when it was confronted with evidence of having betrayed the national movement during the Quit India struggle, and teamed up with the British. 'It has been an old, very old gibe of the reactionary parties and their scribes the world over. It was the main theme the British Prosecutor played up against us in the Meerut Conspiracy Case. If 17 years later you make the same suggestion against us, we cannot but ask you – Is this worthy of you?'[2]

And always, there is the decisive proof – of having been

[2] *Communist Reply to the Congress Working Party Charges,* by the general secretary of the party, P.C. Joshi, Communist Party of India, Calcutta, March 1946, abridged version, pp. 3–4.

vindicated by history! 'All our brother parties had to live down this slander through their work among their own people,' the Communist Party continued. 'And if in the world of today there is any single political force which is growing it is the Communist movement. If any banner has lost ground in every country, it is the bankrupt banner of blind anti-communism.'

Towards the end of 1983, Mr V.M. Tarkunde invited me to deliver the M.N. Roy Memorial Lecture for 1984. The lecture was held on the same day in 1984 as it is every year – the birth anniversary of M.N. Roy. I documented the treacherous role the communists had played during the 1942 movement. Pritish Nandy, then editor of *The Illustrated Weekly,* carried the text in a series. The text contained documents from Indian and British archives – of secret liaisons of the communist functionaries with British rulers, of the reports they furnished detailing the service they were rendering to the British, the requests they were making and the concessions they were being given....

E.M.S. Namboodiripad rushed to Bombay. Shourie is speaking for the forces of reaction, he thundered at a specially convened press conference. These forces have panicked at the growing unity of secular and democratic forces ... They are unnerved that they will get a sound drubbing at the elections which are round the corner...

No elections were round any corner. Mr Tarkunde had given his invitation five months earlier. The communists' role in the Quit India movement had not been the topic I had thought of in the first instance. I had thought that I would speak on 'Ideology as Blinkers', and that I would illustrate my argument with four examples. By the time of the lecture only one example was ready – that relating to the communists during the 1942 movement. And that is how I got to speak on the topic when I did. But 'conspiracy', 'unnerved', 'elections round the corner'... it was!

The Communist Party of India published a series of

pamphlets – *Arun Shourie's Slanders Rebutted: History has vindicated the Communists....*[3]

'This is not the first time that the Quit India movement has been forked out to slander and attack the communist movement in our country,' began the foreword by the general secretary of the Communist Party of India, C. Rajeshwara Rao. 'Whenever the ruling circles and reactionary vested interests are in a tight corner or the communist movement is making headway, they would dig up old fables to whip up anti-Communist prejudices. The pet theme is the so-called "betrayal" of the freedom struggle in 1942 by the united Communist Party of India. Such things have happened a number of times in the past, even as late as 1975, during the days of Emergency imposed by Mrs Indira Gandhi' – that last bit was truly audacious! For it was the general secretary's very own Communist Party which had *supported* Mrs Gandhi's Emergency!

'Now the extreme reaction is worried because of the forging of left unity through the united struggles of the toiling people and also its gathering round of democratic allies,' the general secretary pronounced. 'Hence this resurrection of the ghost of 1942 once again by Mr Arun Shourie in order to isolate the communist movement by fanning anti-communism.'

'One would have ignored these attacks since we know very well that this is not the first time that such attacks have been leveled against us,' the publication declared. 'Arun Shourie, howsoever his journalistic talent may be, stands no comparison to such eminent personalities who have attacked us in the past. The eminent barrister, Langford James, of Meerut Conspiracy Case called us anti-God, anti-family, anti-decent everything with no sense of humour. History vindicated us.

[3] The following illustrative passages are taken from *Arun Shourie's Slanders Rebutted, History has vindicated the Communists,* Communist Party of India, New Delhi, June 1984, and *1942 August Struggle and the Communist Party of India,* Communist Party of India, New Delhi, June 1984.

The Communist Party of India grew from strength to strength since those days of 1929. Today the Communist Movement is a strength to reckon with.' What all this had to do with the facts which I had set out, what I had to do with that barrister of 1929 was and remains a mystery. But 'devastating refutation' it was! And remember the line, 'One would have ignored these attacks....' – it too is a standard one. The facts which have been brought to light, even more so those who have brought the facts to light are always beneath their dignity to answer. Recall Panikkar's lofty self-abnegation: 'The alternative of suing for defamation the likes of Shourie is below one's dignity....'[4]

Apart from everything else, one reason this is so is that the dunce is not going to be able to comprehend the reality in any case. 'It will be a waste of effort and also good space to refute this nonsense which betrays Shourie's utter ignorance of history and world events,' the Communist Party publication continued – recall Shrimali on his nuances being beyond the comprehension of persons like me! 'We do not want to go into his vapid nonsensical utterances in the last installment. They are tarred with the same rotten anti-Communist stuff with the hackneyed claim that communists are but the agents of Moscow (or rather of the Soviet Union) and as such they are to be treated with contempt. [On the contrary, my argument had been that precisely for this reason they ought to be treated with wariness, that their potential for harming the country, for poisoning discourse must not be ignored!] Even a cursory reading of the names of the Communist Party members who have found their way from other streams of the national movement, either of the national revolutionary or of the orthodox Gandhian type [And what about those who saw through the Communist Party, including several of the topmost functionaries of the Party, and left it?] and the whole host of intellectuals who have adored [sic] the ranks of the

[4] *The Asian Age*, 7 July 1998, p. 13.

Communist Party, and the large mass of workers and peasants who have acquired a new stature in their life by joining and working for the Communist Party would belie Arun Shourie's vile slanders.' Suppose for a moment that all the intellectuals of India had fallen to 'adoring' the ranks of the Communist Party, that every worker and peasant had become a devotee of the Party, how would that alter the assistance the Party had rendered to the British?

And the 'this-is-an-old-charge' defence again: 'These slanders themselves are not of Arun Shourie's original imagination either; they are products of a diseased and jaundiced view of the state of affairs which cannot bear the thought of the ordinary worker and peasant, of the ordinary man taking part and having a say in the political life of the country....'

Mockery, derision, scorn, the charge of conspiracy, of secret funds being pumped in by unnamed forces, the charge that the critic is privilege personified and therefore cannot stand the fact that, because of the struggles put up by the Left, the masses are coming into their own – an avalanche to scare everyone from doing what this fellow has done. 'The argument would be similar to say, "When did you last stop beating your wife?" This pearl of wisdom which Shourie seems to be bestowing cannot just be called a fool's paradise in which he may be lurking. It is a dangerous game to sow dissensions in the minds of the young political workers. And there are many other interests in the country who are financing it as is evident from various translations and other media coverage that have gone with it.'

But hope, confidence too – lest the rank and file lose heart: 'But truth is truth and must stand out, even when Shourie indulges in making a lot of "*shor*" (noise), but with a purpose no doubt.'

The great names who saw the light and acknowledged that the communists are the ones who had been right... 'They all did this out of a process of understanding of national events in the context of international developments which is beyond the mental horizon of Arun Shourie or similar other anti-Communist scribes who have slandered us in the past....' Two key points in that – the ones who criticize them are deficient in understanding, and they are congenitally anti-communist.

'It is difficult for Arun Shourie to realise this, devoid as he is of any political perspective' – the person in question can be said to have 'political perspective' only when and if he reaches the same conclusions as the communists!

As the man lacks elementary political understanding, it is always pointless to check up the facts which such a person has adduced: I had published extensive extracts from a 120-page report which the Communist Party had submitted to the British narrating the assistance its members were rendering by sabotaging the Quit India movement. 'The so-called 120-page document,' the publication scoffed, 'unfortunately I thought it a waste of time to count whether it was actually 120-pages as Shourie seems to have done.'

Hence, the confidence in the future: 'We are aware that the four articles by Arun Shourie both in English and other languages are designed particularly to create a rift between the left and the other democratic forces. We have every confidence that this will fail and our healthy national movement will work steadily towards the goal of bringing about the social transformation through the path of peace, consolidation of national freedom, and socialism.'

Arun Shourie's series, began another publication which the Communist Party put out, 'is a long chain of distortions, canards and slander against the Communist Party of India, the international communist movement and the Soviet Union....' 'From 1944 onward (and even earlier) paid pen-pushers and agents of imperialism and the bourgeoisie have repeatedly run slander campaigns against the CPI and the USSR....' Hansraj Vohra.... Langford James, the barrister again..., 'the notorious Minoo Masani and later on his worthy "disciple" Sitaram Goel'....

'Naturally enough questions are being asked by people all over India: why has Shourie started this foul campaign *now*?....' That is always a useful question to ask: when you can't answer a person on facts, ask: 'But why *now*?' India carries out its first nuclear explosion on 18 May 1974 at Pokhran. And what does the redoubtable representative of the communists ask in the Lok Sabha?

> We have been told that we have [had] the capability for a long time, we could have set off this blast much earlier, if we wanted to. Well, if we could have set it off much earlier, we could have set it off much later also. My question is about the timing of it. There must be some reason behind the timing of this, this particular timing of 18th May. I am not clear about it.[5]

Redouble authority by quoting each other! That is twice-blessed: it doubles the weight of your assertion, and, as the comrade is being cited as an authority, it doubles his weight for the future! And so the publication fortifies the question it has posed – the hardy perennial, 'But why *now?*' – by citing what E.M.S. Namboodiripad has asked! 'Reputed Communist leader and General Secretary of the CPI(M) E.M.S. Namboodiripad,' it says, 'has queried: "Why should Arun Shourie have taken up the shop-soiled wares of Communist Betrayal in 1942, 40 years after the Quit India struggle started?"' And the answer too is fortified by citing E.M.S. once again: 'The seasoned anti-Communist Minoo Masani promptly jumped into the fray, in defence of Shourie...' E.M.S. sharply retorts: 'What Mr. Shourie himself and Mr. Masani are afraid of is thus the coming together of opposition parties not opposed to the Communists, but cooperating with them. This is exactly what I suspected in my Bombay press conference...' 'Thus the cat is out of the bag,' the publication proclaimed in triumph taking EMS's assertion as proof. 'Large segments of the non-Communist non-left

[5] *Lok Sabha Debates*, 8 August 1974, Column 223.

opposition parties have repeatedly joined hands with the Communist-led left opposition, both against the authoritarian forces led by Indira Congress as well as against right-wing communal and divisive forces like the BJP and others. This has alarmed both Indira Gandhi and her entourage, as well as the BJP, RSS and their allies. Shourie and Masani have come out as their spokesmen and in their desperate efforts to drive a wedge between the Communists and the non-Communist opposition parties. In this foul effort, what better weapon can they take up than the shop-soiled ware of anti-Communist, anti-Soviet canard?' Thus, congenitally anti-communist, vile motives, desperation of the critic – all there!

Next, a repeat of denunciation-by-association: 'Let us now have a brief look at the "noble" anti-communist predecessors of Arun Shourie!' the publication proceeds. Hansraj Vohra… Minoo Masani… And now comes Arun Shourie who is supposed to be a talented journalist but who has been exposed as a communalist… And who has published his articles? *The Illustrated Weekly of India* which has also published an article [among the hundreds it would have published in the period!] 'The RSS will stay' by an RSS member. And so the truth manifest: 'The communists must go and the RSS must stay – the "Weekly"-Shourie-Masani tie-up is now crystal clear! This is the basic reason why Shourie has picked up from the dustbin of history the discarded weapon of anti-communism!'

Forty pages of such sterling refutations in one publication, twenty-three pages in another. All leading to the conclusion – at once triumphal and defiant, and comic:

> The CPI is a party of heroes and martyrs of freedom struggle as well as of class battles. The Shouries and Masanis can wear the shop-soiled dirty shirt of anti-communism as long as they like, but their place is in the dung-heap of history! The combined imperialist armies tried to destroy the young Soviet State. They failed. Hitler tried it too and was destroyed in turn. Today the Reagans and Thatchers are again trying

> to play the same dirty game. They too will meet the fate of Hitler and Mussolini! So also will their paid henchmen, who spatter mud at the communists! Like old man Galileo facing the inquisition and like our own Dimitrov, facing the butcher Goering, we Indian communists also hurl defiance at the face of all our reactionary detractors and persecutors and with rock-like conviction, resolutely declare: Nonetheless, the Earth goes forward, and all roads lead to Communism!

Amen!

Twin lessons in that. To roll back their untruth, we must immunize ourselves against their verbal terrorism. And among the easy prophylactics is to cut out and store their vituperation – in less than no time it mutates into the ridiculous. The press conferences and pamphlets were hurled at me in 1984. In 1986 in his *A History of Indian Freedom Struggle,* E.M.S. Namboodiripad acknowledged that communists had collaborated with the British during the 'Quit India' movement.[6] In 1984, as we have just seen, the communists were proclaiming, 'Nonetheless, the Earth goes forward, and all roads lead to Communism.' In 1989 the Berlin Wall was pulled down....

[6] Social Scientist Press, Trivandrum, 1986. Even at this stage Namboodiripad proffered convoluted explanations for the collaboration: cf. my *'The Only Fatherland'*, ASA, 1991, pp. 3–11. Soon he was saying it had been a mistake!

Their Line

7

A circular

Manoj Raghuvanshi had invited K.M. Shrimali, one of this group of eminences, and me to discuss on ZEE Television's *Aap ki Adalat, Aap ka Faisala* the charge that history was being rewritten in communal colours. Raghuvanshi read out what *Outlook* had reported – that the West Bengal Board of Secondary Education had issued instructions in 1989 that 'Muslim rule should never attract any criticism. Destruction of temples by Muslim rulers and invaders should not be mentioned.'

Raghuvanshi asked Shrimali, whether this did not amount to distortion? True, that was a painful period of our history, Raghuvanshi said, but should it be erased from our history books? Would that be objective history, rational history? Shrimali's response was the well-practised script: firstly, he did not know that such an instruction had ever been issued; if it had been issued, he said, he was against it; but one must see what the context was in which the instruction had been issued...

Concerned teachers in West Bengal have been so kind as to send me the circular relating to textbooks for Class IX. Dated 28 April 1989, it is issued by the West Bengal Secondary Education Board. It is in Bengali, and carries the number 'Syl/89/1'.

'All the West Bengal Government recognised secondary school Headmasters are being informed,' it begins, 'that in

History textbooks recommended by this Board for Class IX the following amendments to the chapter on the medieval period have been decided after due discussions and review by experts.'

'The authors and publishers of Class IX History textbooks,' it continues, 'are being requested to incorporate the amendments if books published by them have these *aushuddho* [impurities, errors] in all subsequent editions, and paste a corrigendum in books which have already been published. A copy of the book with the corrigendum should be deposited with the Syllabus Office (74, Rafi Ahmed Kidwai Road, Calcutta-16).' Signed, '....Chattopadhyay, Secretary.'

The accompanying pages contain two columns: *aushuddho* – impurity, or error – and *shuddho.* One has just to glance through the changes to see the objective the progressives are trying to achieve through their 'objective', 'rational' approach to the writing of history. Here are some of the changes.

Book: *Bharat Katha,* prepared by the Burdwan Education Society, Teachers Enterprise, published by Sukhomoy Das:

> *Page 140: Aushuddho* – 'In Sindhudesh the Arabs did not describe Hindus as *Kafir.* They had banned cow-slaughter.' *Shuddho* – 'Delete, "They had banned cow-slaughter".'
>
> *Page 141: Aushuddho* – 'Fourthly, using force to destroy Hindu temples was also an expression of aggression. Fifthly, forcibly marrying Hindu women and converting them to Islam before marriage was another way to propagate the fundamentalism of the *ulema.' Shuddho:* though the *ashuddho* column reproduces the sentences only from 'Fourthly....,' the Board directs that the entire matter from 'Secondly.... to *ulema'* be deleted.
>
> *Page 141: Aushuddho* – 'The logical, philosophical, materialist Mutazilla disappeared. On the one hand, the fundamentalist thinking based on the Quran and the *hadis....' Shuddho* – 'Delete, "On the one hand, the fundamentalist thinking based on the Quran and the *hadis*"....'

Book: *Bharatvarsher Itihash,* by Dr Narendranath Bhattacharya, published by Chakravarty and Son:

Page 89: Aushuddho – 'Sultan Mahmud used force for widespread murder, loot, destruction and conversion.' *Shuddho* – 'There was widespread loot and destruction by Mahmud.' That is, no reference to killing, no reference to forcible conversions.

Page 89: Aushuddho – 'He looted valuables worth 2 crore dirham from the Somnath temple and used the Shivling as a step leading up to the *masjid* in Ghazni.' *Shuddho* – 'Delete "and used the Shivling as a step leading up to the *masjid* in Ghazni."'

Page 112: Aushuddho – 'Hindu-Muslim relations of the medieval ages constitute a very sensitive issue. The non-believers had to embrace Islam or death.' *Shuddho* – All matter on pages 112–13 to be deleted.

Page 113: Aushuddho – 'According to Islamic law non-Muslims will have to choose between death and Islam. Only the Hanafis allow non-Muslims to pay *jaziya* in exchange for their lives.' *Shuddho* – Rewrite this as follows: 'By paying *jaziya* to Alauddin Khalji, Hindus could lead normal lives.' Moreover, all the subsequent sentences 'Qazi....', 'Taimur's arrival in India....' to be deleted.

Page 113: Aushuddho – 'Mahmud was a believer in the rule of Islam whose core was "Either Islam or death".' *Shuddho* – Delete.

Book: *Bharater Itihash,* by Shubhankar Chattopadhyay, published by Narmada Publishers:

Page 181: Aushuddho – 'To prevent Hindu women from being seen by Muslims, they were directed to remain indoors.' *Shuddho* – Delete.

Book: *Itihasher Kahini,* by Nalini Bhushan Dasgupta, published by B. B. Kumar:

Page 132: Aushuddho – 'According to Todd [the famous chronicler of Rajasthan annals] the purpose behind Alauddin's

Chittor expedition was to secure Rana Rattan Singh's beautiful wife, Padmini.' *Shuddho* – Delete.

Page 154: Aushuddho – 'As dictated by Islam, there were three options for non-Muslims: get yourself converted to Islam; pay *jaziya;* accept death. In an Islamic State non-Muslims had to accept one of these three options.' *Shuddho* – Delete.

Page 161: Aushuddho – 'The early Sultans were eager to expand the sway of Islam by forcibly converting Hindus into Islam.' *Shuddho* – Delete.

Book: *Bharater Itihash,* by P. Maiti, Sreedhar Prakashani:

Page 117: Aushuddho – 'There is an account that Alauddin attacked the capital of Mewar, Chittorgarh, to get Padmini, the beautiful wife of Rana Rattan Singh.' *Shuddho* – Delete.

Page 139: Aushuddho – 'There was a sense of aristocratic superiority in the *purdah* system. That is why upper-class Hindus adopted this system from upper-class Muslims. Another opinion has it that *purdah* came into practice to save Hindu women from Muslims. Most probably, *purdah* came into vogue because of both factors.' *Shuddho* – Delete.

The most extensive deletions are ordered in regard to the chapter on 'Aurangzeb's policy on religion'. Every allusion to what he actually did to the Hindus, to their temples, to the very leitmotif of his rule – to spread the sway of Islam – are directed to be excised from the book. He is to be presented as one who had an aversion – an ordinary sort of aversion, almost a secular one – to music and dancing, to the presence of prostitutes in the court, and that it is these things he banished. The only allusion to his having done anything in regard to Islam which is allowed to remain is that 'By distancing himself from Akbar's policy of religious tolerance and policy of equal treatment, Aurangzeb caused damage to Mughal rule.'

Book: *Swadesh O Shobhyota,* by Dr P.K. Basu and S.B. Ghatak, Abhinav Prakashan:

Page 126: Aushuddho – 'Some people believe that Alauddin's Mewar expedition was to get hold of Padmini, the wife of Rana Rattan Singh.' *Shuddho* – Delete.

Page 145: Aushuddho – 'Apart from this, because Islam used extreme, inhuman means to establish itself in India, this became an obstacle for the coming together of Indian and Islamic cultures.' *Shuddho* – Delete.

Book: *Bharat Katha,* by G. Bhattacharya, Bulbul Prakashan:

Page 40: Aushuddho – 'Muslims used to take recourse to torture and inhuman means to force their religious beliefs and practices on Indians.' *Shuddho* – Delete.

Page 41: Aushuddho – 'The liberal, humane elements in Islam held out hope for oppressed Hindus.' *Shuddho* – The entire paragraph beginning with 'the caste system among Hindus.... was attacked' is to be deleted. Instead write, 'There was no place for casteism in Islam. Understandably, the influence of Islam created an awakening among Hindus against caste discrimination. Lower caste oppressed Hindus embraced Islam.'

Page 77: Aushuddho – 'His main task was to oppress non-believers, especially Hindus.' *Shuddho* – This and the preceding sentence to be deleted.

Book: *Bharater Itihash,* by A.C. Roy, published by Prantik:

Page 102: Aushuddho – 'There is an account that Alauddin attacked Chittor to get the beautiful wife of Rana Rattan Singh, Padmini.' *Shuddho* – Delete.

Page 164: Ashuddho – 'It was his commitment to Islam which made him a fundamentalist.' *Shuddho* – Delete.

Book: *Bharat Kahini,* by G.C. Roychoudhury, published by A.K. Sarkar and Co:

Page 130: Aushuddho – 'That is why he adopted the policy of converting Hindus to Islam – so as to increase the number of Muslims. Those Hindus who refused to discard their religion were indiscriminately massacred by him or his generals.' *Shuddho* – Delete.

In a word, no forcible conversions, no massacres, no destruction of temples. Just that Hinduism had created an exploitative, casteist society. Islam was egalitarian. Hence the oppressed Hindus embraced Islam!

Muslim historians of those times are in raptures at the heap of kafirs who have been dispatched to hell. *Muslim* historians are forever lavishing praise on the ruler for the temples he has destroyed, for the hundreds of thousands he has got to see the light of Islam. Law books like *The Hedaya* prescribe exactly the options to which these little textbooks alluded. All whitewashed away.

Objective whitewash for objective history. And today if anyone seeks to restore truth to these textbooks, the shout, 'Communal rewriting of history'.

But there isn't just whitewash of Islam. For, after Islam, came another great emancipatory ideology – Marxism-Leninism.

The teachers in Bengal furnish extracts from the textbook for Class V:

> '.... in Russia, China, Vietnam, Cuba and in other East European countries, the workers and peasants are ruling the country after capturing power, whereas in U.S.A., England, France and Germany the owners of mills and factories are ruling the country.'
>
> '.... after the Revolution in Russia the first exploitation-free society was established.'
>
> '.... Islam and Christianity are the only religions which treated man with honour and equality....'

Thus, not just whitewash, hogwash too.

8

Devices to further the circular

As we have seen, the explicit part of the circular issued by the West Bengal government in 1989 in effect was that there must be no negative reference to Islamic rule in India. Although these were the very things which contemporary Islamic writers had celebrated, there must be no reference to the destruction of the temples by Muslim rulers, to the forcible conversion of Hindus, to the numerous other disabilities which were placed on the Hindu population. Along with the circular, the passages which had to be removed were listed and substitute passages were specified. The passages which were ordered to be deleted contained, if anything, a gross understatement of the facts. On the other hand, passages which were sought to be inserted contained total falsehoods: that by paying *jizyah* Hindus could lead 'normal lives' under an Islamic ruler like Alauddin Khalji!

A closer study of the textbooks which are today being used under the authority of the West Bengal government shows a much more comprehensive, a much deeper design than that of merely erasing the cruelties of Islamic rule.

Of course, there is no reference to those cruelties. But in addition, the growth of the Aligarh movement and its objectives, the role of Sir Syed Ahmad in founding this movement, the role of the Muslim League, its close ['association with the British, its espousal of the Two Nation doctrine – all these are almost entirely erased in the half a dozen books which teachers in Calcutta have been so kind as to send.

It was only in one book, *Sabhyatar Itihash* by Dr Atul Chandra Ray, Prantik, 1998, for Class VIII, that there was a reference to the Muslim League, the Lahore Resolution, the Two Nation theory, and Jinnah's 'Direct Action'. Even in this book the only reference to Sir Syed Ahmad was one that projected him as a great, progressive religious reformer: 'All his life he struggled against blind faith and tradition, conventional rituals, practices and ignorance.' That he founded the Aligarh movement, that he was the original proponent of the Two Nation theory, that he exhorted Muslims to stay away from the Congress, that he wrote essays followed by books followed by essays to establish in the eyes of the British how loyal Muslims had been through the 1857 uprising, how loyal they were and would always be to the British because of their nature and their religion, that he gave very special 'interpretations' to passages from the Quran to establish that it was the religious duty of Muslims to support and stand by the British rulers – to the point that if the British asked them to eat pork, they were by their religion duty-bound to do so in good cheer:[1] not a word on any of this.

Similarly, while Ram Mohan Roy is mentioned, while Keshab Chandra Sen – in whom Max Muller had seen such hope for Christianizing India! – is mentioned, while Debendranath Tagore is mentioned in this 'History of Civilisation', Bankimchandra is *not* mentioned! After all, for the constituency which our progressives have been wooing, Bankimchandra, being the author of '*Bande Mataram*', of *Ananda Math,* is anathema. Many would think it natural that as such 'Histories of World Civilisation' are written in and for Bengal, Bengali personages – including K.C. Sen! – should

[1] For illustrative extracts from Sir Syed's writings on these points see my *Indian Controversies,* ASA 1991, HarperCollins 1997, Chapter VII.

figure more prominently than reformers and leaders from outside Bengal. But even they would be surprised by what the teachers point out in regard to the most widely used textbook: that while Swami Vivekananda gets one line, Karl Marx gets forty two!

In regard to our religion, the trick is threefold. The textbooks denigrate religion, attributing to it the evils which it serves the progressives' purpose to highlight. Second, in each of these instances the examples they give are linked by them to Hinduism. Third, among religions, Islam is always presented as the one, progressive, emancipatory religion. Of course, the final emancipation comes in the form of the Soviet Revolution of 1917!

Itihash o' Bhugol, Pratham Bhag, West Bengal Shiksha Adhikar, Calcutta, 1993, is a book for Class III, that is for children of seven or eight. It has the customary section on *'Vyaktigata Sampatti o' Das Pratha'* and it sets out the customary Marxist exposition. The emergence of two classes, rich and poor, is attributable to personal property and the profit motive..., to augment its growth, one class of society fights another class....; some lose out their property; others grab everything of theirs...; those who lose out are made prisoners and employed as labourers; they become slaves; they are absolute paupers...; those who make them work like this become their *malik....;* gradually those maliks, without working, start enjoying the fruits of the labour of slaves...; thus society gets divided into rich and poor, owners and slaves; the rich and the owners and craftsmen class of people start fleecing these slaves; not only are the latter denied their dues, they are also subjected to *atyachar....;* sometimes these poor, these slaves used to rebel when they could no longer bear the atyachar; to discipline them the rich created law, police and courts.... A proper preparation of the Class III child for abiding by the law!

On the next page this account is merged into the account

of 'rituals and ceremonies of society'. The illustration on the page shows Hindu pundits around a fire with the caption '*Rishis* performing *Yajna*'. Having described the emergence of two classes, the oppression of one class and its being pushed into becoming slave labour, having described law, police and courts as instruments of this oppression, the textbook now tells the Class III student 'these priests devised and got busy in creating laws and rituals for worship. That is how scriptures were written. And they started teaching the children from these scriptures, and they themselves became the teachers. Gradually they established themselves at the top of the social ladder. That is how they became leaders of society. And they became the allies of those who were ruling the world'. Not just the usual Marxist claptrap, the Marxist rendition of the Macaulay-missionary design: make them ashamed of the things they revere – their gods, their scriptures, their language, Sanskrit; and make them hate the one group which has been charged with the task of continuing their religion and culture.

The theme is continued and the association of Hinduism with everything evil is deepened in the textbook, *Itihash o' Bhugol,* Part II (West Bengal Vidyalaya Shiksha Adhikar, 1995, Calcutta), meant for the Class IV students. On page 10 the standard account is given – one which has been called into serious question by current scholarship. Aryans come from the north-west.... They institute four castes, the Shudras are consigned to be the lowest caste. They were the original inhabitants of this land, of dark complexion.... No right to education....

That is on page 10. On page 17 we learn of the great emancipatory event. Muhammad is born. He establishes Islam....It creates a great civilization, a civilization educationally, culturally advanced. It establishes a vast empire – but because of internecine fighting in various parts, this empire yields to the emergence of different states.

Two pages later again: Muhammad is born ..., a great *mahapurush*...., his religion Islam means 'Peace'. He taught all to give alms to the poor, and to pay the worker his legitimate due. He taught, 'Do not cause pain or suffering to slaves, do not take interest on loans.' He stopped idolatry. These are the principal doctrines of Muhammad. Many accepted Muhammad's religion.... And then the insinuation slipped in: 'All great men have taught peace... but people have forgotten their message and are quarrelling and fighting. The rich, instead of helping the poor, duped them, and added to their own wealth. They indulged in loot, bloodletting in the name of religion. When Jainism and Buddhism spread in India, the Brahmin pundits saw danger. They thought that if men did not follow the rituals, they might not obey and care for them. Therefore, on the pretext of saving Hindu religion and to maintain their hold on society, they became desperate. They were helped by many kings. Thus, the influence of Jainism and Buddhism declined and the influence of Hinduism increased.'

That much is on page 20. On pages 25 and 26 this superimposition is carried further. The standard Marxist 'thesis' is once again driven into the child. Peasants exploited.... surplus appropriated.... his cattle, land expropriated..., suffering.... progressive immiserization day by day..., and then, 'in the name of god, the pundits extracted gifts for puja and festivals. The pundits became oppressive and began living off the labour of others, becoming exploiters and oppressors. They were helped by kings and landlords. Shudras, slaves and the poor suffer most from religious persecution. This is how the stratification of society between high and low started. Shudras became untouchables; there was no restriction on exploiting their services and every excuse was good enough for the men of higher castes to exploit and persecute the Shudras.... The upper-caste men used to kill Shudras and wipe out entire villages on any excuse whatsoever.'

And there is an illustration on the page to reinforce the

message into the child's mind. Captioned *Dharmiya Utpidan,* 'Religious Persecution', it shows a man in a bush-shirt, flogging a poor person with a whip. In the foreground is a Brahmin in a dhoti, with a *chutia,* a menacing frown, directing him to do so.

By predictable contrast, *Itihash* (*Prachin*), West Bengal Shiksha Parishad, 1994, on page 94 gives an illustration of the ruins of Nalanda. It says how important these seats of learning were. But it is studiously silent on who it was that destroyed them! After all, alluding to that would violate the circular!

The Class III textbook, *Itihash o' Bhugol, Pratham Bhag,* on page 32, teaches the child, 'With the emergence of personal property one section has been depriving the other. The differences between rich and poor have grown. Suffering has been created. The downtrodden have lost all their rights. They have been subjected to many indignities. Even now people are killing each other, even now a man exploits a fellow being, even now there are wars, battles. If peace ever comes to this earth, if exploitation and oppression are stopped, if every man can enjoy equal happiness and peace, how wonderful this earth would become.'

This pattern – of sowing anger against the state of things and attributing that condition to the entities the communists want to target – continues from one year to the next. *Itihash,* Part III, West Bengal Shiksha Adhikar, 1996, after giving the same sequence and 'theses' of exploitation, of division of society, of religion as a handmaiden of exploitation, turns to 'the emergence of new consciousness'. An exploitative order.... Brahmins wielding great influence.... Those of the working class, the Shudras pushed down..., no rights or dignity.... Shudras not even to perform religious rituals.... Exploitation.... Rebellion of Christian slaves.... Spartacus.... Shakes the very foundation of the Roman Empire.... After 600 years of Christ, a new religious creed that every man has equal rights, this religious creed was preached by Hazrat Muhammad.... Ideas of great men abandoned.... Exploitation continues.

At last! Lenin, the Bolshevik Party.... 'This is how the common man's revolt took place in November 1917 and an exploitation-less [*shoshan-mukt*] society of the working class was established. Tagore visited Russia in 1930 and said that if he had not visited Russia, he would have missed out on the most sacred place of pilgrimage....' The Chinese Revolution....

The Industrial Revolution in England.... Proprietors expropriate.... Labour is progressively immiserised.... Country becomes rich but is controlled by a few; the rest sink into misery, getting hardly anything, not even two square meals a day.... And then, on page 32, the Russian Revolution: 'In November 1917 before the end of the First World War, the workers and peasants of the Russian Empire led by Lenin and his Bolshevik Party staged the Revolution and uprooted the Czarist Empire and thus established the first exploitation-less [*shoshan-mukt*] rule of Workers and Peasants in Soviet Russia....'

And then the Second World War: Hitler, Japan and Italy combined. Japan also was very greedy and ambitious, and planned to set up an empire in Asia. The Axis came into conflict with 'Britain, France and the American imperialists.' 'The issue,' it tells the student, 'was who will exploit and plunder the world. That is how the Second World War started....' Bengal Famine.... In 1941 Germany attacked Soviet Russia. The Russian people fought to defend the Motherland and finally defeated Hitler's Germany. Bombing of Hiroshima and Nagasaki.... After the end of the Second World War, the movement for freedom in colonies became vigorous.

Like this book, *Sabhyatar Itihash,* 'The History of Civilisation', 1998, also presents the Russian Revolution as the culmination of that evolution. A remarkable, comprehensive revolution....

While these books are published in 1995,1998, etc., there is not a word in them about the purges under Stalin, about the fact that under him millions of Soviet citizens were killed, nor of the fact that millions more were killed under Maoist rule in China, there is not a word of the slave labour camps of these regimes. And, of course, there is not a word about what has happened to the Soviet Union, to eastern Europe since then, nor about the great leap which China has executed away from the bankrupt communist economic system.

Hence the design is not just what was set out in that circular – to erase the evil that Islamic rulers heaped upon India and Indians. It is to attribute evil to the religion of our country, Hinduism; it is to present Islam as the great progressive force which arose; it is to lament the fact that humanity did not heed the teachings of progressive men like Muhammad – till the 'remarkable and comprehensive' Russian Revolution of 1917!

In Kerala the same sorts of efforts have been on, say the teachers. It is just that as parties have been alternating in forming governments, it has not been possible to push one line for long. The recent fracas over the Minimum Levels of Learning project illustrates the position, they say.

The 1986 National Education Policy emphasized the need to urgently lay down minimum levels of competence which children completing different stages of education must achieve. A committee was set up in 1990. It specified the competencies which students must acquire in Standards I to V. The state government revised the curriculum and textbooks accordingly. The new curriculum and textbooks were introduced in larger and larger number of schools from 1993.

In 1996 the Marxists came to power again. They once again revised the texts and curricula for Standards I to IV. The textbooks and curricula which had been introduced just three years earlier and which were in the process of being extended over the state were dumped. The textbooks were prepared by teachers who were actively associated with the Sasthra Sahitya Parishad, a Marxist-sponsored organization. 'Public educationists and teachers' organizations strongly criticised the new textbooks,' teachers write. 'The main criticism was that the textbooks were silent in regard to national leaders, social reformers, ancient poets and Indian culture. Stories and poems relating to Ramayana and Mahabharatha were left out in the name of secularism.'

As is usual with sclerotic movements, things are often taken to ridiculous lengths. The teachers give an example. A poem by the leading poet of Kerala, Mahakavi Ikkitham Achuthan Namboodiripad, was prescribed for study, they write. In it, anxious and pining for her son, the mother asks whether anyone has seen her son, *'Ambadi kannante niramane'* – my son, the colour of Krishna, which is dark. This line has been deleted, and substituted' by *'Njaval pazhathinte chelane'* – Njval pazham is a fruit, which, the teachers point out, is red in colour. 'This change was done without the prior permission of the renowned poet,' they write. 'It was done to ensure that the name of Lord Krishna does not occur in the poem.' Furthermore, they point out, the 1986 National Education Policy had identified a set of core components. In preparing the new curriculum the ones related to the history of the Indian freedom movement, the content essential to nurture a national identity, the items dealing with India's common cultural heritage, as well as those relating to the removal of social barriers, were all erased from the curriculum. In the lesson on Gandhiji in the textbook for Class IV, he is not represented as the leader of the struggle for freedom, but merely as one who loved the poor. For this an incident from his days in South Africa is recalled. And, the teachers say, he is deliberately referred to as *ayal,* which means 'he'. The word is a disrespectful one, they write. It is not used for an honourable person, an elder.

With the sway which Marxists have ensured over the education department, each facet at every level will be subjected to the same sort of alterations and substitutions that we have encountered in Bengal – all that is necessary is that the progressives' government remains in power, and that the rest keep looking the other way.

9

'Let us look forward to the positive aspects'

The position of these 'academics' in Bengal has, of course, been helped by the fact that the CPI(M) has been in power there for so long. But their sway has not been confined to the teaching and 'research' institutions of that state. It is no surprise, therefore, to see the same 'line' being poured down the throats of students at the national level. And so strong is the tug of intellectual fashion, so lethal can the controlling mafia be to the career of an academic that often, even though the academic may not quite subscribe to their propositions and 'theses', he will end up reciting those propositions. Else his manuscript will not be accepted as a textbook by the NCERT, for instance, it will not be reviewed....

S.N. Jha's *Society, State and Government* is an NCERT textbook for Class XI students.[1] This author too is from that citadel of the 'committed writing' which we are considering, the Jawaharlal Nehru University. Working in that institution, among those controllers, whatever his views, the text he produces for acculturating the young fits the pattern.

The book does deign to mention that the Soviet Union has

[1] National Council of Educational Research and Training, Delhi, 1996. Unless indicated otherwise, page numbers in this chapter refer to this publication.

collapsed, that East Germany has merged with West Germany. But even in 1996 it regurgitates rationalizations for the Soviet system, and when it cannot avoid mentioning the collapse of the Soviet Union and of other 'socialist' states, it dutifully puts the word 'collapse' within inverted commas!

There is the great breakthrough, as always: 'Socialism argued and elaborated so eloquently by a number of scholars..., remained in the realm of ideas till 1917, when the ideas formed the concrete basis for the Russian Revolution,' the Professor tells the students. 'It provided an opportunity to organise the State and the government in a way that the ideals of socialism could be attained. The Chinese Revolution in 1949 was another landmark in the organisation of socialist States. They provided the models for many States that adopted the socialist form.'[2]

The subliminal association so well known to propagandists and advertisers: 'The decade[s] of the Russian and Chinese Revolutions were also the period of decolonisation.... The experiment with socialism found favour in the Third World.'[3]

The phenomenal spread: 'Authentic surveys published in 1984 suggested that the 15 socialist States accounted for about a quarter of the world's territory and about a third of the world's population. They spread in almost all the continents of the world. Many of them made a place for themselves in the world on the basis of achievements in different fields – economic, social, political and military....'[4]

The economic basis of society and governance: hence, the nationalization of the means of production, leading to workers' control over the forces of production....

The special ways of organizing socialist states, the jettisoning of institutions and mores which are appurtenances of non-socialist states – states that are not organized around

[2] p. 83.
[3] p. 83.
[4] p. 83.

an agreed ideology – and they have not done the things that socialist-states have ensured. Thus, the special way of organizing political parties in socialist states:

> Since socialist societies will have achieved a stage where, in place of multiplicity of classes, there will be only one class, i.e. the proletariat, there is no place for multiplicity of political parties. There is also a single ideology to be pursued. Socialist societies usually have a single political Party. In some such states the number of parties had been more than one.[5]

True, some socialist states had two or more parties, the textbook says, but the other parties were adjuncts of the main party and strove to further the same ideology. Moreover, the political party in such a state does not work only for 'short-term electoral gains in electoral field'. 'One important role,' the textbook says, 'is to act as a vanguard of the socialist ideals and not only represent it, but also ensure that it is reflected in society and polity' – in any other system a party performing this kind of a role would be denounced as a 'thought-police', as being the informer and enforcer of a totalitarian State. But our text gilds the role in words that would probably embarrass even a citizen who had been all-commitment in the days of the Soviet Union! The party ensures 'a personal liaison' between the party leadership and the armed forces. It also 'influences the decisions about appointment of people in important institutions…'[6]

With a role such as this to be performed, the party cannot allow itself to be hobbled by bourgeois notions of loose, unfocussed functioning. Hence, says our textbook, in words that seem to have been taken straight out of Stalin's manual:

[5] p. 85.
[6] p. 85.

> Such a conception of the role of the Party will naturally require a strong and firm leadership to pursue its goals. In order to promote its ideology and serve the interests of the society, it requires a disciplined and unified, rather than a fragmented and loose structure. The Party has a monolithic structure.[7]

Stalin ensconced, Lenin is to be recalled! And so, the standard accompaniment to the monolith:

> Requirements of Party structure and participation of Party members are reconciled by the Principle of Democratic Centralism, enunciated by Lenin. Firm leadership and a unified structure of the Party, however, do not mean that the participation of the members of the Party, i.e. the workers, is in any way restricted....[8]

Elections are held at all levels within the party. There is freedom to air one's views.... 'Thus the Party organisation combined the participation of members and units of the Party with strict discipline and united structure,' says the text. 'The cadre could "thus act as transmitters of central policy and mass demands, familiarise the members with the day-to-day problems of the villages, help create Party branches and participate in a mass education movement".'[9]

Nor is that all to democracy within the party. 'The individual members can bypass the leadership in the organisation and can appeal and complain to higher bodies in the Party,' says the text – the mountains of evidence of what happened to individuals who tried to do anything of the sort notwithstanding. 'Individual appeals and complaints can be made to the highest level, right up to the Chairman of the Central Committee....' Almost as welcoming as the *darbar-i-am* of Mughal rulers![10]

[7] pp. 85–86.
[8] p. 86.
[9] p. 86.
[10] pp. 86–87.

This much having been internalized, it is time to make a little concession to reality. Hence, the theory having been adumbrated at such length, the flaw that arose in implementation is noted!

> Such an organisation of a Party is highly centralised from top to the bottom, as perhaps it is intended to be. In actual working, this arrangement does not encourage participation from lower levels, that it seeks to do in theory. The higher levels of the Party get isolated from the realities of the society and is [sic] not quite sensitive to the socio-economic and cultural changes taking place in society. The Party organisation becomes rigid and also top-heavy. In such a situation, the political Party is unable to perform the important function of acting as a link between the people and the government. Party becomes part of the government. Many other kinds of aberrations (such as corruption and arrogant leadership) also occur, that are typical of a top-heavy organisation which is not subject to popular control. After the collapse of the USSR many weaknesses in the working of CPSU have come to light.[11]

Next, elections as we know them, turn out to be as out of sync, if not as out of place, as democratic political parties:

> Since the socialist society claims to have a single economic class, that of the proletariat (i.e. the working class), there is no competition among different economic classes. The single ideology serves the interests of the single class. Actual process of elections, therefore, is within the different units of the Party organisation. Once such electoral choice is ensured in elections to governmental institutions, like the legislature, are limited to the Party candidates [sic]. There is no contest between candidates of different parties....[12]

[11] p. 87.
[12] p. 87.

For the same reason all this claptrap of countervailing institutions, of checks and balances, of separation of powers which mars bourgeois democracies is done away with:

> Since the organisation of power is based upon strong commitment to [a] single ideology, there is no apprehension about concentration of power. State power is vested in the representative bodies at each level of the State organisation. Representative bodies have all the powers, at least formally, and it is [sic] not shared by the executive and judicial branches of the government....[13]

'Strong commitment to [a] single ideology' is put in a fashion that would make it seem to be a voluntary commitment by the citizenry at large! And those bodies elected in that way, special to socialist states, become '*representative* bodies'! Eliminating even the '*apprehension* of concentration of power'!

What holds for notions such as separation of powers, holds, a fortiori, for an institution such as the judiciary. The whole populace having committed itself to that ideology, the ideology having found in the party an instrument for its realization, the party having ensured democracy within itself, the whole arrangement cannot be put to the mercy of a bourgeois institution such as the judiciary! Hence,

> According to Marxist analysis, law and justice, along with other functions and organs of the State, reflect socio-economic conditions of the society. In a socialist society, therefore, the judiciary also takes part in 'building of socialism and communism'. According 'to this conception, judiciary is the protector of the ideology. Law serves to 'enforce political decisions'. States' policies are more important than law. Instead of protecting the rights and freedom of the individual, law protects the social interests. The State and the party is [sic] the protector of the rights of citizens and the institutions of government represent the interests of the society. Under this system, the judiciary does

[13] p. 87.

> not act as the 'guardian' of the Constitution, as it is in the case of India, or the US.[14]

That leaves the judges free to concentrate on 'the other function' of the judiciary!

> The other function of the judiciary is to ensure that whatever laws and rules are made by the government are enforced properly. The judiciary is a part and parcel of the set of institutions that are responsible for protecting the socialist society and State system. Thus it is the rule enforcement function of the judiciary that is emphasised more.[15]

The logic subsumes the apex of the structure:

> 'There is no such highest court of justice in the socialist State to perform such functions of acting as the 'guardian' of the Constitution (except in Yugoslavia where a court existed). As we have seen above, the socialist State does not advocate 'separation of powers' as is the case with a [sic] Constitution of USA. Only institution [sic] that has powers to decide on question of 'constitutionality' is [sic] the representative assemblies or their presidiums. Representative bodies in Rumania and Hungary set up special bodies to perform this function. Socialist States have an institution called procuracy which supervises the observance of the Constitution in terms of 'socialist legality'. This is a centralised body and is responsible to the representative bodies or their presidiums.'[16]

Vishinsky would acclaim that portrayal! Notice the academic neutrality: *both* 'constitutionality' and 'socialist legality' are put within inverted commas! Notice too the characterization of socialist legislatures and presidia as 'representative bodies'!

As the book is being put out in the 1990s, and that too in Delhi, one cannot entirely ignore the fate which has overtaken

[14] p. 88.
[15] p. 88.
[16] p. 89.

the Great Experiment. But in spite of everything that is known about the states which were founded in its name, our academic deems it fit not to rush to any hasty conclusion about the collapse. He remarks:

> Why did this disintegration take place? Which forces were responsible for it? These are complex questions that will be analysed by commentators. It is enough to note here that the socialist state and form of government has [sic] suffered a serious set back.[17]

In any event, he counsels the student in the end:

> Let us not be carried away by the recent developments but look forward to the positive aspects of the Socialist form of State. With the growth of the Socialist Block as an alternative framework, the consciousness about the socialist concerns was high all over the world. Even the non-socialist block had to bring about changes in its policies and became sensitive to social concerns. The socialist State presented a new picture of hope to the countries of the Third World when they gained independence. The Socialist Block helped maintain a balance in international politics, that helped the states of the Third World in the process of consolidation in the initial phases, when it was needed most. The Soviet-help that India received, both politically and economically, is well known in the context of consolidation of democracy, as well as for the protection of its external frontiers. After the collapse of the USSR as a country and as a balancing force, there are apprehensions about the impact of a Uni-Polar World that has emerged.[18]

Woe to the gods that the Utopia has receded, or rather, 'has suffered a serious setback'!

[17] p. 90.
[18] p. 90.

10

Insinuate falsehood, explain away the truth

The closer one gets to Delhi, or the greater the chances that the student would have been exposed to general information, the more delusive these propagandists are. But the 'Party Line' they hawk remains the same: there is no such thing as Hinduism, it is Brahmanism; Brahmanism equals intolerance and persecution – of Buddhists, Jains, and of course the Shudras; Islam equals peace, equality, brotherhood, the ascent towards monotheism; the Left, means equality, freedom and everything nice; Revolution means the rule of Workers and Peasants!

'The Brahmanical reaction began as a result of the policy of Ashoka,' says one of the more important of these 'eminent historians', R.S. Sharma in *Ancient India,* the NCERT textbook for Class XI students.[1] 'There is no doubt that Ashoka adopted a tolerant policy and asked the people to respect even the brahmanas. But he prohibited the killing of animals and birds, and derided superficial rituals performed by women. This naturally affected the income of the brahmanas. The anti-sacrifice attitude of Buddhism and of Ashoka naturally brought loss to the brahmanas, who lived on the gifts made to them

[1] National Council of Educational Research and Training, Delhi, 1996.

in various kinds of sacrifices. Hence, in spite of the tolerant policy of Ashoka, the brahmanas developed some kind of an antipathy to him. Obviously they were not satisfied with his tolerant policy. They really wanted a policy that would favour them and uphold the existing interests and privileges. Some of the new kingdoms that arose on the ruins of the Maurya empire, were ruled by the brahmanas....'[2]

'Naturally', 'obviously', 'they really wanted', and all that yielding just 'some kind of an antipathy'! How are the propositions 'natural' and 'obvious'? Because they are repeated – thrice even in these few lines! And because they are tautologies: Brahmins lived off gifts made to them at sacrifices; Ashoka prohibited sacrifices; obviously, this would have affected the income of the Brahmins; therefore, naturally, the Brahmins would have had 'some kind of an antipathy' towards Ashoka! What proportion of the income of Brahmins came from gifts made at sacrifices – no word on that. If they really had become that addicted to sacrifices, what proportion of the people would have obeyed a prohibition; how, given the primitive modes of communication and transport, given the extremely thin veneer of the state's presence 2,300 years ago, how Ashoka would have had his prohibition enforced – no word on that either. But 'obviously', 'naturally', 'really', it is!

Evidence apart, notice the denunciation-by-juxtaposition. Hinduism equals 'Brahmanism'. Brahmins are fixated on their incomes. Incomes come from sacrifices. Hence, the 'antipathy' to Ashoka is inherent in Brahmanism-equals-Hinduism. And what about the destruction by Islamic invaders and zealots of every Buddhist structure in sight – in India, of course, but also in Central Asia and Afghanistan? R.S. Sharma has all of two sentences on that:

> For their riches the monasteries came to be coveted by the Turkish invaders. They became special targets of the invaders'

[2] R.S. Sharma, *Ancient India*, NCERT, New Delhi, 1996, p. 112.

greed. The Turks killed a large number of Buddhist monks in Nalanda, although some of the monks managed to escape to Nepal and Tibet.[3]

Full stop! First, by attributing the destruction to the usual explanation – 'the economic motive' – this 'eminent historian' glides over the fundamental religious impulse which spurred the Turk – Buddhism had become synonymous with idolatry in spite of the Buddha, and Islam obligated the believer to destroy the places of worship of other religions, in particular to pulverize their idols. Second, by gliding over this basic belief, the eminent historian puts the Turk at par with the Brahmin – the former was acting out of his greed just as the latter had done before him: QED!

And invariably there is another kind of 'balancing' also. These two sentences about the Turks covering three lines in the textbook are preceded by an entire paragraph, six times the length, about the persecution of Buddhists by Hindu rulers! And in that paragraph the motivation of the Hindu rulers is entirely religious!

Now, it is not that this historian erases the internal corruption which had sapped Buddhism. The Buddhist monks had got cut off from the mainstream of the people's life, he says – 'they gave up Pali, the language of the people, and took to Sanskrit, the language of the intellectuals.' They took to idol worship. The rich offerings of devotees supplemented by royal grants led the monks to adopt the easy life – and then there were women in monasteries: all in all, the monasteries became 'centres of corrupt practices which Gautama Buddha had strictly prohibited':[4] another of those unfortunate 'failures in implementation' – like Stalin's massacres in the case of Marxism-Leninism perhaps?

[3] Ibid., p. 78.
[4] Ibid., pp. 121–22.

But even in regard to this degeneration, guess who is to blame, guess what this degeneration was? 'We find that in the beginning every religion is inspired by the spirit of reform,' the historian tells us, 'but eventually it succumbs to rituals and ceremonies it originally denounced. Buddhism underwent a similar metamorphosis. *It became a victim to the evils of brahmanism against which it had fought in the beginning.*'[5] Hence: the original seed of evil is in 'brahmanism', indeed it is evil per se; and Buddhism lost out because it fell back into that cesspool... The standard mode of argument on every controversy today: for 150 years, missionaries denounced Hinduism on the charge that it demarcates people by caste, they exalted Christianity for exorcising caste from among its followers; and now, when they fear that their flock is deserting them because they have in fact continued all those distinctions – separate pews for the lower castes, few OBCs in the hierarchy, etc., – and they must demand reservations for 'Dalit Christians', a category they were saying did not exist by definition, guess who is to blame: it is all the result of the enveloping Hinduism, they allege!

The same 'line' is peddled by Sharma's comradely historian, Satish Chandra, in his companion NCERT textbook, for Class XI students, titled *Medieval India*.[6] Here also we learn that 'not only were the tenets of Buddhism and Jainism challenged at the intellectual level, there was on occasions outbreak of violence and forcible occupation of Buddhist and Jain temples.' Satish Chandra also talks of the 'internal developments in Buddhism' – the reversion to speculation about metaphysical questions, to the recitation of mantras, the relapse into mysticism, to secret rites, etc. The sum total of it all? 'Thus,' says Satish Chandra, 'Buddhism did not so much

[5] Ibid., p. 78.

[6] National Council of Educational Research and Training, New Delhi, 1996.

decline, as *it assumed forms which made it indistinguishable from Hinduism*!'[7]

In a word, both corruption and evil on the one hand and exploitation on the other are germane to, they are inherent in, Hinduism: Hinduism is Brahmanism; Brahmanism is that 'ism' which serves the interests of the Brahmins; these interests can only be served by the exploitation and oppression of people of lower castes. Hence, Hinduism is necessarily an arrangement for the exploitation and oppression of the mass of people. QED!

By contrast, the aggression, the butchery, the devastations committed by Islamic rulers are sanitized through a three-layered filter. First, the devastation is attributed to individuals and not the religion. Among individuals, it is made out that just a few individuals – a few isolated exceptions – indulged in it. Third, that they committed aggression, destroyed temples, pulverized idols, not because of some religious belief but because, being rulers, they had to put down their opponents who happened to be Hindus; and because they were motivated by mundane considerations like greed for the riches of temples, the need to establish political sway over the conquered territory, etc.

Thus Class XI students reading Satish Chandra's *Medieval India* learn that 'in the early phase of the conquest many cities were sacked and temples formed a special target *partly to justify the conquest and partly to seize the fabulous treasures they were supposed to contain.* During this period, a number of Hindu temples were converted into mosques....'[8] Allah forbid that Islam might have had something to do with any of this!

Satish Chandra goes on to gild the shariat itself! He says, 'Their policy towards temples and places of worship of the Hindus, Jains, etc., rested on the Muslim law (*Sharia*) which

[7] Satish Chandra, *Medieval India,* NCERT, New Delhi, 1996, p. 32.
[8] Ibid., p. 85.

forbade new places of worship being built "in opposition to Islam". But it allowed the repair of old temples "since buildings cannot last for ever". This meant that there was no ban on erecting temples in the villages since *there were no practices of Islam there.* Similarly temples could be built within the privacy of homes. But this liberal policy was not followed in times of war. Thus the enemies of Islam, whether human beings or Gods, were fought and destroyed. In times of peace, however, within the Turkish territories and in those areas where the *rajas* had submitted to the Muslim rule, the Hindus practiced their religion openly and ostentatiously.'[9]

Notice the sleight of hand. The repair of temples is allowed! Temples can be constructed in villages! Temples can be constructed 'within the privacy of homes'! Thus 'liberal policy' is the norm which is departed from only in times of war! And the ones who are fought and destroyed at such times are in any case 'the enemies of Islam'! In times of peace, which are the times that prevailed normally, the norm prevails – that is, 'the Hindus practice their religion openly and ostentatiously!'

Each of these assertions is a blatant falsehood. But these historians, having, through their control of institutions, set the standards of intellectual correctness, the one who questions the falsehoods, even though he does so by citing the writings of the best known Islamic historians of those very times, he is the one who is in the wrong.

Satish Chandra continues. 'Despite the pressure of a section of the orthodox theologians, this policy of broad toleration was maintained during the Sultanate,' he says, 'though with occasional lapses.'[10] Three insinuations in that brief sentence: first, that the pressure for aggression came only from theologians, only from orthodox theologians, only from a section of the orthodox theologians; the policy during sultanate was of 'broad

[9] Ibid., p. 85.
[10] Ibid., pp. 85–86.

toleration'; third, that such aggression as took place was one of those 'occasional lapses'.

And then the customary balancing: 'sometimes, prisoners of war were converted, or criminals exempted from punishment if they accepted Islam,' says Satish Chandra. 'Firuz executed a Brahmin for abusing the Prophet of Islam [an assertion which is itself belied by the contemporary accounts – the Brahmin was executed, not for abusing the Prophet of Islam but, as we shall see, for not converting to Islam and stopping the observances of his own religion]. On the other hand, there were some instances of conversion of Muslims to Hinduism. Thus, Chaitanya, the great Vaishnava reformer, converted a number of Muslims. The theologians, of course, considered apostasy from Islam to be a capital crime.'[11]

How many did Chaitanya convert? And how does that number compare with the lakhs upon lakhs of Hindus whose conversion the Muslim historians of the time celebrated? Do only 'theologians' consider apostasy from Islam to be a capital crime? Is that not something mandated by the Prophet himself? Do hadis after hadis not recount how the Prophet himself dealt with the persons who, having accepted Islam, went back to their traditional observances? Does Allah Himself not command,

> Then, if they turn their backs, take them, and slay them wherever you find them.[12]

Did the Prophet leave any doubt about the duty of believers when he said, 'Whoever changes his Islamic religion, kill him'?[13] And does hadis after hadis not testify that the Prophet enforced this injunction? Recall what happened to members of the tribe of Ukl. Some persons from the tribe came to the Prophet and embraced Islam. The climate of Medina did not

[11] Ibid., p. 86.
[12] Quran, 4.91.
[13] *Sahih Bukhari,* 84.57.

suit them. The Prophet ordered them to go to the herd of milch camel and drink the milk and urine as medicine. After recovering from their illness, they reverted from Islam, killed the shepherd and ran off with the camels. The Prophet had them caught. He then ordered their hands and legs to be cut off, their eyes to be branded with heated pieces of iron. He ordered that the cut hands and legs should not be cauterized so that they bleed to death. 'And when they asked for water to drink,' records the hadis, 'they were not given water.'[14]

The Prophet having himself acted and commanded thus is that not the Sunnah which it is mandatory for every Muslim to follow? On the other hand, is there any injunction to that effect in any Hindu text? Is there any Hindu religious teacher who acted that way towards those who chose some other religion? Have the Hindus honoured, to say nothing of following any of their saints on the ground that he acted that way? But parity it is!

And in regard to the killing of that Brahmin which our eminent historian Satish Chandra attributes to the Brahmin having abused the Prophet of Islam – the *Tarikh-i-Firuz Shahi* of Shamsu'd-Din bin Siraju'd-Din, the courtier of Firuz Shah himself, describes the execution as follows:

> A report was brought to the Sultan that there was in Delhi an old Brahman *(zunar dar)* who persisted in publicly performing the worship of idols in his house; and that people of the city, both Musulmans and Hindus, used to resort to his house to worship the idol. The Brahman had constructed a wooden tablet (*muhrak*), which was covered within and without with paintings of demons and other objects.... An order was accordingly given that the Brahman, with his tablet, should be brought into the presence of the Sultan at Firozabad. The judges and doctors and elders and lawyers were summoned, and the case of the Brahman was submitted for their opinion.

[14] *Sahih Bukhari,* 82.794–97; *Sahih Muslim,* 4130–37.

> Their reply was that the provisions of the Law were clear: the Brahman must either become a Musulman or be burned. The true faith was declared to the Brahman, and the right course pointed out, but he refused to accept it. Orders were given for raising a pile of faggots before the door of the *darbar*. The Brahman was tied hand and foot and cast into it; the tablet was thrown on top and the pile was lighted. The writer of this book was present at the *darbar* and witnessed the execution. The tablet of the Brahman was lighted in two places, at his head and at his feet; the wood was dry, and the fire first reached his feet, and drew from him a cry, but the flames quickly enveloped his head and consumed him. Behold the Sultan's strict adherence to law and rectitude, how he would not deviate in the least from its decrees!

'On the whole,' says Satish Chandra, 'conversions to Islam were not effected with the strength of the sword. If that was so, the Hindu population of the Delhi region would have been the first to be converted. The Muslim rulers had realised that the Hindu faith was too strong to be destroyed by force. Shaikh Nizamuddin Auliya, the famous Sufi saint of Delhi, observed, "Some Hindus know that Islam is a true religion but they do not embrace Islam." Barani also says that attempt to use force had no effect on the Hindus.'[15]

Satish Chandra's explanation for conversions is as follows: 'Conversions to Islam were due to political gains or economic advantages, or [to] improve one's social position. Sometimes when an important ruler or a tribal chief converted, his example was followed by his subjects.' Satish Chandra says that sometimes 'Sufi saints' also played a role, 'though they were generally unconcerned with conversions, and welcomed both the Hindus and Muslims to their discourses' – if only this eminent historian were to read the accounts of these Sufis, he would learn how they acted as the advance scouts of the armies

[15] Satish Chandra, op. cit., p. 86.

of Islam! Hence Satish Chandra's exculpatory conclusion: 'conversions were thus due to personal, political, and in some cases, to regional factors, as in the Punjab, East Bengal etc.'[16] How do these assertions compare with what Islamic historians themselves said at that time? What was the extent according to them of these 'occasional lapses'? Most important, what did they say was the motivation which spurred the rulers of the time?

[16] Satish Chandra, op. cit., p. 86.

11

Were all these authors also communalists?

'There can be no doubt that the fall of Buddhism in India was due to the invasions of the Musalmans,' writes the author. 'Islam came out as the enemy of the "*But*". The word "*But*", as everybody knows, is an Arabic word and means an idol. Not many people, however, know that the derivation of the word "*But*" is the Arabic corruption of Buddha. Thus the origin of the word indicates that in the Moslem mind idol worship had come to be identified with the religion of the Buddha. To the Muslims, they were one and the same thing. The mission to break the idols thus became the mission to destroy Buddhism. Islam destroyed Buddhism not only in India but wherever it went. Before Islam came into being Buddhism was the religion of Bactria, Parthia, Afghanistan, Gandhar and Chinese Turkestan, as it was of the whole of Asia....'

A communal historian of the RSS school?

But Islam struck at Hinduism also. How is it that it was able to fell Buddhism in India but not Hinduism? Hinduism had state patronage, says the author. The Buddhists were so persecuted by the 'Brahmanic rulers', he writes, that, when Islam came, they converted to Islam: this swelled the ranks of Muslims but in the same stroke drained those of Buddhism. But the far more important cause was that while the Muslim invaders butchered both – Brahmins as well as Buddhist monks – the nature of the priesthood in the case of the two religions was different – 'and the difference is so great that it contains the whole reason why Brahmanism survived the attack of Islam and why Buddhism did not.'

For the Hindus, every Brahmin was a potential priest. No ordination was mandated. Neither was anything else. Every household carried on rituals – oblations, recitation of particular mantras, pilgrimages – each Brahmin family made memorizing some Veda its very purpose.... By contrast, Buddhism had instituted ordination, particular training, etc., for its priestly class. Thus, when the invaders massacred Brahmins, Hinduism continued. But when they massacred the Buddhist monks, the religion itself was killed.

Describing the massacres of the latter and the destruction of their viharas, universities, places of worship, the author writes:

> The Musalman invaders sacked the Buddhist Universities of Nalanda, Vikramshila, Jagaddala, Odantapuri to name only a few. They raised to the ground Buddhist monasteries with which the country was studded. The monks fled away in thousands to Nepal, Tibet and other places outside India. A very large number were killed outright by the Muslim commanders. How the Buddhist priesthood perished by the sword of the Muslim invaders has been recorded by the Muslim historians themselves. Summarising the evidence relating to the slaughter of the Buddhist Monks perpetrated by the Musalman General in the course of his invasion of Bihar in 1197 AD, Mr Vincent Smith says, '....Great quantities of plunder were obtained, and the slaughter of the "shaven headed Brahmans", that is to say the Buddhist monks, was so thoroughly completed, that when the victor sought for someone capable of explaining the contents of the books in the libraries of the monasteries, not a living man could be found who was able to read them.' 'It was discovered, we are told, that the whole of that fortress and city was a college, and in the Hindi tongue they call a college Bihar.'

> Such was the slaughter of the Buddhist priesthood perpetrated by the Islamic invaders. The axe was struck at the very root. For by killing the Buddhist priesthood, Islam killed Buddhism. This was the greatest disaster that befell the religion of the Buddha in India....

The writer? B.R. Ambedkar.[1]

But today the fashion is to ascribe the extinction of Buddhism to the persecution of Buddhists by Hindus, to the destruction of their temples by the Hindus. One point is that the Marxist historians who have been perpetrating this falsehood have not been able to produce even an iota of evidence to substantiate the concoction. In one typical instance, Romila Thapar had cited three inscriptions. The indefatigable Sita Ram Goel looked them up. Two of these turned out to have absolutely no connection with Buddhist viharas or their destruction, and the one that did deal with an object being destroyed had been held by authorities to have been a concoction; in any event, it told a story which was as different from what the historian had insinuated as day from night.

Some Jain priests had taken over a place where a Shivalinga was worshipped; the Shaivite priests had asked them to vacate the place; the Jain priests had said they would do so if the Shaivites could perform a miracle; the miracle had been performed; the Shaivite priests had thereupon reoccupied the place and reinstalled their idol; the case had been referred to the Jain king who ruled over the area, and he had upheld what the Shaivites had done. Goel repeatedly asked the historian to point to any additional evidence or to elucidate how the latter had suppressed the import that the inscription in its entirety conveyed. He waited in vain.

Marxists cite only two other instances of Hindus having

[1] B.R. Ambedkar, 'The decline and fall of Buddhism,' *Dr Babasaheb Ambedkar: Writings and Speeches,* Volume III, Government of Maharashtra, 1987, pp. 229–38.

destroyed Buddhist temples. These too, it turns out, yield to completely contrary explanations. Again Marxists have been asked repeatedly to explain the construction they have been circulating – to no avail. Equally important, Sita Ram Goel invited them to cite any Hindu text which orders Hindus to break the places of worship of other religions – as the Bible does, as a pile of Islamic manuals does. He asked them to name a single person who has been honoured by the Hindus because he broke such places – the way Islamic historians and lore have glorified every Muslim ruler and invader who did so. A snooty silence has been the only response.[2]

But I am on the other point. Once they had occupied academic bodies, once they had captured universities and thereby determined what will be taught, which books will be prescribed, what questions would be asked, what answers will be acceptable, these historians came to decide what history had actually been! As it suits their current convenience and politics to make out that Hinduism also has been intolerant, they will glide over what Ambedkar says about the catastrophic effect that Islamic invasions had on Buddhism, they will completely suppress what he said of the nature of these invasions and of Muslim rule in his *Thoughts on Pakistan*,[3] but insist on reproducing his denunciations of 'Brahmanism', and his view that the Buddhist India established by the Mauryas was systematically invaded and finished by Brahmin rulers.

Thus, they suppress facts, they concoct others, they suppress what an author has said on one matter even as they insist that what he has said on another be taken as gospel truth. And when anyone attempts to point out what had in fact happened,

[2] The exchanges are reproduced in Appendix 4 of Sita Ram Goel's *Hindu Temples: What Happened to Them: The Islamic Evidence,* Voice of India, 1993.

[3] B.R. Ambedkar, *Thoughts on Pakistan,* Thacker and Company, Bombay, 1941.

they rise in chorus: a conspiracy to rewrite history, they shout, a plot to distort history, they scream. But they are the ones who have been distorting it in the first place – by suppressing the truth, by planting falsehoods.

And these 'theses' of their's are recent concoctions. Recall the question of the disappearance of Buddhist monasteries. How did the grandfather, so to say, of present Marxist historians, D.D. Kosambi, explain that extinguishing?[4] The original doctrine of the Buddha had degenerated into lamaism, Kosambi wrote. And the monasteries had 'remained tied to the specialised and concentrated long-distance "luxury" trade of which we read in the *Periplus*. This trade died out to be replaced by general and simpler local barter with settled villages. The monasteries, having fulfilled their economic as well as religious function, disappeared too.' And the people lapsed! 'The people whom they had helped lead out of savagery (though plenty of aborigines survive in the Western Ghats to this day), to whom they had given their first common script and common language, use of iron, and of the plough,' Kosambi wrote, 'had never forgotten their primeval cults.'

The standard Marxist 'explanation' – the economic cause, the fulfilling of historical functions and thereafter disappearing, right to the remorse at the lapsing into 'primeval cults'. But today, these 'theses' won't do. Today the need is to make people believe that Hindus too were intolerant, that Hindus also destroyed temples of others…

Or take another figure – one saturated with our history, culture, religion. He also wrote of that region – Afghanistan and beyond. The people of those areas did not destroy either Buddhism or the structures associated with it, he wrote, till one particular thing happened. What was this? He recounted:

[4] For the following, D.D. Kosambi, *Myth and Reality,* Popular Prakashan, Bombay, 1962, 1983 reprint, p. 100.

> In very ancient times this Turkish race repeatedly conquered the western provinces of India and founded extensive kingdoms. They were Buddhists, or would turn Buddhists after occupying Indian territory. In the ancient history of Kashmir there is mention of these famous Turkish emperors – Hushka, Yushka, and Kanishka. It was this Kanishka who founded the Northern School of Buddhism called Mahayana. Long after, the majority of them took to Muhammadanism and completely devastated the chief Buddhistic seats of Central Asia such as Kandhar and Kabul. Before their conversion to Muhammadanism they used to imbibe the learning and culture of the countries they conquered, and by assimilating the culture of other countries would try to propagate civilisation. But ever since they became Muhammadans, they have only the instinct of war left in them; they have not got the least vestige of learning and culture; on the contrary, the countries that come under their sway gradually have their civilisation extinguished. In many places of modern Afghanistan and Kandhar etc., there yet exist wonderful Stupas, monasteries, temples and gigantic statues built by their Buddhist ancestors. As a result of Turkish admixture and their conversion to Muhammadanism, those temples etc. are almost in ruins, and the present Afghans and allied races have grown so uncivilised and illiterate that, far from imitating those ancient works of architecture, they believe them to be the creation of super-natural spirits like the Jinn etc....

The author? The very one the secularists have tried to appropriate: Swami Vivekananda.

And look at the finesse of these historians. They maintain that such facts and narratives must be swept under the carpet in the interest of national integration: recalling them will offend Muslims, they say, doing so will sow rancour against Muslims in the minds of Hindus, they say. Simultaneously, they insist on concocting the myth of Hindus destroying Buddhist temples. Will that concoction not distance Buddhists from Hindus? Will that narrative, specially when it does not have the slightest basis in fact, not embitter Hindus?

Swamiji focussed on another factor about which we hear little today: internal decay. The Buddha – like Gandhiji in our times – taught us first and last to alter our conduct, to realize through practice the insights he had attained. But that is the last thing the people want to do, they want soporifics: a few words to chant, a pilgrimage, an idol which may deliver them from the consequences of what they have done. The people walked out on the Buddha's austere teaching – for it sternly ruled out props. No external suppression, etc., were needed to wean them away: people are deserting Gandhiji for the same reason today – is any violence or conspiracy at work?

The religion became monk- and monastery-centric. And these decayed as closed groups and institutions invariably do. Ambedkar himself alludes to this factor – though he puts even this aspect of the decay to the ravages of Islam. After the decimation of monks by Muslim invaders, all sorts of persons – married clergy, artisan priests – had to be roped in to take their place. Hence the inevitable result. Ambedkar writes: 'It is obvious that this new Buddhist priesthood had neither dignity nor learning and were a poor match for the rival, the Brahmins whose cunning was not unequal to their learning.'

Swami Vivekananda, Sri Aurobindo and others who had reflected deeply on the course of the religious evolution of our people, focussed on the condition to which Buddhist monasteries had been reduced by themselves. The people had already departed from the pristine teaching of the Buddha, Swamiji pointed out: the Buddha had taught no God, no ruler of the universe, but the people, being ignorant and in need of sedatives, 'brought their gods, and devils, and hobgoblins out again, and a tremendous hotchpotch was made of Buddhism in India'. Buddhism itself took on these characters: and the growth that we ascribe to the marvelous personality of the Buddha and to the excellence of his teaching, Swami Vivekananda said, was due in fact 'to the temples which were built, the idols that were erected, and the gorgeous ceremonials that were put before the nation'.[5] Soon the 'wonderful moral strength' of the original message was lost 'and what remained of it became full of superstitions and ceremonials, a hundred times cruder than those it intended to suppress', of practices which were 'equally bad, unclean, and immoral....'

Swami Vivekananda regarded the Buddha as 'the living embodiment of Vedanta'. He always spoke of the Buddha in superlatives. For that very reason, Swami Vivekananda raged all the more at what Buddhism became: 'It became a mass of corruption of which I cannot speak before this audience....;' 'I have neither the time nor the inclination to describe to you the hideousness that came in the wake of Buddhism. The most hideous ceremonies, the most horrible, the most obscene books that human hands ever wrote or the human brain ever conceived, the most bestial forms that ever passed under the name of religion, have all been the creation of degraded Buddhism....'[6]

With reform as his life's mission, Swami Vivekananda reflected deeply on the flaws which enfeebled Buddhism, and his insights hold lessons for us to this day. Every reform movement, he said, necessarily stresses negative elements. But if it goes on stressing only the negative, it soon peters out. After the Buddha, his followers kept emphasizing the negative, when the people wanted the positive that would help lift them.

'Every movement triumphs,' he wrote, 'by dint of some unusual characteristic, and when it falls, that point of pride becomes its chief element of weakness.' And in the case of Buddhism, he said, it was the monastic order. This gave it an organizational impetus, but soon consequences of the opposite kind took over. Instituting the monastic order, he said, had 'the evil effect of making the very robe of the monk honoured',

[5] Swami Vivekananda, *Collected Works,* for instance, Volume II, p. 139; Volume III, pp. 216–17.

[6] *Collected Works,* for instance, Volume III, p. 265.

instead of making reverence contingent on conduct. 'Then these monasteries became rich,' he recalled, 'the real cause of the downfall is here.... some containing a hundred thousand monks, sometimes twenty thousand monks in one building – huge, gigantic buildings...' On the one hand this fomented corruption within, it encoiled the movement in organizational problems. On the other it drained society of the best persons.[7]

From its very inception, the monastic order had institutionalized inequality of men and women even in sanyasa, Swami Vivekananda pointed out. 'Then gradually,' he recalled, 'the corruption known as *Vamachara* (unrestrained mixing with women in the name of religion) crept in and ruined Buddhism. Such diabolical rites are not to be met with in any modern Tantra....'[8]

Whereas the Buddha had counselled that we shun metaphysical speculations and philosophical conundrums – as these would only pull us away from practice – Buddhist monks and scholars lost themselves in arcane debates about these very questions.[9] The consequence was immediate: 'By becoming too philosophic,' Swami Vivekananda explained, 'they lost much of their breadth of heart.'

Sri Aurobindo alludes to another factor, an inherent incompatibility. He writes of 'the exclusive trenchancy of its [Buddhism's] intellectual, ethical and spiritual positions,' and of how 'its trenchant affirmations and still more exclusive

[7] *Collected Works,* for instance, Volume III, pp. 533–34; Volume V, p. 230.

[8] *Collected Works,* for instance, Volume IV, p. 326; Volume V, p. 317; Volume VI, pp. 224–25; Volume VII, pp. 119, 215–16.

[9] Hence a truth in Kosambi's observation, but in the sense opposite to the one he intended: Shankara's refutations show that Shankara knew nothing of Buddha's original doctrine, Kosambi asserted [Kosambi, op. cit., p. 14]; Shankara was refuting the doctrines which were being put forth by the Buddhists in his time. And *these* had nothing to do with the original teaching of the Buddha.

negations could not be made sufficiently compatible with the native flexibility, many-sided susceptibility and rich synthetic turn of the Indian religious consciousness; it was a high creed but not plastic enough to hold the heart of the people...'[10]

We find in such factors a complete explanation for the evaporation of Buddhism. But we will find few of them in the secularist discourse today. Because their purpose is served by one 'thesis' alone: Hindus crushed Buddhists, Hindus demolished their temples...

In regard to matter after critical matter – the Aryan-Dravidian divide, the nature of Islamic invasions, the nature of Islamic rule, the character of the freedom struggle – we find this trait – *suppresso veri, suggesto falsi. This* is the real scandal of history writing in the last thirty years. And it has been possible for these 'eminent historians' to perpetrate it because they acquired control of institutions like the ICHR. To undo the falsehood, the control has to be undone.

[10] Sri Aurobindo, *The Foundations of Indian Culture,* Sri Aurobindo Ashram, Pondicherry, 1968, pp. 75, 160–61, 192–93.

12

The policy of 'broad toleration'!

'Despite the pressure of a section of the orthodox theologians,' the eminent historian Satish Chandra assures the Class XI student, 'this policy of broad toleration was maintained during the Sultanate.' Really?

What policy do we find narrated in the accounts of Islamic historians of the time, in the accounts, that is, of the very authorities on whose books our distinguished historians would have to construct their 'theses'? What events do they celebrate? What do those Islamic authorities say were the motives which impelled the rulers of the time?

Fortunately, the intrepid Sita Ram Goel has set out four hundred pages of extracts and evidence from the leading Islamic historians of those days in his decisive work, *Hindu Temples: What Happened to Them, The Islamic Evidence,* Volume II.[1] Even a small sample from that mountain of evidence will be sufficient to indicate how much it is that our eminent historians conceal.

Sultan Jalalu'd-Din Khalji (1290–96): *Tarikh-i-Firuz Shahi* of Ziau'd-Din Barani (born 1285–86):

> *Jhain (Rajasthan):* 'In the year AH 689 (AD 1290), the Sultan led an army to Rantambhor.... He took....Jhain, destroyed the idol temples, and broke and burned the idols....'

[1] Voice of India, Delhi, 1993. All citations in this chapter are taken with his permission from Goel's meticulous and unimpeachable study.

Vidisha (Madhya Pradesh): 'Alau'd-din at this time held the territory of Karra, and with the permission of the Sultan he marched to Bhailsan (Bhilsa). He captured some bronze idols which the Hindus worshipped and sent them on carts with a variety of rich booty as presents to the Sultan. The idols were laid before the Badaun gate for true believers to tread upon…' (Report to the same effect in Nizamu'd-Din Ahmad bin Muhammad Muqim al-Harbi, Tabqat-i-Akbari.)

Sultan Alau'd-Din Khalji (1296–1316), in *Tarikh-i-Firuz Shahi*, op. cit.:

Somnath (Gujarat): 'At the beginning of the third year of the reign, Ulugh Khan and Nusrat Khan, with their amirs and generals, and a large army marched against Gujarat.... All Gujarat became a prey to the invaders, and the idol, which after the victory of Sultan Mahmud and his destruction of (the idol) of Manat, the Brahmans had set up under the name of Somanat, for the worship of the Hindus, was carried to Delhi where it was laid for the people to tread upon…' (Report to the same effect in *Tabqat-i-Akbari,* op. cit., and Mulla Abdul Qadir Badauni's *Muntakhabu't-Tawarikh;* the latter also mentions that at the site of the temple a mosque was constructed.)

Sultan Firuz Shah Tughlaq (1351–88): *Tarikh-i-Firuz Shahi* of Shamsu'd-Din bin Siraju'd-Din, a courtier of Firuz Shah:

Puri (Orissa): 'After the hunt was over, the Sultan directed his attention to the Rai of Jajnagar, and entering the palace where he dwelt he found many fine buildings. It is reported that inside the Rai's fort, there was a stone idol which the infidels called Jagannath, and to which they paid their devotions. Sultan Firoz, in emulation of Mahmud Subuktigin, having rooted up the idol, carried it away to Delhi where he placed it in an ignominious position…'

Jajnagar (Orissa): 'The victorious standards set out from Jaunpur for the destruction of idols, slaughter of the enemies

> of Islam and hunt for elephants near Padamtalav... The Sultan saw Jajnagar which had been praised by all travelers... The troops which had been appointed for the destruction of places around Jajnagar, ended the conceit of the infidels by means of the sword and the spear. Wherever there were temples and idols in that area, they were trampled under the hoofs of the horses of Musalmans.... After obtaining victory and sailing on the sea and destroying the temple of Jagannath and slaughtering the idolaters, the victorious standards started towards Delhi....'

This achievement in the service of Islam is also narrated in *Sirat-Firuz Shahi* as follows:

> Allah, who is the only true God and has no other emanation, endowed the king of Islam with the strength to destroy this ancient shrine on the eastern sea-coast and to plunge it into the sea, and after its destruction, he ordered the nose of the image of Jagannath to be perforated and disgraced it by casting it down on the ground. They dug out other idols, which were worshipped by the polytheists in the kingdom of Jajnagar, and overthrew them as they did the image of Jagannath, for being laid in front of the mosques along the path of the Sunnis and way of the *musallis* (the multitude who offer prayers) and stretched them in front of the portals of every mosque, so that the body and sides of the images may be trampled at the time of ascent and descent, entrance and exit, by the shoes on the feet of the Muslims.

In *Futuhat-i-Firuz Shahi* written by Sultan Firuz Shah Tughlaq himself, he records how he decreed that the names and titles of 'those sovereigns of Islam under whose happy fortune and favour infidel countries had been conquered, whose banners had waved over many a land, under whom idol-temples had been demolished, and mosques and pulpits built and exalted' should be recited in the *khutba,* and prayers offered for the remission of their sins.

On the steps he took for erasing idolatry in Delhi and its surroundings, Sultan Firuz Shah records,

> The Hindus and idol-worshippers had agreed to pay the money for toleration (*zar-i-zimmtya*) and had consented to the poll-tax (*jizya*) in return for which they and their families enjoyed security. These people now erected new idol-temples in the city and the environs in opposition to the Law of the Prophet which declared that such temples are not to be tolerated. Under divine guidance I destroyed these edifices and I killed those leaders of infidelity who seduced others into error, and the lower orders I subjected to stripes and chastisement, until this abuse was entirely abolished. The following is an instance: In the village of Maluh there is a tank which they call *kund* (tank). Here they had built idol-temples and on certain days the Hindus were accustomed to proceed thither on horseback, and wearing arms. Their women and children also went out in palankins and carts. There they assembled in thousands and performed idol-worship.... When intelligence of this came to my ears my religious feelings prompted me at once to put a stop to this scandal and offence to the religion of Islam. On the day of the assembly I went there in person and I ordered that the leaders of these people and the promoters of this abomination should be put to death. I forbade the infliction of any severe punishments on Hindus in general, but I destroyed their idol-temples, and instead thereof raised mosques. I founded two flourishing towns (*kasba*), one called Tughlikpur, the other Salarpur. Where infidels and idolaters worshipped idols, Musulmans now, by God's mercy, perform their devotions to the true God. Praises of God and the summons to prayer are now heard there, and that place which was formerly the home of the infidels has become the habitation of the faithful, who there repeat their creed and offer up their praises to God.... Information was brought to me that some Hindus had erected a new idol temple in the village of Salihpur, and were performing worship to their idols. I sent some persons there to destroy the idol temple, and put a stop to their pernicious incitements to error.

And about neighbouring Gohana, Firuz Shah narrates,

> *Gohana (Haryana):* 'Some Hindus had erected a new idol-temple in the village of Kohana, and the idolaters used to assemble there and perform their idolatrous rites. These people were seized and brought before me. I ordered that the perverse conduct of the leaders of this wickedness should be publicly proclaimed, and that they should be put to death before the gate of the palace. I also ordered that the infidel books, the idols, and the vessels used in their worship, which had been taken with them, should all be publicly burnt. The others were restrained by threats and punishments, as a warning to all men, that no *zimmi* could follow such wicked practices in a Musulman country.'

In his *Tarikh-i-Firishta,* Muhammad Qasim Hindu Shah Firishta gives an account of Sultan Firuz Shah Tughlaq at Nagarkot, Kangra in Himachal Pradesh:

> .... From thence the King marched towards the mountains of Nagarkot, where he was overtaken by a storm of hail and snow. The Raja of Nagarkot, after sustaining some loss, submitted, but was restored to his dominions. The name of Nagarkot was, on this occasion, changed to that of Mahomedabad, in honour of the late king... Some historians state, that Feroze, on this occasion, broke the idols of Nagarkot, and mixing the fragments with pieces of cow's flesh, filled bags with them, and caused them to be tied round the necks of Brahmans, who were then paraded through the camp. It is said, also, that he sent the image of Nowshaba to Mecca, to be thrown on the road, that it might be trodden under foot by the pilgrims, and that he also remitted the sum of 100,000 *tunkas,* to be distributed among the devotees and servants of the temple.

Do the accounts leave any doubt about the motivation which spurred these sultans? Do these glowing and triumphant accounts leave any ground for maintaining that the sultans of Delhi followed a policy of 'broad toleration'?

Sultan Shamsu'd-Din Altutmish (1210–36) in *Tarikh-i-Mubarak Shahi* of Yahya bin Ahmad bin Abdu'llah Sirhindi:

> ....Next he turned towards Ujjain and conquered it, and after demolishing the idol-temple of Mahakal, he uprooted the statue of Bikramajit together with all other statues and images which were placed on pedestals, and brought them to the capital where they were laid before the Jami' Masjid for being trodden under foot by the people. (Reports to the same effect in *Tabqat-i-Akbari,* op. cit., in *Muntakhabu't-Tawarikh,* op. cit., and in *Tarikh-i-Firuz Shahi,* op. cit.)

Sultan Nasiru'd-Din Mahmud Shah Tughlaq *(1389-1412)* in *Tarikh-i-Muhammadi* of Muhammad Bihamad Khani:

> Historians have recorded that in the auspicious year AH 792 (AD 1389–90) Sultan Nasiru'd-Din got founded a city named Muhammadabad, after the name of Prophet Muhammad, at a place known as Kalpi which was a home of the accursed infidels, and he got mosques raised in place of temples for the worship of Allah. He got palaces, tombs and schools constructed, and ended the wicked ways of the infidels, and promoted the *Shariat* of Prophet Muhammad....

Sultan Sikandar Lodi (1489–1517) in Ahmad Yadgar's *Tarikh-i-Shahi:*

> Sultan Sikandar led a very pious life.... Islam was regarded very highly in his reign. The infidels could not muster the courage to worship idols or bathe in the (sacred) streams. During his holy reign, idols were hidden underground. The stone (idol) of Nagarkot, which had misled the (whole) world, was brought and handed over to butchers so that they might weigh meat with it.

Shaykh Rizqu'llah Mushtaqi's *Waqiat-i-Mushtaqi* carries a report to the same effect. It also records the following regarding Sikandar Lodi's pious deeds at Mathura:

He got the temples of the infidels destroyed. No trace of infidelity was left at the place in Mathura where the infidels used to take bath. He got caravansarais constructed so that people could stay there, and also the shops of various professionals such as the butchers, *bawarchis, nanbais* and sweetmeat sellers. If a Hindu went there for bathing even by mistake, he was made to lose his limbs and punished severely. No Hindu could get shaved at that place. No barber would go near a Hindu, whatever be the payment offered....

In *Tabqat-i-Akbari*, op. cit. we have Sultan Sikander Lodi at *Mandrail* (Madhya Pradesh):

Thereafter he himself laid siege to the fort of Mandrail. Those inside the fort surrendered the fort to him after signing a treaty. The Sultan got the temples demolished and mosques erected in their stead.... and then after the rainy season was over, he led an expedition towards the fort of Udit Nagar in AH 912 (AD 1506–07).... Although those inside the fort tried their utmost to seek a pardon, he did not listen to them, and the fort was breached at many points and conquered.... The Sultan thanked Allah in the wake of his victory.... He got the temples demolished and mosques constructed in their stead....

In Abu'llah's *Tarikh-i-Da'udi:* Sultan Sikandar Lodi at Mathura (Uttar Pradesh):

He was so zealous a Musalman that he utterly destroyed diverse places of worship of the infidels, and left not a vestige remaining of them. He entirely ruined the shrines of Mathura, the mine of heathenism, and turned other principal Hindu places of worship into caravansarais and colleges. Their stone images were given to the butchers to serve them as meat-weight, and all the Hindus in Mathura were strictly prohibited from shaving their heads and beards, and performing their ablutions....

And then at Dholpur (Madhya Pradesh):

In that year the Sultan sent Khawas Khan to take possession of the fort of Dhulpur. The Raja of that place advanced to give battle, and daily fighting took place. The instant His Majesty heard of the firm countenance shown by the *rai* of Dhulpur in opposing the royal army, he went there in person; but on his arrival near Dhulpur, the *rai* made up his mind to fly without fighting.... He (Sikandar) offered up suitable thanksgiving for his success, and the royal troops spoiled and plundered in all directions, rooting up all the trees of the gardens which shaded Dhulpur to the distance of seven *kos*. Sultan Sikandar stayed there during one month, erected a mosque on the site of an idol-temple, and then set off towards Agra....

Sultan Mahmud bin Ibrahim Sharqi (AD 1440–57): in *Tabqat-i-Akbari*, op. cit.:

After some time he proceeded to Orissa with the intention of *jihad*. He attacked places in the neighbourhood of that province and laid them waste, and destroyed the temples after demolishing them....

Sultan Mahmud Khalji of Malwa (AD 1436–69): in *Tabqat-i-Akbari*, op. cit.:

Chittaurgarh (Rajasthan): 'After he had crossed the river Bhim, he started laying waste the country and capturing its people by sending expeditions towards Chittor every day. He started constructing mosques after demolishing temples. He stayed 2-3 days at every halt.'

Jalalu'd-Din Muhammad Akbar Padshah Ghazi (AD 1556–1605) in *Muntakhabu't-Tawarikh*, op. cit.:

The temple of Nagarkot, which is outside the city, was taken at the very outset.... On this occasion many mountaineers became food for the flashing sword. And that golden umbrella, which was erected on the top of the cupola of the temple, they riddled with arrows.... And black cows, to the number of 200, to which they pay boundless respect, and actually worship, and present to the temple, which they look upon as an asylum, and let loose there, were killed by the Musulmans. And, while arrows and bullets were continually falling like drops of rain, through their zeal and intense hatred of idolatry they filled their shoes full of blood and threw it on the doors and walls of the temple....

And the same sequence was being enacted in the south.

Sultan Alau'd-Din Mujahid Shah Bahmani (AD 1375–78): the account in *Tarikh-i-Firishta*, op. cit.:

Vijayanagar (Karnataka): 'Mujahid Shah, on this occasion, repaired mosques which had been built by the officers of Alla-ood-Deen Khiljy. He broke down many temples of the idolaters, and laid waste the country; after which he hastened to Beejanuggur.... The King drove them before him, and gained the bank of a piece of water, which alone divided him from the citadel, wherein the *Ray* resided. Near this spot was an eminence, on which stood a temple, covered with plates of gold and silver, set with jewels: it was much venerated by the Hindoos, and called, in the language of the country, Puttuk. The King, considering its destruction a religious obligation, ascended the hill, and having razed the edifice, became possessed of the precious metals and jewels therein....'

Sultan Ahmad Shah I Wali Bahmani (AD 1422–35): in *Tarikh-i-Firishta*, op. cit.:

Vijayanagar (Karnataka): 'Ahmud Shah, without waiting to besiege the Hindoo capital, overran the open country; and wherever he went put to death men, women, and children, without mercy, contrary to the compact made between his uncle and predecessor, Mahomed Shah, and the *Rays* of Beejanuggur. Whenever the number of slain amounted to twenty thousand, he halted three days, and made a festival celebration of the bloody event. He broke down, also, the idolatrous temples, and destroyed the colleges of the brahmins. During these operations, a body of five thousand Hindoos, urged by desperation at the destruction of their religious buildings, and at the insults offered to their deities, united in

> taking an oath to sacrifice their lives in an attempt to kill the King, as the author of all their sufferings....'

Sultan Muhammad Shah II Bahmani (AD 1463–82): in *Tarikh-i-Firishta*, op. cit.:

> Komdapalli (Andhra Pradesh): 'The King having gone to view the fort, broke down an idolatrous temple, and killed some brahmins, who officiated at it, with his own hands, as a point of religion. He then gave orders for a mosque to be erected on the foundation of the temple, and ascending a pulpit, repeated a few prayers, distributed alms, and commanded the *Khootba* to be read in his name. Khwaja Mahmood Gawan now represented, that as his Majesty had slain some infidels with his own hands, he might fairly assume the title of *Ghazy*, an appellation of which he was very proud. Mahmood Shah was the first of his race who had slain a brahmin....'

And so on – among the highest piles of rubble in the world of the sacred temples of another religion, among the highest piles of corpses of those venerated by another religion. Yet, in the reckoning of our eminent historians a policy of 'Broad Toleration'! A policy of toleration guided by purely secular motivations!

Having presented voluminous evidence about the destruction of temples, Sita Ram Goel remarks:

> Starting with Al-Biladhuri who wrote in Arabic in the second half of the ninth century, and coming down to Syed Mahmudul Hasan who wrote in English in the fourth decade of the twentieth, we have cited from *eighty* histories spanning a period of more than *twelve hundred years*.. Our citations mention *sixty-one* kings, *sixty-three* military commanders and *fourteen* Sufis who destroyed Hindu temples in *one hundred and fifty-four* localities, big and small, spread from Khurasan in the West to Tripura in the East, and from Transoxiana in the North to Tamil Nadu in the South, over a period of *eleven hundred years*. In most cases the destruction of temples was followed by erection of mosques, *madrasas and khanqahs*, etc., on the temple sites and,

> frequently, with temple materials. Allah was thanked every time for enabling the iconoclast concerned to render service to the religion of Muhammad by means of this pious performance.[2]

And the destructions were not because of a lust for plunder or a determination to impose political hegemony alone. Their impulse was religious – that is, to carry out the command of Allah and to follow the Sunna of the Prophet. Goel correctly observes:

> The destruction of Hindu temples at the hands of Islamised invaders continued for more than eleven hundred years, from the middle of the seventh century to the end of the eighteenth. It took place all over the cradle of Hindu culture, from Sinkiang in the North to Tamil Nadu in the South, and from Seistan in the West to Assam in the East.
>
> All along, the iconoclasts remained convinced that they were putting into practice the highest tenets of their religion. They also saw to it that a record was kept of what they prized as a pious performance. The language of the record speaks for itself. It leaves no doubt that they took immense pride in doing what they did.
>
> It is inconceivable that a constant and consistent behaviour pattern, witnessed for a long time and over a vast area, can be explained except in terms of a settled system of belief which leaves no scope for second thoughts. Looking at the very large number of temples, big and small, destroyed or desecrated or converted into Muslim monuments, economic or political explanations can be only a futile, if not fraudulent, exercise. The explanations are not even plausible.[3]

In an entire chapter – Chapter 16 of his book – Goel recalls instances after instances set out with great pride by the biographers of the Prophet, describing the destruction of temples by the Prophet himself. What the Prophet did

[2] Sita Ram Goel, op. cit., p. 245.

[3] Ibid., p. 255.

is by definition the Sunna – along with the Quran, it is one of the two principal sources in accordance with which every believer must order his conduct. Sita Ram Goel's conclusion is unassailable. He writes:

> Thus the practice of the Prophet or his *Sunnah* vis-a-vis idols and idol-temples was added to prescriptions of the Quran in this respect, and the Islamic theology of iconoclasm stood completed. Ever since, iconoclasm has been a prominent as well a permanent part of the theology of Islam.
>
> Allah had denounced the idols and their worship as abominable. His Prophet got the idols broken or burnt, and their temples destroyed.
>
> The Prophet added a few nuances on his own. He got the sites and materials of pagan temples used in the construction of mosques that replaced them. In many cases, idols were placed on the footsteps of the mosques so that the faithful could trample upon them while entering and coming out of Allah's abodes. These acts, too, became pious precedents and were followed by Islamic invaders wherever they came across idols.[4]

In a word, what was done was no fortuitous 'error'. Allah had decreed that the houses of worship of other religions be destroyed. The Prophet had carried out the command at every occasion on which it had been necessary and prudent to do so. And what the Prophet did is the Sunna, which, alongwith the Quran, is the model on which believers are to order their conduct. That is what these rulers, invaders, and 'saints' did. That is what they and their historians said they were doing.

And that is precisely what our eminent historians conceal.

[4] Ibid., p. 371.

13

The litmus test

The same pattern continues throughout the textbook, *Medieval India,* written by one of the more eminent among these historians, Satish Chandra, and published by the NCERT for Class XI students. 'Thus, there was no atmosphere of confrontation between the Sikhs and the Mughal rulers during this period,' says Satish Chandra. 'Nor was there any systematic persecution of the Hindus, and hence, no occasion for the Sikhs or any group or sect to stand forth as the champion of the Hindus against religious persecution. The occasional conflict between the gurus and the Mughal rulers was personal and political rather than religious. Despite some display of orthodoxy by Shah Jahan at the beginning of his reign and a few acts of intolerance, such as the demolition of 'new' temples, he was not narrow in his outlook which was further tempered towards the end of his reign by the influence of his liberal son, Dara.'[1]

That being the case, what do these eminent historians have to say about what is enshrined in the *Granth Sahib,* about Guru Nanak, and his searing cry:

Khurasan khasmana kiya Hindustanu daraiya
Aapae dosu na deyi karta jamu kari mughlu chadhaiya

[1] Satish Chandra, *Medieval India,* National Council of Educational Research and Training, Delhi, 1996, p. 223.

Aiti maar payi karlande tain ko dardu na ayiya
Karta tu sabhna ka soi
Je sakta sakte kayu mare, taa mani rosu na hoyi
Sakta sihu maare paye vagaye khasme sa pursai
Ratan vigadi vigoye kuttin muiya saar na koyi....

[*Mahla* 1.360]

Having lifted Islam to the head, You have engulfed Hindustan in dread.... Such cruelties have they inflicted, and yet Your mercy remains unmoved.... Should the strong attack the strong, the heart does not burn. But when the strong crush the helpless, surely the One who was to protect them has to be called to account.... O' Lord, these dogs have destroyed this diamond-like Hindustan, (so great is their terror that) no one asks after those who have been killed, and yet You do not pay heed....

What do they say of Guru Nanak's account of the young brides whose youth, jewels, honour have been snatched away by the invaders on the orders of Babar? What of his wail,

Ikna vakhat khuvai ahi iknaha pooja jayi
Chauke vinu hindvandiyan kiyu tike kadhayi nayi
Ramu na kabhu chetiyo huni kahni na mile khudai....

[*Mahla* 1.417]

Hindus have been forbidden to pray at the time of the Muslim's namaz, Hindu society has been left without a bath, without a tilak. Even those who have never uttered 'Ram', even they can get no respite, not even by shouting '*Khuda, Khuda*'.... The few who have survived Babar's jails wail.... The desolation which has come over the land .... The entire races which have been exterminated, which have been humiliated....[2]

[2] The passages are merely illustrative, they can be multiplied many times over. For a comprehensive treatment of the subject see K. P. Agarwal, *Guru Granth Sahib aur Islam*.

The account not of some merely eminent historian, but of Guru Nanak. Not some account written by looking at records of centuries ago, but testimony of the moment, of what Guru Nanak had been witness to himself….

Let us hear these eminent secularists, then declare that this cry of Guru Nanak was a concoction. And that the entire life and campaign of Guru Govind Singh was born of 'personal and political' factors rather than from a profound religious impulse, and that, therefore, all his own explanations, his impassioned, soul-stirring explanations in this regard are that much deception.

Akbar is the epitome of tolerance, Shah Jahan 'despite some display of orthodoxy …. at the beginning of his reign and a few acts of intolerance' remains broad-minded.[3] The only opposition to this liberalism comes from 'orthodox elements'. But here too Satish Chandra executes the 'balancing'. The orthodox elements in question are always of 'the two leading faiths, Hinduism or Islam', together![4] Both sides strive to undo the liberality of the Islamic rulers out of the same mundane motivation – that is, they oppose the liberal policy because it threatens their entrenched interests.

Aurangzeb's orthodoxy cannot, of course, be entirely denied. Therefore, explanations upon explanations – secular explanations! – are invented. 'Later, in the eleventh year of his reign (1669),' remarks Satish Chandra, 'Aurangzeb took a number of measures which have been called puritanical, but many of which were really of economic and social character, and against superstitious beliefs …. Many other regulations of a similar nature, some of a moral character and some to instill a sense of austerity, were issued….'[5]

The destruction of temples upon temples by Aurangzeb

[3] Satish Chandra, op. cit., p. 223.

[4] Ibid., p. 223.

[5] Ibid., pp. 229–30.

naturally comes in for the longest explanations! Firstly, we are told that all that Aurangzeb did was to reiterate the old order of the shariat – that no new temples shall be built, and that this 'order regarding temples was not a new one' – it merely reaffirmed the position which had existed during the sultanate period, the period, remember, of 'broad toleration'! Satish Chandra adds a second explanation: 'In practice, it [the order] left wide latitude to the local officials as to the interpretation of the words "long standing temples".'[6]

A third extenuating circumstance is then invented. Having noted the destruction of temples in Gujarat by Aurangzeb when he was the governor of that province, and having noted his reiteration of the standing order under the shariat, Satish Chandra says, 'however, it does not seem that Aurangzeb's order regarding ban on new temples led to a large scale destruction of temples at the outset of the reign.' It is only when Aurangzeb 'encountered political opposition from a number of quarters, such as the Marathas, Jats etc.,' that he 'seems to have adopted a new stance'. When he now came in 'conflict with local elements', he began to consider it 'legitimate to destroy even longstanding Hindu temples as a measure of punishment and as a warning'.[7] Thus, first, the order was just an old one! Second, the order left wide latitude to the local officials! Third, even this order was not implemented 'at the outset of the reign'! Fourth, it is only when he encountered political opposition and when he came in conflict with local elements that Aurangzeb began to consider it legitimate to destroy Hindu temples! Fifth, this 'new stance' – a mere stance – too is only something which *seems to have been adopted!*

Moreover, Aurangzeb did so, Satish Chandra tells us, because 'he began to look upon temples as centres of spreading subversive ideas, that is ideas which were not acceptable to

[6] Ibid., p. 230.
[7] Ibid., 231.

the orthodox elements. Hence the destruction of the Kashi Vishwanath Temple at Banaras and the temple, at Mathura.' 'The destruction of these temples had a political motivation as well....,' Satish Chandra emphasizes, and continues, 'it was in this context that many temples built in Orissa during the last 10 to 12 years were also destroyed.' And then, 'but it is wrong to think that there were any orders for the general destruction of temples.' Lest anyone come up with citations from contemporary historians, another sentence to explain away what was actually done: 'however, the situation was different during periods of hostilities.'[8]

The general conclusion: what Aurangzeb did 'was a setback to the policy of broad toleration followed by his predecessors'![9] And even he did it for secular reasons! And even though compelled by these reasons, he did it only for the shortest time, for the years marked by hostilities instigated by 'local elements'! And, finally, concludes Satish Chandra, 'it seems that Aurangzeb's zeal for the destruction of temples abated after 1679, for we do not hear of any large scale destruction of temples in the South between 1681 and his death in 1707.'[10]

Yes, Aurangzeb introduced the jazyah, but, cautions Satish Chandra, 'it was not meant to be an economic pressure for forcing Hindus to convert to Islam, for its incidence was to be light.' For this assertion Satish Chandra gives two bits of proof, so to say. First, 'women, children, the disabled, the indigent, that is, those whose income was less than the means of subsistence, were exempted as were those in government service.'[11] How could even Aurangzeb have exacted a tax from those 'whose income was less than the means of subsistence?' And why would he exact a discriminatory and humiliating tax from those who were in government service, that is, from

[8] Ibid.
[9] Ibid.
[10] Ibid.
[11] Ibid. p. 232.

those who were already serving his interests and those of the Islamic State? The second proof that Satish Chandra gives is that 'in fact, only an insignificant section of Hindus changed their religion due to this tax'[12] – but could that not have been because of the firm attachment of Hindus to their faith, because of their tenacity rather than because of the liberality of Aurangzeb?

The jazyah was not meant either to meet 'a difficult financial situation'. Its reimposition was in fact, says Satish Chandra, 'both political and ideological in nature.' Political in the sense that 'it was meant to rally the Muslims for the defence of the State against the Marathas and the Rajputs who were up in arms, and possibly against the Muslim States of Deccan, especially Golconda, which was in alliance with the infidels.'[13] A parity twice over – one, that Aurangzeb was only trying to rally the Muslims just as those opposing him had rallied the Marathas and Rajputs! And, in any case, the ones who were opposing him were 'infidels'!

And what about the 'ideological' impulse? 'Ideological', yes, but the 'ideology' was everything except Islam!

Furthermore, Satish Chandra explains, '*jaziya* was to be collected by honest, God-fearing Muslims who were specially appointed for the purpose and its proceeds were reserved for the *Ulema*.'[14] As the proceeds went to the ulema, there was a secular reason for exacting the tax – it was to be 'a type of bribe for the theologians among whom there was a lot of unemployment', and, second, as the tax was being collected by 'honest, God-fearing Muslims', one can be certain that they were considerate and, like Allah in the Quran, would have never imposed upon anyone a burden which he could not bear!

Some modern writers, Satish Chandra says, are of the

[12] Ibid.
[13] Ibid.
[14] Ibid.

opinion that Aurangzeb's measures were designed to convert India into *Dar-ul-Islam* but, in fact, 'although Aurangzeb considered it legitimate to encourage conversions to Islam, evidence of systematic or large scale attempts at forced conversions is lacking.'[15]

And finally a piece of evidence which is a favourite with the secularists – recall Shrimali in the TV programme: 'Nor were Hindu nobles discriminated against. A recent study has shown that the number of Hindus in the nobility during the second half of Aurangzeb's reign had steadily increased, till the Hindus, including Muslims, formed about one-third of the nobility as against one-fourth under Shah Jahan.'[16] Correspondingly, one can claim on behalf of the British Empire that close to 98 per cent of the titles it conferred – Rai Sahib, Rai Bahadur, Knighthoods and so on – were conferred on Indians! That they were conferred because these Indians were serving the British Empire faithfully, just as Aurangzeb was taking into his nobility those who were serving his purposes faithfully, is a matter of detail by which naturally Class XI students would not like to be confused!

The final assessment of our secularist eminence could not be more empathetic! First, Satish Chandra emphasizes that 'Aurangzeb's religious beliefs could not be considered the basis of his political policies.' Aurangzeb was an 'orthodox Muslim', true; he was 'desirous of upholding the strict letter of the law', true; but he was also a ruler and was 'keen to strengthen and expand the empire'. The former required that he be tough with the Hindus. The latter, on the other hand, required that he retain 'the support of the Hindus to the extent possible'. The two impulses – his religious ideas and beliefs on the one hand and the requirements of empire on the other – sometimes 'led him to adopt contradictory policies which harmed the empire'.[17]

[15] Ibid., pp. 232–33.
[16] Ibid., p. 233.
[17] Ibid.

Our eminent historian then proceeds to give an account of the Marathas, the Jats, the campaigns against Golconda and Bijapur. At every turn he labours to show that the religious impulse did not have much to do with Aurangzeb's attitude towards any of these 'rebellions'. Indeed, Aurangzeb's religious policy must be seen in the context of the rebellions which were challenging his empire, we are told! Thus, Satish Chandra's final conclusion:

> Aurangzeb's religious policy should be seen in the social, economic and political context. Aurangzeb was orthodox in his outlook and tried to remain within the framework of the Islamic law. But this law was developed outside India in vastly dissimilar situations, and could hardly be applied rigidly to India. His failure to respect the susceptibilities of his non-Muslim subjects on many occasions, his adherence to the time-worn policy towards temples and re-imposition of *jizyah* as laid down by the Islamic law did not help him to rally the Muslims to his side or generate a greater sense of loyalty towards a state based on Islamic law. On the other hand, it alienated segments of the Hindus and strengthened the hands of those sections which were opposed to the Mughal empire for political or other reasons. By itself, religion was not a point at issue. *Jizyah* was scrapped within half a dozen years of Aurangzeb's death and restrictions on building new temples eased.[18]

'In the ultimate resort,' Satish Chandra concludes, 'the decline and downfall of the empire was due to economic, social, political and institutional factors' – notice, no religious factors! Akbar held the forces of disintegration in check for some time. But it was impossible for him to effect fundamental changes in the structure of society, says our author, and therefore:

[18] Ibid., p. 255.

> By the time Aurangzeb came to the throne, the socio-economic forces of disintegration were already strong. Aurangzeb lacked the foresight and statesmanship necessary to effect fundamental changes in the structure or to pursue policies which could, for the time being, reconcile the various competing elements.
>
> Thus, Aurangzeb was both a victim of circumstances, and helped to create the circumstances of which he became a victim.[19]

Empathy personified!

The first thing that strikes one, of course, is the double standard. We shall soon see how, with next to no evidence, our eminent historians pressed the most far-reaching assertions about ancient India – about its having been a period riddled with tensions, inequity and oppression. And how, in cases such as Aurangzeb and the sultanate, these very historians shut their eyes to what stares them in the face. In a word, their histories are set to a formula: pre-Islamic India must be presented as a land of discord, a land in the grip of a social and political system marked by injustice, extreme inequities and oppression – evidence or no evidence; and the Islamic period must be presented – evidence or no evidence – as a period in which 'the composite culture' flowered, a period in which the policy of 'broad toleration' was the norm, and such departures from it as took place were just the aberrations of individuals, aberrations which themselves can be tracked down to wholly secular causes.

The second point which strikes one is reach and consistency! Recall the deletions which the West Bengal Secondary Board had decreed in regard to Aurangzeb, and the portrait that it had ensured would reach the students: a ruler who banned music, etc., out of ordinary, secular aversion; who, when he moved against others, did so for the eminently understandable and wholly secular reason – that of protecting his empire.

[19] Ibid., p. 255.

Recall that the Board had ensured that any mention of his policy towards Hindus would be accompanied by a reminder – that this was an exception to the general rule, in particular to Akbar's policies of religious tolerance and equal treatment. How faithfully our eminent historian in Delhi has followed the guidelines issued for elementary textbooks in Bengal!

The third thing that strikes one in these accounts and explanations is how closely they parrot the volumes of a person like Ishtiaq Husain Qureshi; as is well known, Qureshi taught history at the Delhi University and then migrated to Pakistan. There he became one of the early and ardent proponents of Islamization: he is credited with, he credited himself with having been one of the principal drafters of the 'Objectives Resolution' which was passed by the Pakistan Constituent Assembly in 1949, and became the fount of Islamization; he became a minister in the government of Liaqat Ali Khan and later the president of the Pakistan Historical Society. He was eventually decorated with the high honour, *Sitara-i-Pakistan.*

In his volume *The Muslim Community of the Indo-Pakistan Subcontinent,* Qureshi remarks about the reimposition of jizyah by Aurangzeb as follows:

> When Alamgir I reimposed *jizyah* after a lapse of 115 years, no sudden spurt in the number of conversions is recorded. Without the availability of statistics a definite conclusion is difficult to reach; but even in the epistles of such an ardent advocate of the reimposition of *jizyah* as the Mujaddid-i-alf-i-Thani, the argument that the abolition of *jizyah* had in any way affected the propagation of Islam was not advanced; nor does Bada'uni, who bewailed Akbar's lapse from orthodoxy and disapproved not only of the abolition of *jizyah* but also of the growth of Hindu influence in the affairs of the Empire, say that the abolition of *jizyah* had hampered the spread of Islam. There is no record of any significant difference in the rate of conversion either as the result of the abolition of *jizyah* or of its reimposition. If there had been a change such a development

could not have escaped the notice of the chroniclers, especially of men like Bada'uni, who has included in his history all that could be said against Akbar's religious policies.

If *jizyah* had been a crushing burden upon the non-Muslims, it could have led to conversions, but it was not too heavy a burden. It was levied only on able-bodied male adults who had a surplus of income after meeting the necessary expenses of maintaining themselves and their families. The religious classes like priests and monks were exempt. The rates charged were the equivalent in local currency of twelve, twenty-four and forty-eight dirhams, depending upon the income of the assessee. The assessment seems to have been lenient because at no time did *jizyah* form an important source of revenue, and a very large percentage of the non-Muslim population was exempt for one reason or another. Even if a tax is heavy but bearable, people are averse to changing their religion to escape it; but when it is not heavy, there is little inducement for conversion. Therefore, it does not seem likely that *jizyah* helped, in any significant manner, conversion to Islam.[20]

And our eminent historian says:

We are told that after accession to the throne, Aurangzeb contemplated revival of the *jizyah* on a number of occasions but did not do so for fear of political opposition. Ultimately, in 1679, in the twenty-second year of his reign, he finally re-imposed it. There has been a considerable discussion among historians regarding Aurangzeb's motives for the step. Let us first see what it was not. It was not meant to be an economic pressure for forcing the Hindus to convert to Islam for its incidence was too light – women, children, the disabled and the indigent, that is those whose income was less than the means of subsistence were exempted, as were those in government service. Nor, in fact, did any significant section of

[20] I.H. Qureshi, *The Muslim Community of the Indo-Pakistan Subcontinent,* reprinted by Renaissance Publishing House, Delhi, 1985, pp. 80–81.

> Hindus change their religion due to this tax. Secondly, it was not a means of meeting a difficult financial situation. Although the income from *jizyah* is said to have been considerable, Aurangzeb sacrificed a considerable sum of money by giving up a large number of cesses called *abwabs* which were not sanctioned by the *shara* and were hence considered illegal. The re-imposition of *jizyah* was, in fact, both political and ideological in nature. It was meant to rally the Muslims for the defence of the state against the Marathas and the Rajputs who were up in arms, and possibly against the Muslim states of the Deccan, especially Golconda which was in alliance with the infidels. Secondly, *jizyah* was to be collected by honest, God-fearing Muslims, who were especially appointed for the purpose, and its proceeds were reserved for the *ulama.* It was thus a big bribe for the theologians among whom there was a lot of unemployment.[21]

The historian then notes the infirmities in implementing the tax, but his final verdict remains as considerate as that of Qureshi:

> Some modern writers are of the opinion that Aurangzeb's measures were designed to convert India from a *dar-ul-harb,* or a land of infidels, into *dar-ul-Islam,* or a land inhabited by Muslims. Although Aurangzeb considered it legitimate to encourage conversion to Islam, evidence of systematic or large-scale attempts at forced conversion is lacking. Nor were Hindu nobles discriminated against....[22]

Similarly, Qureshi emphasizes in the same volume that Aurangzeb had no option but to wage his campaigns against Golconda and Bijapur. He remarks:

> The Sultanates were incapable of even keeping peace within their territories. The Marathas got their sinews of war by plundering them. Besides, the sultanates, in spite of the growth

[21] Satish Chandra, op. cit., p. 232.
[22] Ibid., pp. 232–33.

> of Maratha power at their expense, were secretly in alliance with them and helped them with money and supplies. The situation in Golconda was even worse because the real power was in the hands of two Brahmin officials, Madanna and Akanna, whose obnoxious rule was resented by the Muslim population of the sultanate and who were even more enthusiastic supporters of the Marathas. Under such circumstances it would have been foolish to leave the sultanates alone.[23]

In his volume *Ulema in Politics,* Qureshi reverts to the same matter and remarks:

> The Sultanates of the Deccan had been so weakened by the Marathas that they were fast sinking into a state of anarchy. They, because of this weakness, became almost the storehouse of Maratha resources who grabbed whatever they needed from their territories. Besides they were in alliance with the Marathas, because they perversely thought that after the threat from the Mughuls had been averted, the Marathas could be dealt with more easily. This was a gross underestimate of the potentialities of the Maratha activities. So far as Alamgir was concerned, he had no choice. The Marathas and the Sultanates constituted a single problem and could not be detached from each other. Those who suggest that the Sultanates could be persuaded to act against the Marathas or could become a bulwark against Maratha expansion ignore the realities of the situation.[24]

The verdict of our eminent historian is identical. He says:

> Aurangzeb has been criticised for having failed to unite with the Deccani states against the Marathas, or for having conquered them thereby making the empire 'so large that it collapsed under its own weight.' A unity of hearts between Aurangzeb

[23] I.H. Qureshi, *The Muslim Community of the Indo-Pakistan Subcontinent*, op. cit., p. 185.

[24] I.H. Qureshi, *Ulema in Politics,* reprinted by Renaissance Publishing House, Delhi, 1985, pp. 105–06.

> and the Deccani states was 'a psychological impossibility' once the treaty of 1636 was abandoned, a development which took place during the reign of Shah Jahan himself. After his accession, Aurangzeb desisted from pursuing a vigorous forward policy in the Deccan. In fact, he postponed as long as possible the decision to conquer and annex the Deccani states. Aurangzeb's hand was virtually forced by the growing Maratha power, the support extended to Shivaji by Madanna and Akhanna from Golconda, and fear that Bijapur might fall under the domination of Shivaji and the Maratha-dominated Golconda. Later, by giving shelter to the rebel prince Akbar, Sambhaji virtually threw a challenge to Aurangzeb who quickly realised that the Marathas could not be dealt with without first subduing Bijapur and possibly Golconda.[25]

And though Satish Chandra is inclined to concede, 'perhaps Aurangzeb might have been better advised to accept the suggestion apparently put forward by his eldest son, Shah Alam, for a settlement with Bijapur and Golconda to annex only a part of the territories and let them rule the South Karnataka which was far away and difficult to monitor,' his understanding of Aurangzeb's compulsions is no less than that of Qureshi!

Qureshi is at pains to emphasize that Aurangzeb did not institute new laws, that, therefore, the collapse of the empire after him cannot be attributed to his religious policies. As he puts it:

> The Muslim Empire had endured in the subcontinent for several centuries. The orthodox laws of Islam had been imposed with varying degrees of thoroughness. Alamgir, I did not bring into existence a new set of laws. In the course of these centuries the *jizyah* had remained in abeyance only for a period of one hundred and fifteen years. The order for the demolition of unauthorised temples had been given under Shah Jahan and

[25] Satish Chandra, op. cit., p. 254.

> Alamgir did not enforce it for the first time. If the Empire collapsed like a house of cards after the death of Alamgir I, the main causes must be sought elsewhere than in the religious policies of that emperor, though these also played some role in its disintegration.'[26]

Our eminent historian emphasises the same point in almost the same words in context after context: 'Aurangzeb's order regarding temples was not a new one. It reaffirmed the position which had existed during the Sultanate period and which had been reiterated by Shah Jahan early in his reign ....' And of course, jizyah was not being imposed for the first time, – it was being re-imposed after a gap of 115 years![27]

And so on. Thus the 'explanations' for Aurangzeb's policies are identical, all that is missing is the adoration that Qureshi holds for Aurangzeb.

The fourth point is the brazenness with which our historians suppress the evidence and, having done so, slip in falsehoods. To take just one example, recall how Satish Chandra concludes the account of Aurangzeb's deeds visa-à-vis temples: The order for destroying temples was not a new one; the order was limited to new temples and not to existing structures; the order left a great deal of latitude to local officials; Aurangzeb adopted 'a new stance' only when he encountered political hostility and when he came to conclude that the temples had become centres from which 'subversive ideas' were being spread; that the destruction of temples was more or less confined to periods of hostilities. And finally that 'it seems that Aurangzeb's zeal for the destruction of temples abated after 1679, for we do not hear of any large scale destruction of temples in the South between 1681 and his death in 1707.'

How does this assertion compare with what the *Akhbarat* of

26 I.H. Qureshi, *The Muslim Community of the Indo-Pakistan Subcontinent,* op. cit., pp. 186–87.

27 Satish Chandra, op. cit., pp. 230, 231–32.

Aurangzeb itself state, as well as other accounts recorded at the time? Here are some of the entries:

> 25 May 1679: 'Khan-i-Jahan Bahadur returned from Jodhpur after demolishing its temples, and bringing with himself several cart-loads of idols. The Emperor ordered that the idols, which were mostly of gold, silver, brass, copper or stone and adorned with jewels, should be cast in the quadrangle of the Court and under the steps of the Jama Mosque for being trodden upon.'
>
> January-February 1680: 'The grand temple in front of the Maharana's mansion (at Udaipur) – one of the wonderful buildings of the age, which had cost the infidels much money – was destroyed and its images broken.' 'On 24 January the Emperor went to view the lake Udaisagar and ordered all the three temples on its banks to be pulled down.' 'On 29 January Hasan Ali Khan reported that 172 other temples in the environs of Udaipur had been demolished.' 'On 22 February the Emperor went to look at Chitor, and by his order the 63 temples of the place were destroyed.'
>
> 10 August 1680: 'Abu Turab returned to Court and reported that he had pulled down 66 temples in Amber'. *2 August 1680:* 'Temple of Someshwar in western Mewar ordered to be destroyed.'
>
> September 1687: 'On the capture of Golkonda, the Emperor appointed Abdur Rahim Khan as Censor of the city of Haidarabad with orders to put down infidel practices and (heretical) innovations and destroy the temples and build mosques on their sites.'
>
> Circa 1690: Instances of Aurangzeb's temple destruction at Ellora, Trimbaakeshwar, Narsinghpur (foiled by snakes, scorpions and other poisonous insects), Pandharpur, Jejuri (foiled by the deity) and Yavat (Bhuleshwar) are given by K.N. Sane in *Varshik Iribritta* for Shaka 1838, pp. 133–135.
>
> 1693: 'The Emperor ordered the destruction of the Hateshwar temple at Vadnagar, the special guardian of the Nagar Brahmans.'
>
> 3rd April 1694: 'The Emperor learnt from a secret news-writer of Delhi that in Jaisinghpura Bairagis used to worship idols, and that the Censor on hearing of it had gone there,

arrested Sri Krishna Bairagi and taken him with 15 idols away to his house; then the Rajputs had assembled, flocked to the Censor's house, wounded three footmen of the Censor and tried to seize the Censor himself; so that the latter set the Bairagi free and sent the copper idols to the local *subahdar.*'

Middle of 1698: 'Hamid-ud-din Khan Bahadur who had been deputed to destroy the temple of Bijapur and build a mosque (there), returned to Court after carrying the order out and was praised by the Emperor.'

'The demolition of a temple is possible at any time, as it cannot walk away from its place.' – Aurangzeb to Zullfiqar Khan and Mughal Khan.

'The houses of this country (Maharashtra) are exceedingly strong and built solely of stone and iron. The hatchet-men of the Government in the course of my marching do not get sufficient strength and power (i.e., time) to destroy and raze the temples of the infidels that meet the eye on the way. You should appoint an orthodox inspector (*darogha*) who may afterwards destroy them at leisure and dig up their foundations.' – Aurangzeb to Ruhullah Khan in *Kalimat-i-Aurangzib.*

1 January 1705: 'The Emperor, summoning Muhammad Khalil and Khidmat Rai, the *darogha* of hatchet-men...., ordered them to demolish the temple of Pandharpur, and to take the butchers of the camp there and slaughter cows in the temple.... It was done.'

The eminent historian did not need to trouble himself by going to the primary sources. He could have found these and other entries in a single compact appendix in Volume III of Sir Jadunath Sarkar's well-known *History of Aurangzib.* That history has been in circulation since 1928![28] Our writer, writing in 1996, is conveniently oblivious of the evidence which even an elementary student of Aurangzeb's period would have come across!

[28] Jadunath Sarkar, *History of Aurangzib,* Volume III, Orient Longman, New Delhi, 1972 reprint, pp. 185–89.

However, there is little mystery. For there are two pillars of progressive history writing in India: first, to fabricate evidence which will establish Hindus to be intolerant; second, to respect and show an empathetic understanding of Islamic communalism.

And the litmus test of whether you are committed to secular history writing is whether you are prepared to stand up for Aurangzeb!

14

Erasure to parity to absolution

Anyone who has the slightest acquaintance with the Quran, with the *Hadis,* with the history of Islamic rule, knows that the separation between believers and non-believers is of the very essence in Islam.[1] The main concern of our eminent historians is to completely absolve Islam of such notions and of campaigns and deeds which flow from them. When they cannot but acknowledge the deeds of Muslim leaders and rulers, they attribute them to the foibles or errors of individuals. Next, as we have just seen, they give elaborate explanations to account for those individuals having taken those steps. Again and again they emphasize that the spurs for many of those actions were the deeds and attitudes of the victims themselves. And whenever they mention the intolerance or bigotry of the Muslims they make sure to generalize the matter and always slip in allusions to the Hindus also.

The history textbook for Class XII published by NCERT, *Modern India*, is by our old friend, the eminent historian, Bipan Chandra.[2] In his Foreword the director of NCERT records

[1] For some illustrative citations see my *The World of Fatwas,* ASA and HarperCollins, pp. 551–82.

[2] Bipan Chandra, *Modern India,* National Council of Educational Research and Training, New Delhi, sixth reprint, January 1998. Unless otherwise indicated, page numbers given in this chapter refer to this book.

that the earlier version of the textbook was prepared by Bipan Chandra under the auspices of an editorial board. The editorial board, you will not be surprised to learn, consisted of the familiar friends – S. Gopal, S. Nurul Hasan, Satish Chandra, and Romila Thapar.

The role of Syed Ahmad Khan in founding the Aligarh movement, his strenuous efforts to ensure that Muslims would remain loyal to the British and shun the Congress and the nascent national movement, his role as the originator in modern times of the Two-Nation Theory – these are all recorded. As is the role of the Muslim League. But in both cases elaborate explanations are given which amount in effect to exculpations. Thus we learn in the case of Syed Ahmad Khan:

> However, towards the end of his life, he began to talk of Hindu domination to prevent his followers from joining the rising national movement. This was unfortunate, though basically he was not a communalist. He only wanted the backwardness of the Muslim middle and upper classes to go. His politics were the result of his firm belief that immediate political progress was not possible because the British Government could not be easily dislodged. On the other hand, any hostility by the officials might prove dangerous to the educational effort which he saw as the need of the hour. He believed that only when Indians had become as modern in their thinking and actions as the English were, could they hope to successfully challenge foreign rule. He, therefore, advised all Indians and particularly the educationally backward Muslims to remain aloof from politics for some time to come. The time for politics, he said, had not yet come. In fact, he had become so committed to his college and the cause of education that he was willing to sacrifice all other interests to them. Consequently, to prevent the orthodox Muslims from opposing his college, he virtually gave up his agitation in favour of religions reform. For the same reason, he would not do anything to offend the government and, on the other hand, encouraged communalism and separatism. This was, of course, a serious political error, which was to have harmful consequences in later years. Moreover,

some of his followers deviated from his broad-mindedness and tended later to glorify Islam and its past while criticising other religions.'[3]

In other words, just a 'political error' – and an error for which there were the highest reasons! Similarly, in the case of the Muslim League, while its rank opportunism, its toeing the British line, its use of religion to instigate the ignorant masses, are all enumerated, its politics is put to British instigation and the point is emphasized repeatedly that it gained strength from the activities of 'Hindu communalists'. Thus we are told:

The Muslim League propaganda gained by the existence of such communal bodies among the Hindus as the Hindu Mahasabha. The Hindu communalists echoed the Muslim communalists by declaring that the Hindus were a distinct nation and that India was the land of the Hindus. Thus they too accepted the two-nation theory. They actively opposed the policy of giving adequate safeguards to the minorities so as to remove their fears of domination by the majority.'[4]

Not only that, Bipan Chandra peddles the standard secularist 'thesis': the two communalisms are put at par in one breath, and, in the next, the point is made that actually Hindu communalism was 'even less justified' and, therefore, one must infer, even more responsible for the outcome. This is how Bipan Chandra puts the matter:

In one respect, Hindu communalism had even less justification. In every country, the religious or linguistic or national minorities have, because of their numerical position, felt at one time or the other that their social and cultural interests might suffer. But when the majority has by word and deed given proof that these fears are groundless the fears of the minorities

[3] Bipan Chandra, op. cit., p. 177.
[4] Ibid., p. 258.

have disappeared, but if a section of the people belonging to the majority becomes communal or sectional and starts talking and working against the minorities, the minorities tend to feel unsafe. Communal or sectional leadership of the minorities is then strengthened. For example, during the 1930s the Muslim League was strong only in areas where the Muslims were in a minority. On the other hand, in such areas as the North-West Frontier Province, the Punjab, the Sindh and Bengal, where the Muslims were in a majority and, therefore, felt relatively securer [*sic.*], the Muslim League remained weak. Interestingly enough, the communal groups – Hindu as well as Muslim – did not hesitate to join hands against the Congress. In the North-West Frontier Province, the Punjab, Sindh and Bengal, the Hindu communalists helped the Muslim League and other communal groups to form ministries which opposed the Congress. Another characteristic the various communal groups shared was their tendency to adopt pro-Government political attitudes. It is to be noted that none of the communal groups and parties, which talked of Hindu and Muslim nationalism, took active part in the struggle against foreign rule. They saw the people belonging to other religions and the nationalist leaders as their real enemies.

The communal groups and parties also shied away from the social and economic demands of the common people which, as we have seen above, were being increasingly taken up by the nationalist movement....[5]

Indeed, the very nature of the nationalist movement, Bipan Chandra emphasizes repeatedly, alienated the Muslims and it was because of that character of the nationalist struggle that the overwhelming majority of Muslims stayed away from the national movement and in the end backed the Muslim League. Therefore, once again it is the Hindus who are to be blamed!

Bipan Chandra notes Syed Ahmad Khan's propaganda: that the Hindus and Muslims were two different nations, that

[5] Ibid., p. 259.

their interests would not coincide, that Muslims would be swamped by Hindus, that their interest lay in siding with the British – Bipan Chandra recalls these and pronounces, 'these views were, of course, unscientific and without any basis in reality.' Muslims and Hindus of the same class and region were closer to each other than they were to co-religionists from other classes and other regions, he notes.[6] He then explains the rise of separatist thinking among Muslims in terms of their backwardness in education, and in trade and industry, and thereby to the dominance among them of 'reactionary big landlords'.[7] Then follows the usual string of propositions. First, he says, 'the manner in which Indian history was taught in schools and colleges in those days also contributed to the growth of communal feelings among the educated Hindus and Muslims.' And the flaw in the contents of these histories was that they did not subscribe to the secular line which these eminences have since made obligatory! To recall our historian's verdict,

> They failed to bring out the fact that ancient and medieval politics in India, as politics everywhere else, were based on economic and political interests and not on religious considerations. Rulers as well as rebels used religious appeals as an outer colouring to disguise the play of material interests and ambitions. Moreover, the British and communal historians attacked the notion of a composite culture in India.[8]

But from the very next sentence the responsibility is loaded, as usual, on to the Hindus. Bipan Chandra writes:

> The Hindu communal view of history also relied on the myth that Indian society and culture had reached great, ideal heights in the ancient period from which they fell into permanent

[6] Ibid., pp. 204–05.
[7] Ibid., pp. 205–06.
[8] Ibid., pp. 206–07.

> and continuous decay during the medieval period because of 'Muslim' rule and domination. The basic contribution of the medieval period to the development of Indian economy and technology, religion and philosophy, arts and literature, culture and society, and fruits, vegetables and dress was denied.[9]

Notice that there is not a word about Muslim historians and what they had written about India. Those history books were the triumphalist literature of the community as were the writings of influential figures such as Shah Waliullah and Sheikh Ahmad Sarhindi. There is not a word about the volumes upon volumes of those who really governed and moulded Muslim thought in late nineteenth and early twentieth century – for instance, of persons like Maulana Ahmad Riza Khan.

Three paragraphs later Bipan Chandra sets his guns not just at some unnamed Hindu communalist historians, but at the character of the entire national movement and of its greatest leaders. This is how he assesses them:

> Unfortunately, while militant nationalism was a great step forward in every other respect, it was to some extent a step back in respect of the growth of national unity. The speeches and writings of some of the militant nationalists had a strong religious and Hindu tinge. They emphasised ancient Indian culture to the exclusion of medieval Indian culture. They identified Indian culture and the Indian nation with the Hindu religion and Hindus. They tried to abandon elements of composite culture. For example, Tilak's propagation of the Shivaji and Ganapati festivals, Aurobindo Ghose's semi-mystical concept of India as mother and nationalism as a religion, the terrorists' oaths before goddess Kali, and the initiation of the Anti-Partition agitation with dips in the Ganga could hardly appeal to the Muslims. In fact, such actions were against the spirit of their religion, and they could not be expected as Muslims to associate with these and other

[9] Ibid., p. 207.

> similar activities. Nor could Muslims be expected to respond with full enthusiasm when they saw Shivaji or Pratap being hailed not merely for their historical roles but also as 'national' leaders who fought against the 'foreigners'. By no definition could Akbar or Aurangzeb be declared a foreigner, unless being a Muslim was made the ground for declaring one a foreigner. In reality, the struggle between Pratap and Akbar or Shivaji and Aurangzeb had to be viewed as a political struggle in its particular historical setting. To declare Akbar or Aurangzeb a 'foreigner' and Pratap or Shivaji a 'national' hero was to project into past history the communal outlook of 20th century India. This was not only bad history; it was also a blow to national unity.[10]

He swiftly hems, and he swiftly haws, 'This does not mean that militant nationalists were anti-Muslim or wholly communal,' he says. 'Far from it,' he says. Most of them, he says, including Tilak, favoured Hindu-Muslim unity. To most of them, he says, the motherland or *Bharatmata* was a modern notion 'being in no way linked with religion': the exact opposite of what Bharat was to them – an ancient, eternal nation, one which had at its core the Hindu religion. On our historian's reckoning, they were almost secularists! Indeed, the inspiration that spurred the most daring among them was so modern as to be foreign! 'Even the revolutionary terrorists,' Bipan Chandra says, 'were in reality inspired by European revolutionary movements, for example, those of Ireland, Russia and Italy, rather than by *Kali* or *Bhawani* cults.' In spite of this, however, the net effect of what they did was to disrupt the sense of national unity. And so, the hemming and hawing disposed of, our historian is back to his original verdict:

> But as pointed out earlier, there was a certain Hindu tinge in the political work and ideas of the militant nationalists. This proved to be particularly harmful as clever British and

[10] Ibid., p. 207.

> pro-British propagandists took advantage of the Hindu colouring to poison the minds of the Muslims. The result was that a large number of educated Muslims either remained aloof from the rising nationalist movement or became hostile to it, thus falling an easy prey to a separatist outlook. The Hindu tinge also created ideological openings for Hindu communalism and made it difficult for the nationalist movement to eliminate the Hindu communal, political and ideological elements within its own ranks. It also helped the spread of a Muslim tinge among Muslim nationalists.[11]

The saving grace was that, in spite of this Hindu colouring of these nationalists, 'quite a large number of advanced Muslim intellectuals' .... joined the *Swadeshi* movement, the revolutionary terrorists as well as the Indian National Congress. How gracious of them to ignore the provocation! The reason? 'This was because the national movement remained basically secular in its approach and ideology,' says our historian.[12]

The effect in this regard of the Hindu reformers was the same, Bipan Chandra teaches us. Recounting their efforts, he says,

> Moreover, the reformers put a one-sided emphasis on the religious and philosophical aspects of the cultural heritage. These aspects were, moreover, not a common heritage of all people. On the other hand, art and architecture, literature, music, science and technology, etc., in which all sections of people had played an equal role, were not sufficiently emphasised. In addition, the Hindu reformers invariably confined their praise of the Indian past to its ancient period. Even a broad-minded man like Swami Vivekananda talked of the Indian spirit or India's past achievements in this sense alone. These reformers looked upon the medieval period of Indian history as essentially an era of decadence. This was not only unhistorical but also socially and politically harmful. It tended to create the notion

[11] Ibid., p. 208.
[12] Ibid., p. 208–09.

of two separate peoples. Similarly, an uncritical praise of the ancient period and religions could not be fully acceptable to the persons coming from lower castes who had for centuries suffered under the most destructive caste oppression which had developed precisely during the ancient period. The result of all these factors was that instead of all Indians taking an equal pride in their past material and cultural achievements and deriving inspiration from them, the past became a heritage of the few. Moreover, the past itself tended to be torn into compartments on a partisan basis. Many in the Muslim middle classes went to the extent of turning to the history of West Asia for their traditions and moments of pride. Increasingly, Hindus, Muslims, Sikhs and Parsis, and later on lower-caste Hindus who had been influenced by the reform movements tended to be different from one another. On the other hand, the Hindu and Muslim masses who followed traditional ways untouched by the reform movements still lived in harmony, practicing their different religious rituals. To some extent the process of the evolution of a composite culture that had been going on for centuries was arrested; though in other spheres national unification of the Indian people was accelerated. The evil aspects of this phenomenon became apparent when it was found that, along with a rapid rise of national consciousness, another consciousness – communal consciousness – had begun to rise among the middle classes. Many other factors were certainly responsible for the birth of communalism in modern times; but, undoubtedly, the nature of the religious reform movements also contributed to it.[13]

When, in response to the chants – 'Islam is the religion of peace,' 'The Quran and the Prophet teach, "To you your religion, to me mine,"' – *ayat*s from the Quran are cited, when hadis are cited and fatwas which direct the believer to shun, ostracize, subjugate, and suppress non-believers till they give up and embrace Islam, what do the secularists declare? No, no, in understanding a tradition we must go by what the believer

[13] Ibid., pp. 181–82.

in that tradition says, they declare. But when it comes to Hinduism, we must go by what *they*, these progressives who flaunt their emancipation from the religion and tradition, say about it!

That 'many in the Muslim middle classes went to the extent of turning to the history of West Asia for their traditions and moments of pride' was the result of our leaders and reformers giving a Hindu colour to the nationalist movement?

Did the believer need to be instigated by these Hindu reformers before he turned five times a day to the Kaba in the West Asia? Did he need instigation from Hindu reformers or nationalist leaders before he came to regard Mecca and Madina as the places that were holy? Did he need the instigation of these reformers and nationalist leaders for holding Arabic to be the language which deserves the highest veneration – is it not Allah Himself who reminds him repeatedly in the Quran that it is in Arabic that He has sent down the Revelation?

Allah says,

> These are The Symbols (or Verses)
> Of the Perspicuous Book.
> We have sent it down
> As *an Arabic* Quran… (12.1,2)

And again,

> Thus have We revealed it
> To be a judgment of authority
> In *Arabic*… (13.37)

And again,

> We know indeed that they
> Say, 'It is a man that
> Teaches him.' The tongue
> Of him they wickedly point to
> Is notably foreign, while this
> Is *Arabic*… (16.103)

And again,
> Thus have We sent this
> Down – an *Arabic* Quran… (20.113)

And again,
> Verily this is a Revelation
> From the Lord of the Worlds:
> With it came down
> The Spirit of Faith and Truth
> To thy Heart and mind,
> That thou mayest admonish
> In the perspicuous
> *Arabic* tongue. (26.192–95)

And again,
> (It is) a Quran
> *In Arabic*… (39.28)

And again,
> A Book, whereof the verses
> Are explained in detail; –
> A Quran in *Arabic*… (41.3)

And again,
> Had We sent this as
> A Quran (in a language)
> Other than *Arabic,* they would
> Have said: 'Why are not
> Its verses explained in detail?
> What! (a Book) not in *Arabic*
> And (a Messenger) an Arab?'… (41.44)

And again,
> Thus have We sent
> By inspiration to thee
> An *Arabic* Quran… (42.7)

And again,
> We have made it
> A Quran in *Arabic*… (43.3)

And again,

And before this, was
The Book of Moses
As a guide and a mercy;
And this Book confirms (it)
In *the Arabic* tongue... (46.12)

When Allah Himself reminds the believer that he has sent him an 'Arabic Quran', that he has sent him 'the Quran in Arabic', what further instigation does the believer need from Hindu reformers for placing that language far above mere Indian languages?

Does he need to be pushed by the 'Hindu colouring' which these reformers and leaders are said to have given before holding the Arabs to be the chosen people, to whom he must hearken, to whom he must look up? Is it not the Prophet who instructed every believer that anyone who hates Arabs hates him, the Prophet himself? Is it not the Prophet who warned that 'he who is treacherous to the Arabs will not be included in my intercession and will not receive my love'? Is it not the Prophet who warned that 'one of the signs of the approach of the last hour will be the destruction of the Arabs'? Is it not the Prophet who admonished all believers, 'love the Arabs for three reasons: because I am an Arab, the Quran is Arabic, and the inhabitants of Paradise will speak Arabic?'[14]

Is it because the Hindus have instigated a believer that he looks to West Asia for inspiration, or does he do so because the *Hadis* instructs him:

> God chose as the best, the children of Ishmael, the son of Abraham. From Ishmael's descendants, God chose the Quraish (the tribe of Prophet) as the best of people; from the Quraish, God chose the Banu Hashim (the clan of the Prophet) the best of people, and from the Banu Hashim, God chose Muhammad as the best of all men ....

[14] *Mishkat Al Masabhi,* Book 26, Chapter 28.

In honouring not just the Arabs, and among Arabs the Quraish, is the believer instigated by these Hindu reformers and nationalist leaders? Is it not enough for him that the Prophet himself declared that believers are to be subservient to the Quraish and that the caliphate is the right of the Quraish?[15] Does he need Hindu reformers and religious leaders to push him to regard the Quraish as pre-eminent when, Allah having said that he has sent the Quran in Arabic, the Prophet makes that declaration specific, and declares that the Quran has been sent in the Arabic *of the Quraish* – that is, in their dialect which is distinct from the Arabic spoken by other tribes?[16]

All this will be evident to anyone who has even a passing acquaintance with Islam. Nor are these esoteric doctrines, these are notions which are fed to the believer with, so to say, his mother's milk from the moment of his conversion. Every observer is struck with this insistence of Islam in wrenching believers away from his land, from his language, from his dress, from his older beliefs and turning him towards the Arabs, towards Arabia, towards Arabic, towards Arabian lore and legend. V.S. Naipaul has recently given a poignant account in *Beyond Belief* of the deep scars this basic insistence has left on the psyche of the converted. Site after sacred site, conversation after conversation etches the truth: Recounting his travels among believers Naipaul gives a heart-rending account of the consequences of this insistence. Reflecting on what the believers tell him, Naipaul remarks: 'Islam is in its origins an Arab religion. Everyone not an Arab who is a Muslim is a convert. Islam is not simply a matter of conscience or private belief. It makes imperial demands. A convert's world view alters. His holy places are in Arab lands; his sacred language is Arabic. His idea of history alters. He rejects his own; he

[15] *Sahih Muslim,* Chapter DCCLIV.

[16] *Sahih Al-Bukhari,* Book LXI, p. 507.

becomes, whether he likes it or not, a part of the Arab story. The convert has to turn away from everything that is his…'

Everyone who has cared to look at all has been struck by this uprooting, this turning to Arabs, Arabia, Arabic, Arabian lore and legend. The Quran and the Hadis demand it. The most extensive Islamic organization in the subcontinent today is the Tablighi Jamaat: its sole purpose is to stamp out every trace of practices, customs, beliefs which Muslims may still share with their non-Muslim neighbours. But to our eminent historian, the turning away from India towards West Asia is not because of Islam – it is something to which Muslims have been pushed by the Hindu colouring which our reformers and leaders gave the national movement!

Does the Indian who has converted to Islam require Hindu reformers or nationalist leaders to instigate him into shunning the kafirs, into giving up every vestige of the ways of the non-believers? From the very advent of Islam into India, Islamic preachers and reformers have had one singular aim: to exorcise every syncretistic notion and practice. From the moment of his conversion, indeed as part of the ceremony of conversion itself, the convert is made to do things which will rupture – violently rupture – his links with his Hindu past. Precisely for the reason that Ali Mian and others have pinpointed – the reason that the Hindus revere the cow – beef has a special place in this rupturing: in the feast that follows, the new convert is forced or, if you prefer, induced to eat beef openly and publicly.

Does the Muslim need to wait for some Hindu reformer or nationalist leader to distance himself from non-believers, from idolaters? Does he not learn from the Quran itself that 'they are the worst of creatures', that they shall be in hellfire to dwell forever therein?[17] Does he not learn from the Quran itself that they are the cause of 'tumult and oppression', that they block his path to Allah, that therefore they must be slaughtered

[17] Quran, 98.6.

because 'tumult and oppression are worse than slaughter', that they shall not cease fighting the believers until they have got believers to turn their back on the faith?[18] Does the Quran not teach him that the only wish of non-believers is 'that you should reject Faith as they do, and thus be on the same footing (as them)', and that therefore the believer must take no friend from among them – till they have given up their own faith and embraced Islam?[19] Does he need to be pushed by some Dayanand or Tilak before he concludes that the believers are conspiring to do him in? Is it not Allah Himself who instructs him in the Quran, 'The unbelievers spend their wealth to hinder (men) from the path of Allah, and so they will continue to spend?'[20]

Does the Muslim not learn from the Quran itself, 'Strongest among men in enmity to the believers you will find the Jews and Pagans?'[21] To shun Hindus as well as the national struggle, does the Muslim need some Hindu nationalist to paint the freedom struggle in a Hindu hue? Does Allah Himself not declare 'O, you who believe! Truly the pagans are unclean…?'[22] Does a Muslim need any instigation from mere Hindu leaders to shun Hindus and everything associated with them when Allah forbade the Prophet to pray even for his deceased mother on the ground that she had died a non-believer?[23]

Would the Muslim have needed some Tilak to paint the nationalist struggle in Ganapati Mahotsava's colour to stay away from it, as these historians would have us believe? Does Allah not tell him Himself that it is He, Allah Himself who has deliberately misled non-believers, that He has done so for a purpose? Is it not Allah who tells him that He, Allah

[18] Quran, 2.217.
[19] Ibid., 4.89.
[20] Ibid., 8. 36–37.
[21] Ibid., 5.85.
[22] Ibid., 9.28.
[23] Ibid., 9.113; 9.84.

has Himself put non-believers in the Muslim's path to test the latter's faith in Allah? Is it not Allah who declares that no good that the unbelievers do shall ever carry any weight with Him?[24]

Would the believer have had to wait upon some Tilak or Aurobindo or Gandhi to decide that this was just the movement of Hindus for Hindus and therefore he should shun it? Does the Prophet not instruct him in hadis after hadis after hadis that he must in every particular and at all times use one criterion to decide what he should do – that is, he must see what the non-believers are doing, and do the opposite?[25]

Every Muslim learns all this from the moment he becomes aware of his faith – after all, this is one of the central themes of the faith, after all these are notions and exhortations which run through the fundamental repositories of the faith, the Quran and the hadis. Our historians shut their eyes tight to all this. Composite culture, composite culture, they chant. The nationalist leaders, by giving the freedom movement, a Hindu colour, the nationalist historians, by the way they were teaching history, drove the Muslims away from the freedom struggle, they charge. In sharp contrast to the way Bipan Chandra treats nationalist leaders, when he comes to talk of the *Ahrar*s, this eminent historian talks of them as 'the *militantly nationalist Ahrar* movement', when he talks of the Dar-ul-ulum of Deoband he reminds us that 'similar *nationalist* sentiments were arising among a section of the traditional Muslim scholars led by the Deoband School.'[26] From such descriptions of the net effect of the Ahrars and of institutions like the Dar-ul-ulum of Deoband, one must infer either deceit or total ignorance of their literature and their politics. The whole attitude of the

[24] Ibid., 9.17; 9.69; 18.102–06; 45.7–10; 47.7–11.

[25] For representative hadis, see my *The World of Fatwas,* ASA and HarperCollins, Delhi, pp. 611–18.

[26] Bipan Chandra, op. cit., p. 210.

Ahrars, of the Deoband school, even of a person like Mufti Kifayatullah was that, by asking for a separate Pakistan, the Muslim League was confining Islam to one corner of the subcontinent, when in fact the whole of the subcontinent was open for establishing the sway of Islam. The Ahrars did not fault Jinnah from some nationalist viewpoint, they did not fault him for being too Islamic. On the contrary – their famous couplet for Jinnah was:

> *Ik kafira ke waste Islam ko chhora*
> *yeh Quaid-i-Azam hai keh hai kafir-i-azam*

But recalling any of that will strain the effort of our eminent historian in establishing a parity between Hindus and Muslims in regard to communalism, and therefore, he just ignores the facts!

This glossing over can be seen at every turn. The book has a paragraph on Iqbal. But for the fact that Iqbal was 'one of the greatest poets of modern India', he would seem to have been, on the reckoning of our historian, a cross between Swami Vivekananda and M.N. Roy! Students are told, 'Like Swami Vivekananda, he emphasised the need for constant change and ceaseless activity and condemned resignation, contemplation, and quiet contentment. He urged the adoption of a dynamic outlook that would help change the world. He was basically a humanist.' And at the end of the paragraph a line is slipped in – 'In his earlier poetry, he extolled patriotism, though later he encouraged Muslim separatism.'[27] If only our eminent historian had deigned to read, if not Iqbal's own political writings and those on Islam, even his *Shikwa,* at least the volumes upon volumes which have been produced about him in Pakistan, if only he had deigned to ask himself why is it that Pakistani historians, political scientists and politicians ascribe such an

[27] Ibid., p. 178.

important place to Iqbal in the creation of Pakistan, if only he had read any of these and asked whether they are doing so without basis!

Similarly, Bipan Chandra instructs students that 'we must distinguish between religion as a belief or system, which people follow as a part of their personal belief, and the ideology of a religion-based socio-political identity, that is, communalism.'[28] But what about all the authorities of Islam from the Prophet onwards who declare that Islam embraces all of life, that Islam is not merely a matter of adhering to some personal beliefs? What about their affirmations over 1,400 years that Islam is an ideology in the most comprehensive sense of the word? That believers are to regulate their political life, that they are to organize their state, that they are to enact their laws in accordance with it as much as they are to regulate other, more personal aspects of their life and that of the Islamic community in accordance with it? By that very distinction which Bipan Chandra furnishes for the students – 'we must distinguish between religion as a belief or system, which people follow as a part of their personal belief, and the ideology of a religion-based socio-political identity' – is Islam not by its own definition, 'communalism'?

It is not only this basic fact which Bipan Chandra glides over, he fudges the matter further. He says, 'Religion is not the cause of communalism, nor is communalism inspired by religion. Religion comes into communalism to the extent that it serves politics arising in non-religious spheres. Communalism has been rightly described as political trade in religion. Religion was used, after 1937, as a mobilising factor by the communalists.'[29]

Notice the last sentence – 'Religion was used, after 1937, as a mobilising factor by the communalists.' Who began using

[28] Ibid., p. 209.
[29] Ibid., p. 209.

it after 1937? It was Jinnah and his Muslim League – in a word, the Muslim communalists. But, given his commitment to parity, our eminent historian uses the word 'communalists' in general, thereby insinuating to the student that communalists from among both Hindus and Muslims began to use religion to mobilize the people after 1937.

Thus, the general 'theses' which are drilled into students are: all religions have an equal potential to generate communalism; communalism among Muslims grew, not because of anything inherent in Islam, but because of fortuitous factors; in particular, it was instigated by communalism of the Hindu reformers and nationalist leaders; and this latter communalism had even less justification than the communalism of Muslim leaders; Hindu communalism was, therefore, both – the first cause as well as the more condemnable.

The accounts of topic after topic – from social reform to the making of the Constitution – are studded with the clichés these fellows have made conventional. Among reformers, Ambedkar gets much space, Narayan Guru not a word. And the Constitution, the student learns, was brought into being by 'the Constituent Assembly under the guidance of Jawaharlal Nehru and B.R. Ambedkar'![30]

And, of course, we would not expect such a committed historian to tell us the truth about the role of the communists in the 1940s. The Cripps Mission comes and fails. The AICC passes the 'Quit India' resolution. The leaders are swept away to jails. The country erupts in spontaneous protest and violence. The British unleash unprecedented repression, says our historian:

> The Government on its part went all out to crush the 1942 movement. Its repression knew no bounds. The Press was completely muzzled. The demonstrating crowds were

[30] Ibid., p. 272.

> machine-gunned and even bombed from the air. Prisoners were tortured. The police and secret police reigned supreme. The military took over many towns and cities. Over 10,000 people died in police and military firings. Rebellious villages had to pay huge sums as punitive fines and the villagers had to undergo mass floggings. India had not witnessed such intense repression since the Revolt of 1857.[31]

But who was cheering this 'unprecedented repression', this repression without bounds, who was assisting it? 'In general,' says our eminent historian, 'the students, workers and peasants were the backbone of the "revolt", while the upper classes and the bureaucracy remained loyal to the Government.' What about the Communist Party of India? Did its top functionaries not hold secret meetings with officers of the British government up to and including Sir Richard Tottenham, the additional secretary in the home department, and Sir Reginald Maxwell, the home member, the two who personally directed this repression which knew no bounds? What about the 'Progress Reports' which the Communist Party of India regularly submitted to the British to report the good work its members were doing to sabotage the 1942 movement?[32] Not one word from our eminence!

Hence is objective history forged!

[31] Ibid., pp. 264–65.

[32] The documents are reproduced in my M.N. Roy Memorial Lecture, *'The Only Fatherland': Communists, 'Quit India', and the Soviet Union,* ASA, 1991.

15

'Maybe perhaps, probably mostly.... *Therefore*'

Lord Indra is 'rowdy and amoral'.[1] The god Krishna has a 'rather questionable personal record'.[2] Lord Shiva is just 'a development of phallic cults'.[3] Bhakti is just the reflection of 'the complete dependence of the serfs or tenants on the landowners in the context of Indian feudal society'.[4]

The fact apart that the 'evidence' for such constructions itself consists of assertions and conjectures, what a desiccated mind such assertions exhibit! That it should see nothing but questionable conduct in Krishna, that even a foreigner – Stella Kramrisch – should see such an effulgence in the concept of Shiva and this eminent historian just the extended phallus, that he should see nothing more in bhakti than a reflection of feudalism – what telling evidence of the success of Macaulay, the missionaries and Marx!

God was made accessible to everybody through bhakti, the historian teaches us, and this, he says, 'was in tune with the social outlook of the times, when the feudatories considered

[1] D.N. Jha, *Ancient India, An introductory outline,* Manohar, New Delhi, 1977, 1997, p. 18. Unless otherwise indicated, all page numbers in this chapter refer to this publication.

[2] p. 91.

[3] p. 90.

[4] p. xviii.

themselves as meditating at the feet of their masters'.[5] Surely, one of the features of feudalism was that the overlord, the monarch, say, was put beyond the reach of common folk – if they were lucky, they might reach the intermediary just above them, hardly ever could they get their wail heard higher up. So why would it not have been as much 'in tune with the social outlook of the times' for the Supreme Deity to be put beyond the reach of all rather than being made accessible to everyone through bhakti?

As one would expect from an eminent historian, the Brahmins and the warriors, he teaches us, had formed a 'class alliance', and, therefore, 'as elsewhere in India from now on the priests began to play the second fiddle to the ruler and strike mephistophelian bargains'.[6] What the evidence is of the 'class alliance', of the priests 'playing second fiddle', of the 'mephistophelian bargains' – not a word. We, the eminent historians, hold these truths to be self-evident...!

Such assertions are standard form for our eminent historians – the widely used book of D.N. Jha, *Ancient India, An introductory outline,* is studded with these. If one were to merely reproduce what, for instance, the Shia scholars and historians say about three of the four 'rightly guided Caliphs' and about some of the members of the Prophet's own family, if one were merely to reproduce what they say without embellishing the account with any of the adjectives and descriptions of the kind these eminent historians paste on Shiva, Krishna and others – they would be the first to jump and shout, 'He is denigrating the revered figures of Islam.' But as these are Hindu gods and goddesses, the adjectives are not only permissible, they are de riguer!

On point after point these eminent historians are forced to acknowledge that there is next to no evidence to support what

[5] p. 106.
[6] p. 24.

they are saying. But in the very next paragraph, sometimes even the next sentence, what is acknowledged to be without basis becomes a fact.

'Gold *may have been* imported from South India....,' says our author. 'Silver was imported *probably* from Afghanistan and Iran. Copper *may have been* brought from South India.... Alabaster *may have been* brought from a number of places both to the east and the west....'[7] But though such is the basis, the author proceeds with complete confidence to present a preconceived picture of Harappan life.

Excavations show that the Harappan civilization covered areas from Musa Khel in the North-West to Kolhapur in southern Maharashtra to locations far to the East. How a few 'groups' of invading Aryans overran this extensive civilization without leaving any archaeological or literary trace is not explained, but the standard 'Aryans-from-Mesopotamia' theory – with an emphasis on their subjugating native Dravidians – is repeated at length.

Aryans race for settlements, cattle, booty – without an iota of evidence. From this, the further extension: 'This often led to conflicts between various Aryan tribes.' The Rig Veda refers to a battle of ten kings, our author says in support of his proposition. And then, *'It is likely that* there took place other inter-tribal wars of this kind, *of which we have no records!'*[8]

It is mandatory in such books to maintain that beef was eaten in ancient India, and so we read, 'It (the cow) was not yet held sacred; both oxen and cows were slaughtered for food. Beef was a delicacy offered to the guest...' 'The cow is described at one or two places in the Rig Veda as not to be killed (*aghanya*),' our author allows. No matter. 'But this *may* only imply its economic importance,' he declares![9]

[7] p. 7.
[8] pp. 12–13.
[9] p. 14.

All the standard clichés: Aryans from outside; subjugate the native Dravidians; strive to maintain their racial purity; hence, the four castes.[10] Proof?: '*Perhaps* most of the ordinary members of the aboriginal tribes were considered as being outside the pale of Aryan life and were reduced to the lowest position in the new society. As the Aryans settled among them, they laid stress on purity of blood and feared that their assimilation with dark-skinned local inhabitants would lead to the loss of their Aryan identity [a certainty that requires no evidence in support!], *though enough non-Aryan blood already flowed in their veins....*'[11] The latter having been the case, would the Aryans still have been striving to maintain 'the purity of their blood'?

'Weaving,' we are told, 'was practiced on a wide scale *but perhaps* remained confined mainly to women...'[12] 'The rise of new arts and crafts,' we are told, 'may have led to rudimentary commodity production and trade. In this period the *vaishyas may* have engaged in trade....'[13] '*Shudras* were meant to serve the three higher *varnas* and formed the bulk of the labouring masses,' we are told. '*Most likely* the community exercised some sort of general control over them; in this sense *they may* be compared with the helots of Sparta.'[14] 'The emergence of the *gahapati* from the *Vedic* householder to a comparatively wealthy head of the household,' we are told, '*may* indicate the growing disparity of wealth within society. Common people, slaves and labourers seem to have coveted his wealth and wished him harm; often he is depicted as keeping a bodyguard to defend himself.'[15] 'The cultural lag of the aboriginals, living mainly as hunters and fowlers,' we are told, 'in contrast to the *varna*-divided society.... *perhaps* led in the *post-Vedic* period to the

[10] pp. 16–17.
[11] p. 17.
[12] p. 21.
[13] p. 21.
[14] p. 21.
[15] p. 31.

growth, of untouchability.'[16] 'The tremendous increase in the military strength and the coercive power of the State,' we are told, '*seems to have* enhanced the prestige and glamour of the Maurya king....'[17]

'How far the *Arthashastra* provisions were actually put into practice *is difficult to ascertain. But there is little doubt that* the needs of the imperial administration prompted the Mauryas to increase the number of officers in their employ. All this, together with the growing importance of the warrior class from pre-Maurya times, *may* have led to the exaltation of the royal power....'[18] 'Kautilya fixes the wages of artisans, who were *probably mostly* shudras. They *seem to have been* the worst paid members of the society.... He recommends the recruitment of vaishyas and shudras in the army; *but their actual enrollment as soldiers is extremely doubtful.*'[19] If some statement of Kautilya supports the thesis of these historians, it is proof. If it goes against the thesis, the absence of empirical evidence – which is neither cited nor available! – leaves one 'extremely doubtful' that reality accorded with that proposition!

On one page we are told in surprise, 'Although a brahmana, Kautilya asks the king to confiscate temple treasures, put up sudden miracles and set up new images to collect money from the credulous.'[20] Just two pages later Kautilya is charged with an anxiety to protect the position of the ex-Arya slaves as distinguished from the non-Arya or shudra slaves and this, Jha says, 'is understandable; Kautilya was a brahmana'.[21]

The social order, Jha says, did not function as smoothly as the brahmanical lawgivers had envisaged. The kshatriyas and vaishyas were chaffing at their lower social position and, of

[16] pp. 31–32.
[17] p. 58.
[18] pp. 58–59.
[19] p. 64.
[20] p. 62.
[21] p. 64.

course, as the theory would lead us to believe, 'The shudras were no less hostile to the upper classes. They were grossly dissatisfied with the conditions of their life and indulged in criminal activities. [Notice the, at this stage surreptitious, invention of the cause: the shudras indulged in criminal activities because they were grossly dissatisfied with the conditions of their life.] Several categories of offenders and suspects, listed by Kautilya, belonged to the shudra order. He ordains that when a shudra calls himself a brahmana, steals the property of gods, or is hostile to the king, either his eyes shall be destroyed by the application of a poisonous ointment, or he shall have to pay a fine of 800 *panas. This implies that some shudras bore hostility to the priestly and ruling classes.*'[22] Could it not be the other way around? That only those who engaged in criminal conduct were dubbed as shudras and consigned to the periphery, and that these were few in number?

The next sentence carries the projection further! 'Our sources indicate the existence of several religious sects,' says the author, 'which *may* have led to tensions and conflicts.'[23]

And, of course, the Hindus could not have done anything original: the gods and goddesses which the Hindus worship too must have been borrowed from others, at the least for authenticity they need mention in books of foreigners! 'The Greek ambassador also speaks of Herakles being worshipped in the Mathura region,' says the author, adding, 'this god *may* have been Krishna of later legends.'[24] Similarly, 'Shri of the *Arthashastra* identified with Shri-Lakshmi (the wife of Vishnu), *may* have originally been non-Aryan fertility goddess who found her way into the brahmanical religion…'[25] As this was the case with the gods and goddesses themselves, one

[22] p. 65.
[23] p. 65.
[24] p. 66.
[25] p. 66.

cannot but believe, 'The main inspiration of Maurya art was *perhaps* derived from Persian imperial art.'[26]

And soon the differences lead to conflict and that leads to social and religious tensions! 'The ideological conflict between the Vedic brahmanas and the followers of the newly-born protestant creeds,' says our author, '*may have* been a potential source of social and religious tension, *though an actual example of this is wanting*.'[27]

Could a leader who did not denounce or pulverize Hinduism ever be good? As is well known, in one of his edicts Ashoka counsels people to desist from extolling their own sect and denigrating that of others. What does our eminent author see in this? The squelching of free speech! 'By not permitting free expression of differences of opinion,' warns our author, 'one may very often aggravate concealed tensions.' 'But Ashoka's insistence on their suppression may be understood in the context of the need for unity in the empire.' Jha recalls that 'Ashoka banned festive meetings or gatherings', and says that this was done, '*perhaps* due to his fear of conflicts arising out of differences of opinion'. While this is just conjecture, by the very next sentence it becomes the basis for an entire construction. 'The measure is in conformity with the strictly centralised administration of the Maurya empire,' says our author. 'Popular meetings *could* be utilised to criticize and attack the king's new ideas. Their suppression *therefore seems to have been* intended to stifle any popular opposition to the king's ideas and administrative measures.'[28] '*Therefore*,' and '*seems to have been*' – both in the same breath, without even a comma to separate them!

In keeping with the teachings of the Buddha, Ashoka exhorted people to shun all 'useless ceremonies and sacrifices'.

[26] p. 70.
[27] p. 67.
[28] pp. 67–68.

Our author's construction? 'Ashoka's attack on rituals and sacrifices was *probably* intended to undermine the influence of the priests, who presided over various ceremonies and thus cashed in on popular superstition.'[29]

Notice the sequence. The eminent historian starts on the assumption that, evidence or no evidence, there must have been tension in the society. Ashoka, being anxious to serve the 'need for unity of his empire' and to squash opposition to his new ideas, bans meetings. He suppresses expression of opinion, he moves to exorcise ceremonies and sacrifices. This step, one must presume from the author's own analysis, could not but have increased social and religious tensions. Nevertheless, Ashoka pressed ahead with the step because of his overriding need to undermine the influence of the priests. His emphasis on non-violence, says our author, 'obviously hit the interests of the brahmanas, for whom animal sacrifice was a source of livelihood.'[30] The circle is thus complete: The brahmins acquire influence; they depend on sacrifices; Ashoka emphasises non-violence, and exorcises sacrifices; thereby he undermines their influence! Circle completed! Theory proved!

The guilds come into being, the variety of professions multiplies. To his discomfiture, our author has to acknowledge that the condition of even the artisans improved. But our author is quick to recover his gloom and censure! 'Artisans and craftsmen were largely drawn in this period from the shudras,' says our author, 'who gained in wealth and status on account of the progress of crafts and commerce.... The economic distinctions between the vaishyas and the shudras thus tended to be blurred....' That, unfortunately, is an unavoidable fact, and so our author moves swiftly to discount it! 'But most of the artisans known from inscriptions were confined to the Mathura region and the western Deccan,' he says. 'It is therefore

[29] p. 68.
[30] pp. 68–69.

difficult to postulate any change in the living conditions of the main body of the shudras.' Could it not be that the condition of the shudras in general did improve but that the relevant inscriptions have yet been discovered only from Mathura and the western Deccan? Indeed, that they have been recovered from areas which, given the primitive modes of transport and communication must be considered to have been far apart, would suggest that the improvement was pervasive.

And notice also how scrupulous and demanding our author is regarding evidence on this point, and how on other matters – those which will enable him to push his prejudice – he is satisfied with 'may have', 'perhaps', 'probably mostly'. And so a few sentences later our author has recovered his composure fully, and we get his firm conclusion: 'Most shudras seethed in discontent. *It is not unlikely that* under such foreign rulers as the Shakas and Kushanas, who were not committed to the varna ideology, they turned against the brahmanas. This *may* explain why Manu provided a number of safeguards against the hostile activities of the shudras!'[31]

A few pages later we are fed the standard line which we have encountered in other books also of these eminent historians – 'The growing popularity of Buddhism and other heterodox sects went against the Vedic sacrifices involving animal slaughter. The heretical attack on Vedic institutions and sacrifices seriously undermined the prestige and authority of the brahmanas....' Thus far the theory with which we have become familiar: Brahmins depended on sacrifices; Buddhism undermined them by weaning the people from sacrifices. Next, its development. To save themselves the brahmins, 'therefore appropriated a number of popular cults with significant following', says the author. 'In the process brahmanical religion underwent some important changes and most of the Vedic gods passed into oblivion,' and their places were taken by Brahma, Vishnu and Shiva.

[31] p. 85.

Of course, the attributes read into these gods could also not have been original to the Hindus! Thus, about the notion that when evil is rampant Vishnu appears in various incarnations to save mankind, says our author, '*perhaps* the idea was borrowed from the bodhisattva doctrine of Buddhism. It *may* have evolved with the identification of Vishnu with Krishna....'[32]

While he is ever so scrupulous in demanding evidence about improvement in the condition of shudras, our author has no difficulty in deciphering the inner workings of the mind of Chandragupta! The author, in his chapter about the Gupta period entitled, 'The Myth of the Golden Age', says, 'After centuries of political disintegration an empire came to be established in AD 319 under the Guptas. Their origin and original home cannot be determined with certainty. But *very likely* they were initially a family of landowners who acquired political control in the region of Magadha. The first Gupta ruler of consequence was Chandragupta I. By marrying a Lichchhavi princess *he sought to gain in prestige* though Vaishali does not appear to have been a part of his kingdom....'[33]

'Perhaps' leads to 'therefore' which proves the theory – by establishing the progressive immiserization of the artisans and peasants and their sinking into being the property of vested interests! 'The weakening of the commercial links with the western world,' says our author, '*perhaps* stopped the movement of artisans and traders from one part of the country to the other.' Next sentence: 'Immobile artisans *therefore* remained attached to villages where they produced for local consumption. In course of time they, like the peasants, were also transferred to the recipients of village endowments.'[34]

In spite of the labours and proclamations of the brahmin lawgivers, 'The varna system did not always function smoothly,'

[32] p. 89.
[33] p. 96.
[34] p. 102.

the student is taught by our eminent historian. 'The *Shanti Parva* of the Mahabharata which *may be* assigned to the Gupta period, contains at least nine verses which stress the need of combination of the brahmanas and the kshatriyas; these *may* indicate *some kind of* concerted opposition from the vaishyas and shudras....'[35]

A verse, says our author, speaks of vaishyas and shudras wilfully uniting themselves with the wives of brahmins. From this one verse the author deduces, 'The shudras seem to have been particularly hostile to the existing social order.' '*The Anushasana Parva* of the Mahabharata represents them as destroyers of the king. Another [unnamed] contemporary work describes them as hostile, violent, boastful, short-tempered, untruthful....' 'All this as well as passages from the legal texts,' declares our author, '*would suggest* a conflict between the shudras and the ruling classes. *But references to actual revolt by the shudras against the upper classes are not recorded.*'[36]

By such reiteration, on the basis of such 'evidence' the eminent historian paints a picture of a society riven by discord, a society in which the masses are pushed into penury and disability. To defang the resulting discontent and revolts of the poorest classes, the clever brahmins set the boa constrictor of Hinduism, to, on the one hand, appropriate local cults and, on the other, inveigle into the minds of the masses doctrines and notions which would reconcile them to their dismal lot.

Having struck a 'class alliance' with the rulers, having struck their 'mephistophelian bargains', the brahmins gird up to counter the twin challenges – of the campaign against sacrifices by Buddhists and by the growing tradition of asceticism. 'The brahmanas *by way of compromise invented a formula,*' says our author, 'by which the life of an Aryan individual was divided into four stages (*ashrams*)....'[37]

[35] p. 105.
[36] pp. 105–06.
[37] p. 26.

Brahmins invent the Theory of Karma to persuade the poor masses that they should serve their masters well in this life so that they may get their reward in some subsequent life. They invent *avataravad* to persuade the suffering masses that they need not do anything in particular, for God himself shall take form and relieve them of the evil which is crushing them. By teaching us that our condition depends on our deeds, does the Theory of Karma induce us to sit helplessly, 'O, what can I do, I must have done something wrong that I am in this condition?' Or does it give us the assurance, 'Arise, awake, do your duty; what you do is what will determine your fate?' As for avataravada, having assured Arjuna that when evil mounts, to annihilate the evil and protect the good, he takes form, does Krishna tell Arjuna to, therefore, leave things to him, Krishna? Or does he exhort Arjuna to act, to fight and uproot evil himself?

What is seen by all to be proof of the inclusive character of Hinduism is to our author proof of its being the boa constrictor. 'The adoption of various deities, beliefs and superstitions by Vaishnavism,' says our author, 'indicates that it assimilated different popular cults and substituted faith for logic. It therefore acted as an effective instrument for reconciling the masses to their lot and maintaining the social division based on *varna*.'[38]

The double standard is as much a hallmark of these books as invention and conjecture. For the very things on account of which they extol Islam, for which they are in raptures about the Soviet Union, for those very things they condemn Hindus, their texts, their teachers, their rulers!

Bhakti is just a reflection of the subservience of the hapless tenant to the landlord under feudalism. The very word 'Islam' means 'surrender', they teach us in the same breath; such an exalted sentiment, they exclaim – total submission to the will of Allah.

[38] p. 108.

The taxes imposed by the Maurya kings were oppressive exactions for maintaining an ever-expanding coercive apparatus of the state, Jha insinuates.[39] But the jazyah exacted by the sultans was, as we have seen, a little something by paying which Hindus were able to lead normal lives! When Aurangzeb revived it, it was not, we have seen, meant to put any economic pressure on Hindus to convert to Islam, it was not imposed to help the empire deal with financial difficulties either. Its incidence was meant to be light, and care was taken to ensure that it would be collected by honest, Allah-fearing Muslims! And there were many exemptions, don't forget – 'women, children, the disabled, the indigent, those whose income was less than the means of subsistence' were exempted, as were those who were being useful to the empire by being in its service!

The Mauryas instituted a centralized, overbearing state. Their army was an instrument for maintaining domination, it was the coercive arm of the state. Their legal and judicial system was, as such systems are, 'an important weapon of coercion in the hands of the ruling class'.[40] The standard line: from the textbook for Class III students in West Bengal to this college guide. Now, that being their standard, firmly held, so oft-repeated thesis, how come our eminences never come to say of Islamic law, the armies of the sultans and of the Mughal rulers that they too are weapons of coercion, domination, control?

The laws enacted by the republican states of ancient India extended the state's tentacles to such an extent that it came to control the private life of individuals and families, charges our author.[41] But Aurangzeb's orders to destroy temples, why, they left a great deal of latitude to local officials, as we have seen, in any case they were not anything new, in any case they were not enforced after 1679, in any case no general order to destroy

[39] pp. 49–50.
[40] pp. 50–51.
[41] pp. 54, 58.

temples seems to have been given, in any case Hindus were left free to worship in the privacy of their homes….!

Propositions from Kautilya and Patanjali are cited – invent cults so as to exact money from the ignorant, stage sudden miracles to garner money from the credulous, break up hostile tribes by using spies, prostitutes, soothsayers, poison, cash… – as proof that this was the pattern of life.[42] This is what Kautilya has written, therefore this is what must have been happening – that is the reasoning. But when I cite the Quran, the hadis, the fatwas, when I adduce five hundred pages of evidence from them, the standard retort is, 'But who follows these texts?'

The pattern works the other way too. Affirmations which do not fit the theory – for instance, the clearest possible statements in the texts that a person is a Brahmin not by virtue of his birth but by virtue of living up to the duties and norms which have been prescribed – are brushed aside: 'But they are just desiderata,' our theoreticians argue. 'There is no proof that life was lived in accordance with these statements of good intentions.' The statements in Manu that provide discriminatory punishments for identical offences are, of course, proof that differential justice was meted out in practice! As the provision in Stalin's 1937 Constitution granting the right of self-determination to nationalities – a provision which these textbooks invariably cite – is proof that the Soviet state in fact granted such an option to nationalities! As the fact that none of the nationalities exercised the option between 1917 and 1985 is proof that the Soviets had solved the nationalities problem!

In this textbook as in others, Hinduism is charged with assimilating local cults. This is a doubly useful charge – on the one hand it is used to argue that there is nothing original in Hinduism, that it is just a piling up of practices taken from local, animist, fertility cults, the emphasis being on the last!

[42] pp. 62–64.

And, on the other, to argue that it is a boa constrictor which does not let any other religious tradition survive. The point is also made that the older traditions and beliefs have survived nonetheless, that the people continued to retain, as they retain today, beliefs in malevolent spirits and the like.[43] Have you ever seen a book by any of these scholars which points out, as Ali Dashti and others do, that the entire ritual associated with the haj, for instance, is a carry-over of pagan practices from pre-Islamic periods? Or that the Quran is full of verses about malevolent djinns and the like?

Ashoka's tolerance is put to his compulsions – he had to adopt this posture of tolerance because of the need to maintain the unity of his empire, we are taught by our author.[44] But those two sentences in the Quran – 'To you your religion, to me mine,' and 'There is no compulsion in religion' – which are flatly overrun by the text itself, to say nothing of the entire history of Islamic rule over 1,400 years, those two sentences are flaunted as proof-positive of Islam being not just committed to peace and tolerance, they are proof that it is *The* Religion of Peace and Tolerance!

Although Kanishka convened the Fourth Buddhist Council, although great Buddhist scholars and teachers were admittedly associated with him, Kanishka's conversion to Buddhism is declared by our eminent historian to have been 'political'. Kanishka went through no profound experience, he says.[45] Have you ever come across any of these eminences looking askance on this ground – the absence of 'profound experience' – at the lakhs of conversions which Islamic invaders and rulers secured at the point of the sword? Or at the mass conversions which Christian missionaries arrange even today? Those are a result of profound inner experiences, are they?

[43] p. 66.
[44] pp. 67–68.
[45] p. 75.

'Simultaneously with the emergence of these gods,' writes the eminent historian, 'Brahmanism was assimilating a variety of popular cults. Animals, trees, mountains and rivers came to acquire divine association. The cow became an object of worship; *the seeds of modern communal politics centering round the "sacred" animal were thus sown....*'[46] He would, of course, not see the seed in the fact that while the Quran does not require the sacrifice of cows,[47] the text has been altered by Islamic authorities in India; he would not see the cause in the fact that 'Muslim divines' like Ali Mian instigate Muslims here to kill cows in India *precisely because cows are revered by the Hindus* – those being their precise words.[48]

In Jha's book as in others of this school, Hindus are invariably condemned for sacrifices 'involving animal slaughter,' they are lampooned for getting their comeuppance in Buddhism and Ashoka who weaned the people away from these sacrifices. Lakhs and lakhs of animals – cows, goats, and the rest – are slaughtered every Eid. Ever heard any of these eminences characterize these sacrifices as 'involving animal slaughter'? And, of course, were a Hindu or Buddhist at a dinner to request vegetarian fare, he would be sneered at as a primitive by these jet-set progressives.

When Manu specifies different tasks for different sections, he is held up as urging this on behalf of an exploitative order. Simultaneously, the Guptas are condemned for demanding the same work as compulsory labour from all sections of society! Our eminent historian fumes: 'In the Maurya period slaves and hired labourers were subjected to forced labour; this was supervised by an officer and was paid for. But in Gupta times it was extended to all classes of subjects, and it came to include all kinds of work.' Of course, that the Soviets demanded 'all

[46] p. 90.

[47] The relevant ayats are the Quran, XXII.34–37.

[48] For illustrative extracts, *The World of Fatwas*, op. cit., pp. 143–64.

kinds of work' from 'all classes of subjects' – specially in the slave-labour camps – is proof positive of their abolishing class distinctions, of their ushering in the egalitarian Paradise!

'The *Kamasutra* of Vatsayana informs us,' our author continues, 'that peasant women were forced to perform unpaid work of various kinds, such as filling the granaries of the village headman, taking things in and out of the house, cleaning the house, purchasing of cotton, wood, flax, hemp and thread, and the purchase, sale and exchange of various articles....'.[49] Not very onerous, I would think, compared to what lakhs like Solzhenitsyn were forced to do in what has been to these eminences 'The Only Fatherland'. And if you point to either fact – either to their double standards in the two cases, or to the fact that Soviet society was characterized by even sharper differences between the haves and the not-in-the-party have-nots than free societies – you are a reactionary-revanchist-communal-fascist!

Jha, like the rest, strains to ensure that every facet from which pride in the past may be derived is tarred. Monarchies were replaced by some republics, and there was some democracy in these new formations, you say? A 'glorified', 'much trumpeted notion', scoffs our historian. True, 'all important issues were placed before the assembly, and no decision was taken in the absence of unanimity among its members,' but the assemblies consisted mostly of kshatriyas – and so these republics were really oligarchies and not true democracies.[50] As the Union of Soviet Socialist Republics and the Peoples Republic of China surely were – true democracies, not oligarchies!

The final chapter is climactic. The nationalist historians have portrayed the Gupta Age as a Golden Age, says Jha. That is a myth, the period was nothing of the sort.

True, the Guptas extended the empire, our historian cannot

[49] D. N. Jha, op. cit., pp. 101–02.
[50] pp. 52–53.

but acknowledge. But it did not cover all of India, he says – he is requiring 'full democracy', he is requiring that the whole of India be one when talking of *fifteen hundred* years ago! The fact that rulers in the south paid tribute to the Guptas, the fact that a southern ruler sought permission of the Gupta king to do something, these do not establish that the Guptas exercised suzerainty over the latter, he says.

Having denounced the Mauryas for setting up a centralized administration, our eminence denounces the Guptas for decentralizing it.

True, he says, philosophy, art, literature flourished – Ajanta, Ellora, Kalidasa, Aryabhatta..., the poor man is forced to acknowledge. But he is not the one to give up. The paintings of Ajanta fall to his searching class analysis! 'Although the theme of paintings at Ajanta is religious,' he pronounces, 'one can see in them a dramatic panorama of the life of princes, nobles, warriors and sages. The general impression one gets is one of affluence of the upper classes; the normal hardships of the village folk are not portrayed in the paintings.'

True, there was an efflorescence of Sanskrit literature, Jha has to admit. But this literature too falls – by the same touchstone, class analysis! 'Sanskrit literature, like art,' he declaims, 'was mainly enjoyed by the court, upper classes and the aristocracy. The uneducated masses could have hardly understood and much less appreciated the ornate court literature. Not surprisingly therefore the leading male characters of high social status in the contemporary plays speak polished Sanskrit, and those of low status and all women speak Prakrit.' And what proportion of 'the uneducated masses', pray, understood Lenin's *Collected Works,* to say nothing of Mao's 'philosophical essays'!

True, the astronomical works of Aryabhatta and Varahamihira were noteworthy, our author admits. But their insights were not followed up, he swiftly adds. In any case, progress represented in the writings of such observers 'owed, only in part, to indigenous tradition...' One of the five astronomical systems dealt with by Varahamihira was Roman, a second one was of Paul of Alexandria, says our author. What of the other three? What of Aryabhatta's insights – among these that the earth revolves around the sun, that it rotates on its axis? The thing that strikes our author about such insights is not that they were so far ahead of Copernicus and Kepler but that they were 'contrary to the established Indian notion'!

So the notion of 'the so-called Hindu renaissance', he says, rests on the writings of Kalidasa alone. 'But the works of Kalidasa,' declares our historian, 'are not indicative of an intellectual rebirth or revival of literary activity; they merely imply a further development of the literary forms and styles which were evolving in the earlier period.' Not just Kalidasa, 'The *Puranas* had existed much before the time of the Guptas in the form of bardic literature, in the Gupta age they were finally compiled and given their present form.' Had the stories Shakespeare used for his plays not existed before? Did his writing not amount, does not virtually all writing amount to 'merely... a further development of the literary forms and styles which were evolving in the earlier period'?

Even the growth of bhakti, the turning to gods and goddesses which these historians usually adduce as evidence of increasing oppression in society is now pooh-poohed lest it become grist for the nationalists. 'Nor does the growing popularity of Vaishnavism and Shaivism mean any religious resurgence,' our author declares. 'The basic tenets of the two religions [notice – not the two sects of Hinduism, but '*the two religions*'!] go back to earlier times; now in the context of emerging feudalism they could attract a greater following.'

What to talk of that 'so-called Hindu renaissance', the term Hindu itself is a misnomer, our historian declares. 'It was first used by the Arabs in the post-Gupta period,' he says, 'to describe the inhabitants of Hindu [*sic.*] (India). Ancient Indians never thought of themselves as Hindus.' What they thought of themselves as is, naturally, a detail so minor that so eminent an authority cannot but leave it for others to work out!

His role is to lay down the line, which he does with the air of finality that we would expect from so exalted an authority: 'The much-publicised Hindu renaissance was, in reality, not a renaissance, much less a Hindu one.'[51]

Jha's triumphal conclusion:

> Some Indian historians have been so enamoured of the Guptas as to tirelessly speak [that is how those whom these eminences disapprove of speak, never the eminences; how do the latter speak? Tiresomely?] of their rule as representing a golden age of Indian history. In an emotionally surcharged multi-volume work [the other man's work is marred by emotion, never their's!] we are told in a vein of romantic lamentation: 'life was never happier'. Yet it was during the period of the Guptas that in certain parts of the country [how much of the country's area or population did these 'certain parts' cover?] serfdom appeared leading eventually to the economic bondage of the peasantry. Women became an item of property and came to live in the perpetual tutelage of man, notwithstanding their idealisation in art and literature [what appears in art and literature, if it runs counter to the theory, is mere 'idealisation'; what appears in Manu, so long as it can be yoked to shore up the theory, is proof of the way things were in real life!]. Caste distinctions and caste rigidity became sharper than ever before; law and justice showed a definite bias in favour of the higher castes. [That on the basis of such 'evidence' as we have seen. And now see what he does to the statement of one of his prime witnesses which goes contrary to the theory.] Fa-hsien, the Chinese Buddhist pilgrim-scholar who came to India during the reign of Chandragupta II, tells us that the people were generally happy. True, the upper classes were happy and prosperous, and lived in comfort and ease, as can be judged from the contemporary art and literature. But this could have

[51] For the foregoing discussion, pp. 112–15.

> been hardly true of the lower orders; the Chinese pilgrim speaks of the plight of the chandalas. The untouchable class as a whole came to be degraded further in the social scale. Social tensions continued. But religion was used as an instrument for maintaining the varna divided society.

The lesson?

> For the upper classes all periods in history have been golden; for the masses none.

Hence, his eminence's final message for our woebegone masses:

> The truly golden age of the people does not lie in the past, but in the future.[52]

In 1917, perchance!

[52] For this concluding peroration, pp. 115–16.

16

Gavah chust, muddayi sust!

So, the gods of the Hindus are 'rowdy and amoral', with a 'rather questionable personal record', they are just developments of primitive cults – animism, fertility and the rest, specially the phallic cult! Ashoka's policy of tolerance grew out of compulsions of state, not conviction. Kanishka's Buddhism too was just politic as it did not spring from any profound inner experience. Aryabhatta's insights can scarcely be reckoned as they were against accepted Indian notions! Kalidas's works were just a development of what was being written. The order as a whole and throughout the recorded history of India has been exploitative, marked by seething tensions. In particular, the Gupta Age was no Golden Age. That Golden Age lies in the future, and that future lies in 1917!

What fidelity to the Commandments! For hath not the First in-the-Trinity warned, 'The tradition of all the dead generations weighs like a nightmare on the brain,' and has he not therefore commanded,

> The social revolution of the nineteenth century cannot draw its poetry from the past, but only from the future. It cannot begin with itself before it has stripped off all superstition in regard to the past. Earlier revolutions required recollections of past world history in order to drug themselves concerning their own content. In order to arrive at its own content, the

> revolution of the nineteenth century must let the dead bury their dead....[1]

Hence, off with the golden age stuff! You say such twisting of facts, the drawing of such definite conclusions from such infirm data is not objective? Had the Third-in-the-Trinity not *shown* that objectivity, like 'freedom' in writing, is just a mask for hiding the *real* interests one is serving? Had he not *shown* that writing 'cannot be a means of enriching individuals or groups', that 'it cannot, in fact, be an individual undertaking, independent of the common cause of the proletariat'? Had he not therefore commanded,

> Down with non-partisan writers! Down with literary supermen! Literature must become part of the common cause of the proletariat, 'a cog and a screw' of one single great Social-Democratic mechanism set in motion by the entire politically conscious vanguard of the working class....

Of course, everyone is free, and will be free to write whatever he wants, 'without any restrictions', he had assured. 'I am bound to accord you, in the name of free speech, the full right to shout, lie and write to your heart's content. But you are bound to grant me, in the name of freedom of association, the right to enter into, or withdraw from, association with people advocating this or that view' – and as I now control the state, and because all you are doing is to shout, lie and write to please and enrich yourself....!

You talk of freedom, objectivity – that is 'sheer hypocrisy'. Had he not *shown*,

> There can be no real and effective 'freedom' in a society based on the power of money, in a society in which the masses of

[1] Karl Marx, 'The eighteenth Brumaire of Louis Bonaparte', Marx and Engels, *Selected Works,* Volume I, pp. 398, 400.

> working people live in poverty and the handful of rich live like parasites. Are you free in relation to your bourgeois publisher, Mr. Writer, in relation to your bourgeois public, which demands that you provide it with pornography in frames and paintings, and prostitution as a 'supplement' to 'sacred' scenic art? This absolute freedom is a bourgeois or anarchist phrase.... One cannot live in a society and *be* free from society. The freedom of the bourgeois writer, artist or actress is simply masked (or hypocritically masked) dependence on the money-bag, on corruption, on prostitution.

As that freedom is just a mask for serving the masters' interests, as it is freedom only to provide pornography and prostitution to the masters, what if it is sacrificed for the good of the masses it serves to exploit and crush? Hence, one twist of the vice after another, hence one writer after another packed off. Hence our duty to rip off the mask and show the reality behind these pretensions to freedom and objectivity:

> And we socialists expose this hypocrisy and rip off the false labels, not in order to arrive at a non-class literature and art (that will be possible only in a socialist extra-class society), but to contrast this hypocritically free literature, which is in reality linked to the bourgeoisie, with a *really* free one that will be *openly* linked to the proletariat....[2]

Recall Panikkar's fuming: 'He [that is, me] cannot hope to remain a virgin after selling himself in the flesh-market.... As for me [that is, Panikkar], unlike him, I do not hunt with the hound and run with the hare. I contribute signed articles to the publications of the Communist Party, because I believe in the ideals it stands for....!'

So, uprooting the moorings of the people, discrediting

[2] For the foregoing passages, V.I. Lenin, *Collected Works*, Volume X, pp. 44–49.

and destroying every element in the past from which the people may derive pride and identity – these are as essential to the purpose of these progressives today as they were to the purposes of the missionaries and Macaulay in the nineteenth century. So, what they do is done towards a high purpose, and is therefore beyond such bourgeois criteria as objectivity and veracity. As what the rest do is to perpetuate the exploitation of the labouring masses, what if we plant a concoction or two to further the Great Cause!

So, writers have to write in service of the Great Cause. And *what* they have to write in regard to the history of a country has all been set down already by the 'classics' as the Great Ones are called. *Marx*: the mode of production determines the relations of production, these in turn determine the social, political, intellectual process in general; at first property is commonly owned, there are no classes, society is egalitarian; with the increasing incapacity of this arrangement to meet the growing requirements of the population, land becomes scarce, falls to private ownership, classes emerge in society....; division of labour, class differences increase....; class antagonisms intensify....; the form of the state, its appurtenances – law, bureaucracy, the coercive apparatus, the ideology that is given currency, religion – are all instruments of the ruling class to perpetuate its hegemony. *Engels:* the sequence goes through five stages: classless primitive society; slave economy; feudalism; capitalism; socialism and finally communism.... *Lenin:* that the book, *The Origin of the Family, Private Property and the State,* in which Engels spells out this sequence is 'one of the fundamental works of socialism every sentence of which can be accepted with confidence, in the assurance that it has not been said at random but is based on immense historical and political material'; that this sequence is a *universal* law, that *all* countries and societies pass through those stages:

> The development of *all* human societies for thousands of years, *in all countries without exception,* reveals a general conformity to law, a regularity and consistency...

And the stages were spelled out by the 'classics', as also the characteristics of each stage:

> ....so that at first we had a society without classes – the original patriarchal, primitive society, in which there were no aristocrats; then we had a society based on slavery – a slave-owning society... The division into slave-owners and slaves was the first important class division. The former group not only owned all the means of production – the land and the implements, however poor and primitive they may have been in those times – but also owned people. This group was known as slave-owners, while those who laboured and supplied labour for others were known as slaves.

You will recall that the very words are reproduced in the books we have been surveying – from the Class IV textbooks of the West Bengal government to the more erudite books of our eminents! And then the next stage, duly discovered as such in ancient India by our eminents:

> This form was followed in history by another – feudalism. In the great majority of countries slavery in the course of its development evolved into serfdom. The fundamental division of society was now into feudal lords and peasant serfs. The form of relations between people changed.... It was not considered that the feudal lord owned the peasants as chattel, but that he was only entitled to their labour, to the obligatory performance of certain services. In practice... serfdom... in no way differed from slavery...

Thence, within feudalism a new class – the capitalist class....

> The economic power of the landowning class declined and the power of the new class – the representatives of capital –

> developed. The reconstruction of society was such that all citizens seemed to be equal, the old division between slaves and slave-owners disappeared, all were regarded as equal before the law irrespective of what capital each owned; whether he owned land as private property, or was a poor man who owned nothing but his labour power – all were equal before the law. The law protects everybody equally; it protects the property of those who have it from attack by the masses who, possessing no property, possessing nothing but their labour-power, grow steadily impoverished and become converted into proletarians. Such is capitalist society.... This society advanced against serfdom, against the old feudal system, under the slogan of liberty. But it was liberty for those who owned property...

Again, the words are repeated verbatim in our books. Intensifying contradictions, breakdown, growing consciousness and consolidation of the proletarians.... And then the golden age...

And so the firm advice, and the singular pair of spectacles through which *everything* must be viewed:

> This fundamental fact – the transition of society from primitive forms of slavery to serfdom and finally to capitalism – you must always bear in mind, for only by remembering this fact, only by examining all political doctrines placed in this fundamental scheme, will you be able to properly appraise these doctrines and understand what they refer to; for each of these great periods in the history of mankind, slave owning, feudal and capitalist, embraces scores and hundreds of centuries and presents such a mass of political forms, such a variety of political doctrines, opinions and revolutions, that this extreme diversity and immense variety (specially in connection with the political, philosophical and other doctrines of bourgeois scholars and politicians) can be understood only by firmly holding, as to a guiding thread, to this division of society into classes, this change in the forms of class rule, and from this standpoint examining all questions – economic, political, spiritual, religious, etc.

Any doubt about the guidelines our historians have been following in writing their textbooks for the NCERT? Can we be surprised when one of these eminents goes to such pains to ensure that the republican states of ancient India are not looked upon too highly when the master has declared,

> In every course on the history of ancient times, in any lecture on the subject, you will hear about the struggle which was waged between the monarchical and republican states. But the fundamental fact is that the slaves were not regarded as human beings – not only were they not regarded as citizens, they were not even regarded as human beings. Roman law regarded them as chattels. The law of manslaughter, not to mention the other laws for the protection of the person, did not extend to slaves. It defended only the slave-owners, who were alone recognised as citizens with full rights. But whether a monarchy was instituted or a republic, it was a monarchy of slave-owners or a republic of slave-owners. All rights were enjoyed by the slave-owners, while the slave was a chattel in the eyes of the law; and not only could any sort of violence be perpetrated against a slave, but even the killing of a slave was not considered a crime. Slave-owning republics differed in their internal organisation, there were aristocratic republics and democratic republics. In an aristocratic republic only a small number of privileged persons took part in the elections; in a democratic republic everybody took part – but everybody meant only the slave-owners, that is, everybody except the slaves. This fundamental fact must be borne in mind, because it throws more light on the question of the state and clearly demonstrates the nature of the state.

Should we have been surprised at the West Bengal textbook teaching the Class III student: the emergence of personal property, the growth of classes, the rich expropriating the poor, the poor being denied their due and in addition to being subjected to atyachar, the slaves rebelling, to discipline them the rich creating law, police, courts…? Should we have been surprised at the extreme labour our eminent friends put in to establish the expansion and consolidation of the Mauryan state as being nothing but the manifestation of the ruling classes acquiring the means of coercion…? Should we be surprised when our eminent historian says that there must have been clashes and tension even though evidence of these is not available…? Had the master not written it to be an axiom that

> The state is a machine for the oppression of one class by another, a machine for holding in obedience to one class other subordinate classes…. Neither under slavery nor under the feudal system could a small minority of people dominate over the vast majority without coercion. History is full of the constant attempts of the oppressed classes to throw of oppression…. In order to maintain their rule and to preserve their power, the feudal lords had to have an apparatus by which they could unite under their subjugation a vast number of people and subordinate them to certain laws and regulations; and all these laws fundamentally amounted to one thing – the maintenance of the power of the lords over the peasant serfs…[3]

The very words repeated again and again – from Class III textbooks of Bengal to the histories of ancient India written by our eminent historians. Stalin set these assertions and periods in stone by making them a part of the text the faithful memorized, *A Short History of the Communist Party of the Soviet Union!* Indeed, the books of our friends on ancient India can be seen as just a padding up with Indian examples a paragraph and a half from this textbook! Just as textbooks for students of Classes III to VI of the West Bengal government can be seen to be the exact facsimiles of the paragraphs! Here

[3] For convenience the preceding statements of Lenin on periodization and the state have all been taken from just one of his lectures: 'The State', delivered at the Sverdlov University in 1919: *Collected Works*, Volume XXIX, pp. 470–88.

is the sum total of what these books teach us expressed in Stalin's gospel:

> ....In primitive society people lived in tiny communities and jointly owned the means of production – the land, minerals, forests, waters and implements of labour. There were neither rich people nor poor; all were equal. But gradually there emerged private ownership of the means of production, and society was divided into the propertied and the non-propertied. The owners of the means of production began to exploit those who had no such means.
>
> Thus, society was split up into slaves and slave-owners in remote antiquity. The slave had no rights at all. He was considered not a human being but simply a 'talking implement' belonging to his master. The slave-owning system was replaced by the feudal system, under which society consisted of feudal lords and serf peasants. The peasants were attached to the land and their status differed little from that of slaves. But they nonetheless had a small personal husbandry on the plots of land given to them by the landowner, and for this they had to work for their lord for a certain number of days. The feudal system gave way to capitalism. In capitalist society all the basic means of production belong to the capitalists and the landowners. As distinct from the slave and the serf, the worker is a free man. But he owns nothing but the skill of his hands. To live he is compelled to hire himself out as a worker to the capitalist, to sell him his labour power. Essentially, capitalism is a system of hire-slavery.[4]

Each repeating the other, and thereby *proving* the proposition.... The Great Ones having laid down the immutable and universal laws which govern history, the Great Ones having set out the stages through which *all* societies invariably pass, the test of fidelity became repeating, and re-re-repeating the

[4] *A Short History of the Communist Party of the Soviet Union,* Progress Publishers, Moscow, 1977 reprint, p. 23.

propositions. It also became the test of scholarship: all one had to do was to excavate some fragment which would 'prove' that the propositions advanced by the 'classics' held true for India also, all one had to do was to weave these statements into one's narrative, indeed to spin one's narrative in such a way that, from time to time, these sentences emerged as if logically. And when in need, one could always affirm, that the situation *must* have been in accord with the propositions 'though an actual example of this is wanting'! And anyone who doubted that would *by that very doubt* be proving that he was objectively working for the interests of the exploiting classes!

Regurgitating these phrases, returning to them every few pages, having become the necessary as well as sufficient condition of scholarship, our historians have done no more: take that single lecture of Lenin, take just that paragraph and a half from Stalin's *Short History,* and you have the sum total of the analytical content of our eminent historians' output on ancient India. That is the pathetic aspect to history writing during the last thirty years. There is a comic aspect too.

As more and more facts became available about the ancient world, Marxist scholarship exerted to 'refine', to 'further develop' the laws and stages which Marx and Engels had set up. This became all the more necessary as more information about regions outside Europe became available. Even in the Soviet Union, even during the blight of Stalin's decades, Marxist scholars tried to go beyond the straitjacket of laws and stages set out by the founders. Often this was the result of individuals falling out of favour with the rulers: one moment M.N. Pokrovsky rules the roost – the exemplar of Marxist historical writing; the next he is accused of having totally misunderstood and misrepresented Marx; in denouncing him, his traducers advance contrary versions of Marxist propositions…., only to be denounced soon for those propositions…. Each somersault created the occasion, it *necessitated* a new version, a new 'interpretation', another 'creative development' of the 'classics'.

It was recognized that new information even about ancient Greece and Rome did not fully accord with the formulations of Marx and Engels: it could not be denied, for instance, that their characterization of earlier Graeco-Roman society as a 'slave-holding' society had been based upon a gross exaggeration – by Engels – of the number of slaves in Greek city states. As more information became available about prehistoric societies, it became more and more difficult to sustain the fiction that these had been characterized by commonly owned property, by egalitarian harmony; indeed, it now became impossible to deny that even in the animal world social structures were stratified.

In the same way, it became difficult to fit Asiatic societies into categories which had, after all, originated from information about the evolution of societies and states in Europe, and that too only from information which was available in mid-nineteenth century. Piles of additional information even about Europe has become known since then, and heaps more about China, India, and other societies. Sub-classifications and sub-periods accordingly were developed.

But here in India a simplistic recitation of the earlier phrases and categories remained enough. It is not just fidelity to the masters, therefore, which characterizes the history writing by these eminences. It is a simple-mindedness!

But there is an additional factor. Whitewashing the Islamic period is not the only feature which characterizes the work of these historians. There is in addition a positive hatred for the pre-Islamic period and the traditions of the country. Over the years entries about India in Soviet encyclopedias, for instance, became more and more ductile. They began to acknowledge ever so hesitantly that the categories and periods might need to be nuanced when they were extended to countries like China and India. They began to acknowledge that at various times there had been an overlapping and coexistence of different 'stages'. And, perhaps for diplomatic reasons alone, they became increasingly circumspect – careful to avoid denigrating our traditions.

In the standard two-volume Soviet work, *A History of India*,[5] for instance, we find more or less the same characterization of the different periods in Indian histories as we do in the volumes of our eminent historians. But the Soviet volumes have none of the scorn and animosity which we have encountered in the volumes of our eminent historians.

Soviet historians also maintain that after Kalinga, Ashoka 'merely changed his methods to some degree', that 'without forgetting his power and using force where necessary, the Mauryan ruler employed in the main ideological and diplomatic weapons', that 'relying on specially appointed officials and on diplomatic missions he went out of his way to consolidate his influence in territories not yet conquered, promising their inhabitants the emperor's affection and good care, fatherly concern and all manner of support'.[6] They too maintain that 'there is reason to believe that Ashoka was to a certain extent obliged to pursue a policy of religious tolerance, for orthodox and heretical teachings (apart from Buddhism) were still too strong for him to do otherwise', that 'it was precisely his policy of religious tolerance combined with skillful control exercised by the state over the life of various religious sects which enabled Ashoka to avoid conflict with the strong stratum of Brahmans, the Ajivikas, the Jains, and at the same time to promote Buddhism so effectively', that 'when Ashoka abandoned this policy of religious tolerance in the last years of his reign and began to pursue an overt pro-Buddhist policy, this gave rise to determined opposition among the adherents of other religions and brought serious consequences for the

[5] K. Antonova, G. Bongard-Levin, G. Kotovsky, *A History of India*, Progress Publishers, Moscow, Volumes I and II, 1973, English translation 1979.

[6] Ibid., volume I, p. 67.

king and his administration'.[7] In a word, in the Soviet volumes also, Ashoka's tolerance is a policy of expedience.

But while our historians concoct the theory that Brahmins, put out of livelihood by Ashoka's moves against sacrifices, undermined his rule, the Soviet historians put the blame on Ashoka himself. They write that 'towards the end of his reign Ashoka bled the state coffers white as a result of the generous gifts he made to the Buddhist Order to promote the propagation of Buddha's teachings'. They say that his officials warned his grandson, Sampadi of the consequences of 'the emperor's excessive gifts to the monks and demanded that they be revoked at once'. 'On Sampadi's orders Ashoka's instructions with regard to the offerings to the Buddhist Order were not carried out,' they write. They say that according to a number of sources Sampadi was an adherent of Jainism and that the queen Tishyarakshita '(who was also an opponent of Buddhism) took part in this conspiracy as well'.[8]

The Soviet historians give an extensive account of the republics. There is none of the scorn, there is none of the effort to cast doubt over the achievement at such an early date of democratic features in governance which we find in our eminent historians. On the contrary. Soviet historians record how these republican unions 'waged a resolute struggle against the monarchies and on a number of occasions secured impressive victories'. 'Buddhist sources even list some republican states among the "great lands",' they write. 'Both classical and Indian sources depict these non-monarchical unions as flourishing lands with a smoothly running system of administration and a high level of culture,' they write. They are, of course, careful to note that in some of these unions 'the real power was concentrated in the hands of the aristocratic council of the *kshatriyas*'. They note the 'internal contradictions' and class struggles within the

[7] Ibid., pp. 77–78.
[8] Ibid., p. 80.

assemblies of these republican unions, but they also note that 'the all-important characteristic of the political organisation to be found in the *ganas* and *sanghas,* which distinguished them from the monarchies, was that broad strata of the population were involved in political affairs, a fact which made them firm and durable unions'.[9]

They talk of Kanishka as 'one of the most famous rulers of ancient India'. They recall his attachment to Buddhism. There is none of the derision about his conversion having taken place without any profound inner experience![10]

The intellectual and spiritual synthesis which the Gita forged, the great and original breakthroughs it marked for instance, in the concept of inaction-in-action – the central importance it came to acquire in the minds of the people, the testimony of its vitality and centrality which is contained in the fact that so many leaders – Tilak, Gandhi, Sri Aurobindo, even Jawaharlal Nehru – hearkened to it – all these are recorded. The importance that the Gita attaches to bhakti is recalled. But there is none of that reductionism – 'bhakti is the handmaiden of feudalism' – which we find in our eminent historians.[11]

The work of Kalidasa is referred to as 'one of the pearls of ancient Indian literature', as 'an illustrious page of history of world's culture'. Kalidasa is credited with moving beyond the 'idealised image of Buddha and his faithful disciples' that one finds in the writings of Ashvaghosha. 'Without swerving from earlier traditions Kalidasa stood out as an innovator in many respects,' the Soviet historians write in contrast to our eminences. 'This explains why his work has been so accessible to the minds and hearts of the people of India throughout many centuries,' they write.[12]

[9] Ibid., pp. 98–100.
[10] Ibid., pp. 118–19.
[11] Ibid., pp. 148–51.
[12] Ibid., p. 169.

Similarly, while our eminent historians pour water even over the work of scientists of ancient India, the Soviet historians write:

> The first centuries AD were marked by major scientific achievement. This was particularly true of such fields as mathematics, astronomy, medicine and chemistry. Scientific treatises relating to a number of disciplines appeared. Requirements of the economy did a good deal to promote the advance of mathematics. Mathematics was important in relation to the construction of religious edifices, and for purposes of worship.
>
> In the ancient period and in the early Middle Ages lived the outstanding mathematicians Aryabhata (fifth and early sixth centuries), Varahamihira (sixth century) and Brahmagupta (late sixth and early seventh centuries), whose discoveries anticipated many scientific achievements of modern times. Aryabhatta knew that *pi* equaled 3.1416. The theorem known to us as Pythagoras' theorem was also known at that time. Aryabhatta proposed an original solution in whole numbers to the linear equation with two unknowns that closely resembles modern solutions.
>
> The ancient Indians evolved a system for calculation using zero, which was later taken over by the Arabs (the so-called Arabic numerals) and later from them by other peoples. The Aryabhatta school was also familiar with sine and cosine.
>
> Aryabhatta's follower, Brahmagupta, put forward solutions for a whole series of equations.
>
> Indian scholars of this period also scored important successes in the sphere of astronomy. Certain astronomical treatises of this period have been preserved, and these *siddhantas* bear witness to the high level of astronomical knowledge attained by the ancient Indians.
>
> Scholars of the Gupta period were already acquainted with the movement of the heavenly bodies, the reasons for eclipses of the Sun and the Moon. Aryabhatta put forward a brilliant thesis with regard to the Earth's rotation on its axis.

> Brahmagupta (many centuries before Newton) suggested that objects fall to the ground as a result of terrestrial gravity.
>
> Interesting material relating to astronomy, geography and mineralogy is found in Varahamihira's work *Brihatsamhita*...[13]

While our eminent historians try to belittle the achievements of Indian art and architecture in the ancient period – by insinuating that it was derived from other countries, by seeing in it only a reflection of the life of the privileged classes – Soviet historians talk of the high standards the Indians attained in these spheres. They talk of its high originality. They talk of 'the true masterpieces of Indian world of art' as exemplified in the Ajanta caves.[14]

Whereas our friends see in bhakti only an instrument which was fashioned in feudalism to ensure the personal fealty of the serf to his lord, Soviet historians see in it at least one redeeming feature! They see it as a device by which the people broke loose of ritual, and found a way to establish direct communion with the object of their worship. In a word, they present bhakti as a device of social protest, and not as an instrument to tighten social bondage.[15]

While our friends whitewash the religious policy of the sultans and fabricate the fiction of a policy of 'general toleration', Soviet historians present a more candid account. After detailing the steps Firuz Tughluq took to roll back the disastrous consequences of Muhammad Tughluq's reign, they write:

> Yet at the same time Firuz was subjecting to cruel suppression all heretical movements, persecuting the Hindus and the Shiah Moslems. During campaigns against Hindu princedoms (in particular Katehr) he made slaves of the local population and would use their labour on the royal estate. Following their Sultan's example, his officers also began to acquire slaves.

[13] Ibid., pp. 170–71.
[14] Ibid., pp. 172–75.
[15] Ibid., pp. 197–98, 225–27.

> According to the historian Barani there was a total of close on 180,000 slaves in the country at the time.[16]

Whereas our friends ascribe a policy of 'general toleration' to the Delhi Sultanate, the Soviet historians write:

> After the Delhi Sultanate had been set up, India found itself within the cultural orbit of the so-called Moslem world. The ideas of Islam started to penetrate Sind in the seventh century and other parts of Northern India in the ninth century. But in the Delhi Sultanate Islam was made the state religion that was foisted upon the local population by force. Various sections of the Hindu population adopted the new religion, a small part under force and others because of the privileges to which it gave them access, since only Moslems were able to hold prominent posts. A third group took this step in order not to pay the *jizya* or poll-tax on non-Moslems, while members of the lower castes did so in the hope of avoiding the disadvantages attendant on their status.[17]

In contrast to the rationalizations upon rationalizations which our eminent historians fabricate to explain away the religious policy of Aurangzeb, the Soviet historians write:

> Aurangzeb's accession to the throne meant that the more reactionary circles of the *jagirdars* now enjoyed decisive influence at court. This cold, calculating politician was a fanatical Moslem and his victory over Dara Shukoh signified the advent of a policy, which stripped Hindus of their rights, and of a drive to persecute Shiah Moslems. In order to bring the life of the country in accordance with the precepts of Islam, Aurangzeb banned Shiah festivals, the drinking of wine, the playing of music, painting, dancing, the sowing of the drug *bhang*, etc. Between 1665 and 1669, he gave orders for Hindu temples to be destroyed and for mosques to be erected from

16 Ibid., p. 208.
17 Ibid., p. 224.

their debris. Hindus were not allowed to wear any marks of honour, to ride elephants, etc.

The heaviest burden of all was the poll-tax on non-Moslems, or *jizya,* introduced in 1679, that had been abolished by Akbar. This led to popular disturbances in Delhi, Gujarat, Burhanpur, etc. The Marathas, Rajputs and Jats all rose up in protest. The Afghan Moslems also rose up in revolt. This urge to achieve independence and freedom from the Moghul yoke serves to reflect the fact that a number of Indian peoples were showing the first signs of national consciousness. They began to perceive the Moghul state as something alien and oppressive, as something that often offended their religious feelings. The popular movements undermined the power of the Moghul empire.[18]

It is only when the Soviet textbook comes to cover the 1930s and later years that it also becomes comic. For these decades, the textbook reads like our newspapers of today! 'The emergence of a communist movement in India and the formation of workers and peasants political organisations',.... 'The left forces assume a strong position in the national movement, struggle for leadership intensifies',.... 'Intensified class struggle',....

But even in regard to this period, even in regard to the record of the Communist Party in 1942, the Soviet textbook is more honest than the histories written by our friends. As we have seen, our history books completely black out what the communists actually did during, say, the Quit India movement. By contrast the Soviet textbook records:

At this particular stage, as was later acknowledged by the Communist Party of India, certain mistakes were made, both with regard to the Party's political platform and also to the implementation of the tactics they adopted, mistakes which served not to promote but rather undermine the unity of the anti-imperialist forces. The CPI's Central Committee took a

[18] Ibid., p. 255.

> negative view of the 'August Revolution' and also supported the 'Lahore Resolution' drawn up by the Muslim League on the setting up of sovereign states in those regions where Moslems constituted the majority of the population. Despite a resolution drawn up by the CPI's Central Committee in September 1942, which put forward demands for the release of Gandhi and other leaders, an end to repressive measures, the legalisation of the National Congress and the creation of a Provisional National Government, relations between CPI members and the Congress leaders continued to deteriorate. This development can also in part be explained by the considerable successes scored by the CPI in 1942-1945 as it succeeded in extending and consolidating its influence within mass-scale public organisations.[19]

Not quite the whole truth, nor the truth alone – it would be too much to expect them to acknowledge that the 'mistakes' the CPI committed at the time, which they mention, were committed at the direct and express instructions of Moscow! But at least a shadow of the truth!

Thus, there are two points to remember. First, our friends are not just Marxists, they are also Macaulayites. Second, they are Marxists in a special sense. They are Marxists in the sense that they have thought of themselves as Marxists, in the sense that they repeatedly regurgitate a handful of Marxist phrases and assertions. But more than being Marxist historians, they have been establishment historians. Their theories and 'theses' have accorded not just with the 'classics' of Marxism-Leninism, they have accorded with the ideology of, which in terms of their theory means, the needs of Congressite rulers.

[19] Ibid., volume II, p. 228.

Context and Consequences

17

The tug of intellectual fashions

History is but one subject. The Indian Council of Historical Research is but one institution. These intellectuals have over the years captured an array of institutions and professions. Through this dominion they have controlled public discourse in general. They have set the intellectual fashion, they have determined what is politically correct and what is not. The effects are all around us. Occurrences that bedevil us every other day provide ready examples. To begin with, the instances seem unconnected. But only, 'to begin with'.

No one in the twentieth century has done as much to rid us of untouchability as Gandhiji. He attached more importance to ridding Hinduism of this accretion than to attaining swaraj. He brought upon himself the hostility of orthodox opinion all over India by his uncompromising stand on the matter. But the other day, speaking during the commemorative session of Parliament, Kanshi Ram asserted that abolishing untouchability was never on Gandhiji's agenda. Not one person stood up to contradict him, not one stood up to point to the record of forty years of our country's recent history.

Similarly, consider what the press would have been saying and doing if some government other than one headed by a 'Dalit' had spent *rupees one hundred crore* on a park, and contrast it with the way it reacted to Mayawati doing so. Or how it would have screamed itself hoarse if a government had used public funds to put up statues of Lord Rama, and contrast that with the silence it so studiously maintained as Mayawati used the very same funds to set up statues of Ramaswami Naicker and Ambedkar.

Take the project she launched towards the end of her six months. She instructed officers to hasten and give gun licences to 'Dalits', in effect to persons her party factotums certified as being the ones who should have guns. Such a venture is bound to spell disaster. When Mulayam Singh comes to power, he would follow this initiative up by ordering officers to give licences to the 'other backwards', that is to cohorts of *his* party. Thus armed, gangs of the two would swiftly plunge UP to the depths of Bihar. No divine foresight was needed to see this sequence. But the press remained completely silent.

From personal knowledge born of his extensive travels in areas where Muslims are congregated and from his intimate acquaintance with them, in his *Indian Muslims, Need for a Positive Outlook*,[1] Maulana Wahiduddin states that as a community Muslims are much better off today than they were, say at the time of Partition. He gives telling instances in support of this fact. But, he says, to acknowledge the fact in public is regarded among Muslims as betrayal of the community.

Till the collapse of the Soviet Union, our communist parties and communists secured 'assistance' of all kinds from the founts in Moscow and elsewhere. From the silence they maintained, it would seem that it was mandatory for liberals to remain silent about the 'assistance'. Not just that. For the communists to take 'assistance' was taken to be entirely legitimate – woe upon the one who hesitated to believe that they were doing so only for a higher cause. On the other hand, in those who were not of that persuasion they condemned honesty as 'puritanism', they lampooned them for making a 'fetish of honesty', an exhibition of it.

[1] Al-Risala Books, New Delhi, 1994.

'I would like to review your book myself,' said the editor of one of our principal newspapers about *Worshipping False Gods*. 'But if I praise it, they will be after me also. I too will be called communal, high-caste and all that.' 'Brilliant, Arun, it was fascinating,' said a leading commentator who had written a review that inclined to the positive. 'But, you'll understand, I couldn't say all that in print. But it really *is* brilliant. How do you manage to put in this much work?'

The very selection of reviewers tells the same story. If there is a book by a leftist, editors will be loath to give it to a person of a different point of view: 'They will say, I have deliberately given it to a rightist,' the editors are liable to explain. On the other hand, if it is a book by a person they have decided is a rightist, they will be loath to give it to a reviewer who also has been branded a rightist: 'They will denounce me for deliberately giving the book to a person who is bound to praise it,' they will bleat. Therefore, in such cases they deliberately give the book to a person who 'is bound to condemn it'!

A newspaper quotes a friend as saying about my book, *Worshipping False Gods*, 'Arun Shourie has quoted verbatim from the five volumes of *Making of the Indian Constitution* vis-à-vis Ambedkar. The mistake he has made is that he has selectively quoted from the book. He hasn't quoted from the part where Dr Ambedkar said that he was the chairman of the Drafting Committee but there were others like Iyer, B.N. Rau and T.T. Krishnamachri, who had helped in framing of the Constitution. This kind of selective omission and to condemn the person and take it in the context of his life is not fair…' I don't understand the latter part of the last sentence; its obscurity, however, may have been the contribution of the correspondent. But on the main point about selective omission, and the example that had been given: it so happened that the friend had actually been among the most helpful in disseminating the volume; and that particular passage he had cited had been reproduced in full at pages 596 and 597 of the book. Now, I have not the slightest doubt that the friend knows me well enough to know that I wouldn't do the kind of thing he was ascribing to me. I had no doubt too that he could have easily located the passage – it had been mentioned in the index itself. 'But he had to say all that so as to be able to continue to sell your book through his shop,' explained a friend who knew us both.

I get evidence every other day of this compulsion to conform. The number of persons who had taken the trouble to reach out and tell me that I had done 'the greatest possible service' to the country by exhuming the facts about Ambedkar, for instance, was overwhelming – among these were persons from several political parties, as well as some very conspicuous names from among non-Mahar 'Dalits'. Indeed, it was not till the Ambedkar book came out that I got to know what the non-Mahar 'Dalits' thought of the idolization of Ambedkar. But all this was in private, much of it furtive. On occasion, the very same persons – having not just thanked me profusely for nailing the myth, but having actually purchased a substantial number of copies of the book for distribution among influentials in their state – denounced it in public, they even joined in the demand that the book be banned!

Or take the even more pervasive phenomenon. As our commentators never tire of reminding us, party publications and a few exceptions apart, our newspapers are owned by capitalists. And yet it is these very newspapers which have for as long as anyone can remember denounced capitalism, which have for decades extolled Naxalism, which enforced the taboo against talking the truth about the Soviet Union, about Mao's China.

The examples seem disconnected at first sight. In fact they testify to the same phenomenon: the force of the intellectual fashion of the times. For the last half-century, in India this fashion has been set by leftists. Now, this is a miracle that needs some explaining, some understanding. For on the face of it, that this lot should have been able to set the standard is a total incongruity. They had been ranged against the freedom movement for most of the preceding decades. They had brazenly been proclaiming that the Soviet Union was to them 'The Only Fatherland'. Every forecast made by their much-vaunted 'theory' had been totally belied by the course events had taken: that the rate of profit would decline in capitalist economies; that the masses would be progressively immiserized; that the capitalist economies would be convulsed by progressively more intense crises; that the toilers would get progressively organized; that they would form behind the phalanx of a communist party; that the exploited would then overthrow the exploiters, that the expropriators would be expropriated...

Everything went the other way. In the end, their proclamations failed on the one test they had said was the only one that mattered – namely, that of practice: the Soviet economies collapsed by the sheer weight of their wooden inefficiencies. But they still set the standard in India!

The explanation consists of several layers. In spite of their record during the independence struggle, it is to the Macaulay-Missionary-Marx class that power devolved after 1947. There were, to begin with, the intellectual fashions in Europe: the new rulers, Pandit Nehru in particular, were much affected by them. More than just 'affected'. As is well known, the communists used to abuse Panditji day in and day out: 'the running dog of imperialism' was one of their milder epithets for him. But the more they abused him, the more, it would seem, Panditji became anxious not to fall further afoul with them. He would overcompensate in other areas. He would extend his umbrella even farther to shield and protect them. Mrs Gandhi, of course, had no inkling at all about theories, evidence regarding theories and the rest. She had adopted the progressive idiom for harvesting votes. These people had taken out the copyright on this kind of sloganeering. She adopted them as her natural allies, always straining to ensure that they would furnish the certificates she needed to continue to convince the poor, and groups such as the Muslims that she had their interests at heart. This anxiety, coupled with her ignorance of their 'theory' and its record in practice, as well as her great faith in her own ability to handle others made it that much easier for the leftist operators to surround her, and occupy positions from which they could place their henchmen in vital posts – in universities, in institutions like the Indian Council of Historical Research.

Tenure has ensured that their evil has continued after them! And that it will continue for a long time as yet. Tenure in the universities, and its counterpart in the press, the Working Journalists Act, will by themselves ensure that it is a decade and more before the grip of that fashion over what is taught, over what appears in print, over the questions and answers on which persons are adjudged for government service will be loosened. So, the initial explanations are historical, almost accidental, followed by institutional inertia. But there is more.

There is specialization for one, and with it a technology honed over decades. While they have always talked in terms of 'the masses', these people have from the beginning realized the importance of the influential, of the fact that decisions in societies even as vast as India are taken by just a few thousands. Among these are the ones who man the apparatus of the state and the opinion makers. Accordingly, they have always paid great attention to these groups. Often getting at one through the other: those who man the state are greatly influenced by the intellectual fashions of the day; those in the media can often be had through the patronage and information which can be doled out through the state. Paying attention to these sections might seem obvious, but other groups, taken in by the notion that 'the masses' are the ones that matter, have not paid the attention to the influential which these progressives have.

The press is a ready example of their efforts, and of the skills they have acquired in this field. They have taken care to steer their members and sympathizers into journalism. And within journalism, they have paid attention to even marginal niches. Consider books. A book by one of them has but to reach a paper, and suggestions of names of persons who would be specially suitable for reviewing it follow. As I mentioned, the editor who demurs, and is inclined to send the book to a person of a different hue is made to feel guilty, to feel that he is deliberately ensuring a biased, negative review. That selecting a person from their list may be ensuring a biased acclamation is talked out. The pressures of prevailing opinion are such, and editors so eager to evade avoidable trouble, that they swiftly select one of the recommended names. This result is made all the more certain by the fact that, realizing the importance of ideas and books, progressives have made it a point over the years to have their kind fill positions which others considered marginal in journalism – such as that of the person looking after the books page, the one looking after the 'Letters to the Editor' columns.

You have only to scan the books pages of newspapers and magazines over the past fifty years to see what a decisive effect even this simple stratagem has had. Their persons were in vital positions in the publishing houses: and so their kind of books were the ones that got published. They then reviewed, and prescribed each other's books. On the basis of these publications and reviews they were able to get each other positions in universities and the like.... Even positions in institutions which most of us would not even suspect exist were put to intense use. How many among us would know of an agency of government which determines bulk purchases of books for government and other libraries. But they do! So that if you scan the kinds of books this organization has been ordering over the years, you will find them to be almost exclusively the shades of red and pink.

Again, you and I would not think this to be an effort of much consequence: so what if one set of publishers is given a leg-up by this agency purchasing a few hundred or even a thousand copies of some book? – we would ask. But that is only because we do not know the publishing business: given the minuscule print runs of our publishers, the fact that a publisher can be sure of selling, say, five hundred copies through this network in the case of one book, and not have this assurance in the case of another book, will prove decisive.

So, their books are selected for publication. They review each other's books. Reputations are thereby built. Posts are thereby garnered. A new generation of students is weaned wearing the same pair of spectacles – and that means yet another generation of persons in the media, yet another generation of civil servants, of teachers in universities....

And books are but the smallest of their activities: 'Letters to the Editor' are orchestrated in the same way. As are 'analyses': one of them asserts, 'The book is nothing but the last war cry of the twice-born.' Writing in another paper, the other says, 'As the leading commentator .... in his trenchant analysis of Shourie's latest diatribe has *shown,* the book is nothing but the last war cry of the twice-born....' Assertion becomes a thing established!

In an unorganized, unsuspecting society such as ours, even these purely organizational manoeuvres prove decisive. But in a sense, even these devices are results, not causes. After all, why is it that those who were in positions of power found this lot so useful? Why did intellectuals gravitate to this world view in spite of the fact that every shred of evidence showed that it had no basis at all?

18

The appeal of 'The Theory', and the antidote to it

'Progressives' of the kind we have been surveying have always recognized the power of ideas and evidence. And, therefore, of those who will generate, garner, broadcast these. They have devoted time and resources to this activity, to inveigling idea-men into their fold, to knitting networks among these 'intellectuals'.

And they have always seen that ideas have to be worked out at two levels. To attract intellectuals, a theory must be, first, The Theory of Everything – that is, it must explain all the phenomena which are of interest to the intellectual in that particular context: Marxism laid claim to doing exactly this. Second, it must be difficult to comprehend, sufficiently obscure at points for the intellectual to fill years trying to 'interpret' it, eventually to 'develop' it further: part of the reason the manuscripts of the early Marx were even more attractive than his later, published writings was that they were even more opaque than the latter. Scholars spent lifetimes fixing what the ratios were which, when measured, would tell the tale Marx had said would unfold, they built careers and repudiated friendships determining what exactly the rate of profit was which was to be declining – for the rate everyone understood it to imply did not show any sign of declining! Mao's essays 'On Contradiction', 'On Practice', 'On Dialectical Materialism', the later one 'On Dialectics' were just as masterly in their opacity and obscurity.

But as far as the 'masses' are concerned, the complexity and incomprehensibility of these ideas serves an entirely different function. They naturally do not comprehend them. But the fact that they can be told that the theory is there, the belief that it has all been worked out, that what is happening – the course history is taking – is entirely in accord with the formulations of the theory, that what the party or its drummer boys – these intellectuals – are proposing to do is what the theory shows ought to be done, that the programme is bound to succeed because it accords with the march of history which the theory has already unravelled to the elect – these are a potent hallucinogen.

Progressives have always seen the value of the theory as stupefacient. Of course, they denounced other priestly classes for keeping the rites and texts of their religions secret, but, as far as their own texts were concerned, they made sure that these remained mysterious. And, to use their favoured expression, if one looks at the question 'objectively', that is if one goes by what the objective effect of the deed was, we notice that the elucidations of the texts – by an Althusser, for instance – were designed to reinforce the notion that the texts were abstruse and deep, that their true meaning could be discerned only by the elect few, that what these worthies had in turn discovered to be the true meaning was itself beyond the comprehension of ordinary mortals. It followed that the masses needed these intellectuals, and even more so the party of which they were, in their own reckoning, guides and counsellors.

But just as valuable as keeping the doctrine complex and esoteric was simplification. Not so much the progressive intellectuals as those who directed them – the controllers of the party, the movement – knew that just as the masses are fortified in their faith once they believe that there is a grand explanation behind everything that is being done, they are averse to going into details. Whether it is a proposition about some event or it is some policy measure, people do not go by the detailed reasons for it, nor by the details of evidence in its favour. They go by the general temper of the times: one group gets branded 'reactionary', the other progressive and secular; a proposal gets stamped 'anti-people' – this branding determines how the people will react to it. And what label will get pasted on to a group or a proposal, the progressives have known, depends not on the merits of the case, but on the skills and effort which are deployed for the purpose. Whether it is an essay of Lenin or an article of one of our present-day hacks, more space and passion are spent for pasting a label on the adversary than in setting out rational arguments and evidence. In fact, pasting the label, putting a colour on the one who is to be refuted is recognized as the principal task. In his *Encounters With Lenin*,[1] Valentinov recounts Lenin telling him, 'Plekhanov once said to me about a critic of Marxism (I've forgotten his name) "First let us stick the convict's badge on him, and then after that we will examine his case." And I think that we must "stick the convict's badge" on anyone and everyone who tries to undermine Marxism, even if do not go on to examine his case. That's how every sound revolutionary should react.' Branding is the special skill these intellectuals have honed.

And what Eric Hoffer called 'religiofication' – the skill to transform mundane pursuits, mere tactical manoeuvres into Holy Causes. In the case of the progressives this was achieved, as Professor Hayek explained, by appropriating the catchwords of the nineteenth and twentieth centuries: 'scientific', 'rational', 'justice', 'equality'. When a value was too obviously associated with the one they were opposing, they made out – again by the same devices of repetition, echo chambers and the rest – that what the other fellow was actually doing under that rubric was the sham of the real thing, that the value in its 'true form' was

[1] Nikolay Valentinov, *Encounters with Lenin,* Oxford, London, 1968.

found only in the Fatherland, in what *they* were striving for. While Gandhi talks of 'freedom', they screamed, his concept of 'freedom' is just a clever ruse, the clever *bania's* ruse to perpetuate the exploitative order. While Western societies have 'democracy' in form – elections, for instance – actually only muscle and money determine the outcome. While they have a so-called independent judiciary, in such societies 'law' itself is an instrument for sustaining the existing order .... In a workers' state, on the other hand, democracy is real, freedom is not just a monopoly of the microscopic ruling minority, it is the common possession of all. The slightest tightening of labour laws in a capitalist country was ipso facto admission of the worsening crises of capitalism, it was proof of the heartless suppression of the toiling masses; but in the Soviet Union and China it was but natural that workers and peasants should forego the right to strike, the right to bargain about the terms and conditions of work, to form their own organizations – because the state itself belonged to them...

This appropriation of values that had a penumbra made 'religiofication' possible. These intellectuals and the party or ideology they served were the only ones who were committed to 'justice', 'equality', 'freedom'. And their commitment to it, the course they had mapped for attaining these, was not based on mere sentimentalism, it was based on a scientific analysis and understanding of history. Therefore, anyone who stood in the way was opposing the liberation of the downtrodden masses, he was an instrument, 'a conscious, chosen instrument' of the exploiters. Accordingly, all means were justified in putting him out of harm's way...

This 'religiofication' was a skill they honed. And, in turn, making the theory itself a religion served many purposes: the votary was liberated from qualms, from 'bourgeois qualms' about ordering mass executions, about conspiring to pull down others, about pasting that convict's badge on them, circulating canards about them, planting forgeries. Everything was in the cause of the Revolution. What a relief this was: the progressive intellectual could indulge the bully in him without inhibition, without limit. The theory became all the more attractive. And with their dexterity at generalization, they 'developed' the theory into new realms: they couldn't get along with their fathers, they denounced family as an instrument of oppression; they wanted to sleep around with other women, they pronounced marriage and morals to be bourgeois hangovers....

The greatest lure of the theory was that it had been adopted by the ones who were seizing power – Lenin, Stalin, Mao – by groups that were about to seize it – the groups in India, for instance, which our intellectuals have baptised as 'resurgent'. Becoming espousers and developers of the theory, they got close to, or could make-believe they were close to power: as leeches on a wrestler may think that they are the ones who are toppling the opponent.

There was also another reason for the theory's attractiveness, one that seems paradoxical at first sight. One side of the picture was that these intellectuals craved for power, for being liberated from norms, from qualms, and the theory did that for them. The other side was that it satisfied the craving of these intellectuals for abasement, for being flogged, so to say. Lenin, and later Stalin and Mao, had made sure that the centrality of the party was built into the theory as its keystone. There scarcely is any body of writing which pours as much abuse and ridicule on intellectuals as the essays of Lenin and Mao. In the course of the revolutions and movements too, waves upon waves of intellectuals were crushed to death and exile. But that only seemed to have made the theory, and of course the revolutions occurring in their Meccas, even more beguiling for our progressives here. This quality of satiating the masochistic urges of our intellectuals was as important a ground for the popularity of the theory as its giving the bully in them free rein.

And, of course, both parts of the exercise – taking up the cause on the one hand, and being flogged – made them feel virtuous. Because they were shouting in the name of the poor, they were *for* the poor. Because they were for the poor, everything they did was justified. Not that they were poor – in fact, one of the things that made the theory attractive was that it justified *their* having a good time: it is but right that we dupe the exploiters, that we do them out of their wealth, their women, the great teachers had said.

The theory enabled them to believe that they were acting on behalf of the poor, and in addition that they alone were acting on behalf of the poor. In particular, the poor themselves were often not acting in their own interest – this was one of the most comforting results of the theory. For the poor were the prisoners of 'false-consciousness', remember? When they opposed the party and its line, they were 'objectively' acting as the unwitting instruments of the very ones who were exploiting them. It was as imperative, therefore, that the wretches be put down – by the million, if that alone would do.

All this has been the longest-running hoax of the last hundred and fifty years. The theory was an empty box into which anything could be stuffed, from which anything could be conjured up. In practice it was failing by the year. The claim to 'Justice' in the face of slave labour camps in the Soviet Union, in China? The claim to 'Equality' in the face of the *nomenklatura?* The claim to 'Freedom' in the face of the *millions* killed in Stalin's Russia and Mao's China? The claim to super-efficiency in the face of the total collapse of those economies?

The intellectuals developed a consequential skill, one that was of the greatest use to the movement: the facility to explain away facts. This was specially so in countries like India, for in the Holy Lands themselves – the Soviet Union, China – no explanations had to be given. The purges in Soviet Russia? Just the aberration of an individual – Stalin. The wooden inefficiency of the country? Just the sclerosis of an individual – Brezhnev...

How the paranoia or stupor of one individual was able to affect an entire system when the theory had insisted all along that the outcome is determined by architectonic factors such as the pattern of ownership of the means of production, and not by individuals – that was never explained. By mental jugglery the existing reality in societies such as ours was compared, not to the real condition of the Soviet societies – facts about that were either 'shown' to be fabrications of capitalist propaganda, or temporary aberrations – but with the Utopia that the theorists had conjured. Why like should not be compared to like, how facts – which after Khruschev's speech to the Twentieth Congress were being acknowledged by the Soviets themselves – did not in actuality exist, these mundane things too were never explained.

In fact, the real skill, the one they perfected was to ensure that such questions never interrupted discourse. The old device – common to all totalitarian ideologies – was sharpened to exclude, not just questions but the questioners themselves: if a progressive asked such questions, that he was asking them itself proved that he had 'crossed the barricade', that he had turned a *murtad,* an apostate, and so his questioning was obviously to an agenda, accordingly there was no need to pay any attention to it; if a non-progressive asked them, then they were questions from one who was a 'sworn enemy' of the Emancipation of the masses, they were from a kafir in any case, and therefore they were contaminants which were not to be allowed to get anywhere near the faithful.

No one talks of the theory as The Theory of Everything nowadays. In fact, nowhere outside India is the theory talked of at all. The complete refutation of the theory in practice by the collapse of the edifice which had been constructed to realize it – the Soviet states – too has been a setback.

In other parts of the world, that collapse has proved lethal for the theory. But here in India it has been, to recall the expression from the textbook, just a setback. The progressives have turned their well-practised skills to other issues: from fabricating critiques of our tradition, history, religion, to waxing insistent on rights of some hitherto undiscovered microscopic group. Moreover, because they continue to occupy pivotal positions in media and the educational structure, they still remain the ones who determine which will be the experts whom the people will regard as authorities they should heed. The fount of poison has been capped, therefore, but there is enough poison circulating in the system to continue to disable us for a decade or two.

And this is where recent history offers – both warning as well as hope. The warning is that their baleful influence will take long to wane on its own: we must record the forecasts they made and how things have turned out in practice, we must puncture the pretensions of their theory. And we must work out the details of the alternative ways – the tiny ways in which the problems may be alleviated: 'one by one, little by little, again and again'.

Intellectual history of the last eighty years shows that towards this objective the work of even a few goes a long way, that the work of a few unknown persons, of persons who are themselves soon forgotten, goes a long way. Of the contributors to *The God That Failed,* how many would be recognized today? And yet what a hole that single compilation had blown in the wall! Of the contributors to *From Under the Rubble,* apart from Solzhenitsyn there is not a name that we would have even heard of: and yet books like that one, typed out in stealth, copy by laborious copy, became an alternative state. In the years following the triumph of the Bolsheviks, the liberal tradition went into eclipse: the successes of planning were bandied about, even intellectual work about some other way of doing things was as good as abandoned. In his tribute to Ludwig von Mises, Professor Hayek listed the names of persons around whose work the liberal tradition was revived in economics.[2] It is such

[2] F.A. Hayek, 'The transmission of the ideals of economic freedom', 1951, in F.A. Hayek, *Studies in Philosophy, Politics and Economics,* Routledge and Kegan Paul, London, 1967, pp. 195–200.

a short list. Each of them working in isolation, neglected if not scorned by the mainline intellectuals. And how many from his list would even our economists recognize today: Edwin Cannan? Theodore Gregory? Arnold Plant? Frank H. Knight? Luigi Einaudi, later president of Italy? Walter Eucken? Even of von Mises, what do we remember except the 'debate' in which, we were taught in college, he had been conclusively demolished by Oskar Lange? Of Hayek himself?

Yet their solitary labours are what laid the foundation for the ways of thought which have such decisive influence today throughout the world. They and their work are what twentieth-century history has vindicated.

Thus: Walk on.

19

Programmed to self-destruct

Going by Marxist theory – which is taught to this day as gospel in the bastions of the eminent scholars we have been getting to know – for instance in so many of our universities – the communist revolution was to have occurred first in societies which had developed farthest along the capitalist path. The reason was that the Revolution was not something that was to be brought about by someone outside or elsewhere. It was to be the explosion, the overturning which factors inherent to, as well as internal to, capitalist development were to cause. What happened in fact? The advanced capitalist economies learnt to handle the crises that struck them. More important, they developed structures and processes which ensured that the economies would continually elude the extremes which Marx had 'demonstrated' would break things down. And such revolutions as occurred – Russia in 1917, China in 1949 – did so in countries in which capitalism had not even spread all that much, to say nothing of its having exhausted its creative potential – which was the point at which the theory had said the Revolution would occur. The other 'Revolutions' were even more of an embarrassment to the theory: the installation of communist governments in every single country of East Europe, for instance, was the result of nothing but conquests and *pustsch*s directed by an external power. Where the upheavals were brought about from within, the groups that acted were ones which the theory had consigned to somnolence: Marx had consigned peasants to being 'sacks of potatoes' for ever, but they were the ones who were in the forefront of the revolutions in China and Vietnam. Worse, they were impelled not by the factors which the theory had said would ignite them – the concentration and centralization of capital, the falling rate of profit, the herding of labour into larger and larger industrial agglomerations and its thereby acquiring increasingly militant 'proletarian class consciousness', etc. They were propelled by the very thing which the theory had denounced as sheer 'false consciousness', that is by plain old nationalism – against the Japanese in China, against the Japanese and then the French and then against the Americans and eventually against the Chinese in Vietnam.

A hundred years of evidence showing that things were not going in the direction which the theory had insisted they would take should have led the faithful to re-examine the theory. But once a theory becomes the gospel, once it becomes the basis of a religion, that things are going in the direction opposite to what the theory had forecast leads to a repudiation not of the theory, but of the facts. This is exactly what happened. An entire industry grew up devoted to reading new meanings into Marx's propositions about 'value', about 'surplus value', about what the rate was which was to fall, about what exactly he had meant by 'capital', by 'concentration', by 'centralisation' about 'capitalism' becoming 'monopoly capitalism', about 'breaking the imperialist chain at its weakest link', about 'surrounding the capitalist metropolis with the countryside which were the colonies' – an industry inventing meanings for these concepts which would enable the faithful to maintain that what was unfolding was in fact in accordance with the forecasts. To this day these constructions are being taught to students in our universities.

But are the other sets for whom these eminences are always speaking up, those who strain to read new meanings into the verses of the Quran and the Hadis on jihad – 'These refer to only the internal struggle between good and evil' – not doing the same thing today? Instead of re-examining the theory – in their case the revelation – are they not trying to contrive new 'meanings' – meanings that have somehow eluded their predecessors for 1,400 years?

There is a warning in this, as well as a clue. The warning is that the moment a book or a doctrine comes to be treated as the revelation, the moment the faithful come to assume that all knowledge is in the book or flows from it, that what is not in the book or does not flow from it is not true or not useful – the standard position of the ulema about the Quran, for instance – from that moment that teaching becomes a shackle. As for the clue, just watch the faithful: when they begin adjusting facts to fit the corset of that theory, it is done for.

The recent history of Marxism-Leninism furnishes other pointers also. First, like all revelations the doctrine was reductionist in the extreme: *everything* – in the physical universe, in the economy, in social relations, in the psychology of individuals, in art and literature – was said to be an unfolding of matter according to an unvarying dialectic – a configuration generating its antithesis and the conflict between the two resulting in a new synthesis. Second, it legitimized the use of all means, as well as a totalitarian set up: originally designed to legitimize the use of force and deceit for the acquisition and control of the state apparatus, it soon encompassed thinking also – for the obvious reason that independent thinking is more lethal to such regimes than grenades. Finally, and just at the time it should have been reassessing its foundations in the light of new evidence, that is in 1917, the teaching – from being just a doctrine – became state religion: entertaining a doubt about it became henceforth not the starting point of an inquiry, it became heresy. And as the doctrine had itself legitimized the use of all means, and the totalitarian boot to achieve the great goal, as this religion was in turn the one way, the only way to that great goal, using all means to stamp out heresy was not just legitimate, it was imperative in terms of the theory itself. An exact correspondence to the case of other, older revelations.

The consequences of these three factors taken together seem ridiculous to us today, we are scarcely able to believe that they could have occurred. But even a cursory glance at the encyclopedias and tracts which were produced in the Soviet Union shows that the consequences were very real and all-encompassing till just the other day.

As dialectical materialism explained everything, Einstein's special and general theories of relativity, for instance, were denounced for decades in the Soviet Union – not because some data had been discovered which controverted them, but because some inferences from them were said to controvert what followed from dialectical materialism. Soviet scientists could not resume working on them till the relativity theories had been rescued – and this became possible not by showing that the theories were vindicated by later evidence, not by showing that whether or not they conformed to dialectical materialism was irrelevant to their validity, but by showing that it was possible to construe them in a manner which would not conflict with dialectical materialism!

The fate that befell relativity demonstrates the other stultifying effect just as well. Is the universe finite and bounded as many a religious cosmology had implied? Or is it finite and unbounded as Einstein had said? You would settle the question by normal scientific methods. But in the Soviet Union scientists had to reckon with the fact that Lenin had happened to say in his *Materialism and Empirio-Criticism* that the universe is infinite, and, what he had said being part of the canon, his statement could not but be taken to settle the question. Do space, time, matter have an existence independent of one another or are the former two but manifestations of the latter? Soviet scientists till the late 1950s could not assess what followed from, for instance, Einstein's theories on the question by itself. They had not just to reckon with, they had to uphold what Engels and Lenin had said on the relationship of the three – and this they had to do even though neither Engels nor Lenin had been a physicist or a philosopher, and even though neither had written any systematic work on time, space or matter!

Such was the consequence in fields so far removed from the subjects on which the prophets had focussed. Naturally, the consequence was much more severe for disciplines which happened to be closer to the subjects on which these oracles had written. For Marx interest was not just, it was not even primarily the price by which scarce capital was rationed between competing uses, it was an illegitimate amount which exploiters extract from the exploited. Using it to choose between technologies in one project or between investments in different sectors was, therefore, taboo in Soviet planning. Capital, though in extreme scarcity, thus became a 'free good' for the planners, with predictably disastrous consequences. But the taboo could not be broken. Economists and planners spent decades trying to fabricate surrogates – 'Periods of Recoupment' and the rest – which would perform the same function: and we in Indian universities grew up memorizing those surrogates as masterpieces of the creative development of Marxism-Leninism! Similarly, as being guided by the market was taboo, there was little basis for setting prices of finished products; decades were accordingly spent trying to derive prices from Marx's propositions on value – on the 'social labour' 'congealed' in the respective commodities and the rest. The grotesque irrationalities and imbalances which resulted have since become common knowledge.

To see the exact parallel one has just to compare the sophistries by which Soviet economists tried to inveigle interest back into the system in the face of these taboos with the sophistries by which Islamic lawgivers try, to this day, to inveigle interest in the face of corresponding taboos in the Quran and the hadis.

In such systems it is necessary to ensure that everything conforms to what the prophet had said. And it is sufficient to do so. And when the prophet has explained everything in terms of one *deus ex tnachina,* of just one cause – the materialist dialectic in this case – all subsequent inquiry is blocked. For a hundred years, Marxist study of religions came to be confined to arriving at the same conclusions about every religion and ritual which Marx and Engels had set out in *The German Ideology* about Christianity. The insights of the Buddha into the working of the mind, the figure of faith which Jesus inspires, all have invariably ended up being reduced to half a dozen cliches. For seventy years Marxist literary criticism came to be confined to arriving at the same conclusions about every author – and later about every artist, and later still about every film-maker – which Lenin had set out about Tolstoy. And these conclusions were simplistic in the extreme: to the extent that the writer portrays the ills of the existing arrangements he is making a contribution, went the critique; to the extent that, having done so, he falls short of concluding that nothing but the Proletarian Revolution is the answer, he is purblind. Marxist history writing, as we have seen, is no different: every configuration is fitted into the corset of Marx's five stages, every occurrence is tracked down to the forces and relations of production, the same cliches are repeated ad nauseum, – 'Brahmins depended on sacrifices', 'Class-alliance of Brahmins and rulers', 'Law as an instrument of the ruling class'; and once that has been done, nothing else need be done. Except of course when it comes to explaining the cruelties and stagnation of communist societies – then everything must be tracked down to the aberrations of one Stalin or one Ceaucescu!

Is what we are told about the ravages which were committed for centuries in the name of jihad any different? For centuries these ravages were the pride of the tradition, they were proof of the tradition being the special favourite of Allah, of the victors being the chosen of Allah. But today we are told that they were just the aberrations of individual rulers. How come that such a grievously wrong construction came to hold the ground for fourteen hundred years? The question the Left never answered was: you say everything is determined by the forces and relations of production, that the individual does not matter; how is it then that one Stalin could account for all that went wrong? The corresponding question in the case of what is sought to be explained away in Islamic history is: as everything happens by the will of Allah, as the Prophet himself had said, 'My ummah will never agree upon an error,' how come that for fourteen hundred years the faithful put a construction on the texts which was so totally wrong?

Once the doctrine has become a Revelation, creativity must wait upon the current heir and prophet – only a Lenin, having proclaimed all along that the Russian Revolution was the beginning of the World Revolution, can turn around and proclaim 'Socialism in one country'; only a Stalin can proclaim that the analyses of Marx and Engels and Lenin are not edicts fixed forever; only a Mao can turn Marx's pronouncements about peasants on their head and still maintain that what he is doing is just the development of the theory. Creativity must wait, that is, upon the sparkle or the compulsions of the current prophet. But he has but to proclaim his new, amended version and that too – as we saw most recently in the case of Mao in both China and India – gets congealed as the new, unalterable gospel.

Furthermore, when a reductionist ideology becomes the state religion, as happened in the case of Marxism-Leninism and as is the case today in every Islamic state, things get even worse. As the ideology is the instrument which will usher in the glorious future, everything must not only be interpreted to conform to it, every interpretation must be an instrument of the future which the ideology is out to realize. Soviet and Chinese writings on Buddhism and Islam illustrate the matter. It was not just that the subtle insights of the Buddha were reduced to ashes, one thing was said about them one day and its opposite the next – according to what would suit the needs of the rulers. A glance at the relevant entries in any handy reference book – for instance, *The Encyclopedia of Marxism, Communism and Western Socialism* – nails the pattern. During 1917–27 the Soviet rulers needed to pacify Buddhists. Therefore, they extolled Buddhism as an ideology of the oppressed masses, they extolled it for what they said was its atheism, for its emphasis on equality; they saw in its monastic orders a forerunner of collectivization – and naturally many an Indian progressive did the same as a consequence. After 1929 when crushing was in order, they portrayed Buddhism as having been an instrument created by feudal lords to keep the working masses in thrall. Once the stamping out began, Stalin declared that it was 'absurd' to 'equate' Buddhism and dialectical materialism.

As instruments vary over time, the *Encylopedia* records, they vary over space. Thus it was perfectly in accord with the theory for Chinese communists to denounce and exterminate Buddhism at home but to proclaim in Thervadin countries such as Sri Lanka and Burma that they were acting against only the Mahayana variant with its deism and its rituals. The writings on Islam, we learn from the same authorities, went through the same cycle. By the 1930s and '40s Soviet writers were portraying the Prophet and the Quran in dark, minatory colours – ridiculing accounts of miracles attributed to the Prophet, questioning not just the spiritual worth, not just the literary worth but even the coherence of the Quran. That *at that very time* the communists in India, whose mentors had written all this about these religions and their founders, should have been projecting themselves as the champions of the adherents of these very religions too was perfectly in accord with the theory.

This ability to adapt the ideology, to always find the proposition or variant which will serve the objective of the moment, seems very clever at first. But over time, everyone sees the somersaulting. Cynicism follows inevitably – about the claims that are being made on behalf of the theory, total distrust of the ones who are making the claims.

These ideologies have a singular aim: to capture power, in particular the state. Once they do so, the ideology becomes not just a state religion, it becomes the religion of a totalitarian state. Whether a theory or a discovery will advance or sink comes to depend, therefore, not on its intrinsic merit, not even on whether or not it conforms to the canon, but on *who* is espousing it: is the person important in and to the party or not? Many a climber in the Soviet Union did a rival in, many an opportunist advanced his career by putting the most far-fetched constructions on, and drawing wild inferences from, the work of scholars and showing that they were in conflict with the uni-causal ideology.

With this goes the related feature of ideologies that claim to be Revelations: as dialectical materialism claimed to be all-encompassing, to explain everything, the most far-fetched constructions could be put on the theory or writings of an individual in fields far away from his particular work, and yet be fatal: physicists were done in, not because what they said conflicted with something that Engels or Lenin had said on *physics,* but because what they were saying on a *question of physics* could, if interpreted to mean such and thus, yield a conclusion in regard to *social organization* which went against the official view. And in such encounters under such regimes the verdict that counts – on the scientific validity of, say, the theory of relativity as much as on these projections of what the implications will be for social organization – is not that of the community of scientists but of the party hatchets.

The fate of genetics is a notorious example. Communism, all the prophets proclaimed, will create the New Man.

This was certain, they said, because man's nature is a result of environment. By overturning the means and relations of production communism is changing the environment. Therefore, the new Soviet man is a certainty. A remark or two of Marx could be cited to show that he too had subscribed to this view. And Stakhanov in the Soviet Union was living proof, as were the Red Guards later in China, that the new regime was indeed giving birth to the new man. Now, the work of several geneticists, specially Mendel, called into question the premise that acquired characteristics are passed on to succeeding generations. The *Encyclopedia* recounts that a simple-minded 'practical' plant breeder, I.V. Michurin, came up with 'results' to show that the characteristics of plants could not only be altered by changing the environment, the altered characteristics would be inherited by subsequent generations. Lenin took a fancy for him – because his results accorded with the new optimism, because he was a Russian, and a communist and a 'practical nursery man' to boot. One of the most notorious operators in the history of science, Lysenko seized upon the ideas, and, by Lenin's and then Stalin's patronage became the czar and terror of these branches of science. By 1949 Mendelian genetics was outlawed and leading geneticists of the country were made to recant their earlier work, and to denounce themselves for having even sought to build on Mendelian results. This single, mediocre man stifled two entire sciences, the *Encyclopedias* record, caused disasters in Soviet agriculture for three full decades, and became a byword for terror among scientists.

The only reason that we in India have not had a Lysenko is that the communists have not had control over the entire country, and that we have remained an open society. But the 'non-violent' pressures in several of our universities, the networking and blackballing have been just as fatal to creativity and independent thinking. One has only to see the blight in the history and the economics departments of our Left-controlled universities.

And the sequence is inevitable: there is the reductionist revelation; every proposition which can be advanced as something which is substantiating this revelation is ipso facto true, every fact or argument which may call the revelation in question is by definition untrue; and the party hatchet, the cleric is the one who will decide whether the proposition advances the cause or not – after all, it is the party which, it is the ulema who alone understand the revelation, it is the party, the cleric who alone is truly committed to it. Moreover, it is the duty of the party, of the ulema to safeguard and vindicate the revelation, and to make sure that it prevails all across the globe. Anyone who refuses to accept it must be put out – for he is blocking the march of history, he is impeding the will of Allah. So, the party, the faithful are perfectly justified in using all means. The party apart, this 'religiofication' of the ideology cannot but smother creative work. After all, what is the necessary condition for scholarship when an ideology or line has been exalted to such status? That everything one digs up and writes confirms that theory and line. And it is sufficient to do so. That is what we see in the textbooks we have encountered. The sole concern of the authors is to adduce 'evidence', to come up with some inference and 'interpretation' which substantiates the theory. And the moment some fragment of a text, some contrived inference has been pushed, some 'interpretation' imagined which does so, the work is done!

This rule of necessity and sufficiency is enough by itself to kill innovative work. All that the scholar has to do is to bring his study every few pages to reiterate some element of the dogma, to 'validate' some sentence or proposition from some book of some master theoretician – the only care he has to exercise is to make sure that the theoretician is still in the good books of the canonizers. And the more often our scholar repeats the proposition in his study, the more of a theoretician he becomes in his own right.

Thus, as we have seen, in his introduction to his *Ancient India,* D.N. Jha asserts:

> ....Religious rituals and practices underwent considerable change. *Bhakti* (devotion), which reflected the complete dependence of the serfs or tenants on the landowners in the context of Indian feudal society, became the essential ingredient of religion....[1]

Just an assertion, no proof. After all, this is just the *introduction.* A hundred pages later the assertion is still an assertion, but it acquires more body in that it gets an entire paragraph to itself and not just a sentence!

> The doctrine of *bhakti,* clearly enunciated first in the *Gita* and a vital force in Vaishnavism and Shaivism, became socially more relevant in the Gupta period. It preached that one could obtain final liberation only through devotion to and faith in god, and not just by performing sacrifices. God was made accessible to everybody through *bhakti.* This new form of piety was in tune with the social outlook of the times, when the feudatories considered themselves as meditating at the feet of their masters. This explains the new stress on the doctrine of *bhakti* in Vaishnavism, Shaivism, and to a degree in Mahayana Buddhism.[2]

The causal connection between feudalism and bhakti is taken to be one of those self-evident truths, and asserted without any evidence. Why sub-lords, who were in the position of 'meditating at the feet of their masters', should promote or even countenance a doctrine which makes the super-lord accessible directly to every serf and tenant is left unexplained – presumably as an exercise for the reader! The sequence in such

[1] D.N. Jha, *Ancient India,* Manohar, New Delhi, 1997, p. xviii.
[2] Ibid., pp. 106–07.

scholarship is not that some evidence – some secret text, for instance – has been discovered in which some sage has set out the uses of bhakti for the lords, his feudatories and the rest; and independently evidence has been discovered which establishes that, around the period when this text was composed, society was transiting to a feudal arrangement. The sequence is that the theory has proclaimed that societies transit through feudalism. That therefore scraps of 'evidence' are snatched which can be used to assert that the period, say the Gupta period, was one in which feudalism had come to prevail. A doctrine is then held up as helping perpetuate that feudalism!

The assertion gains instant acclaim as it is a repetition of what some theoretical ancestor has said! In this case, D.D. Kosambi himself! But when we read Kosambi we see that he himself had just strung together a string of assertions, and thus built a Theory about the Gita! As an exercise, count the number of assertions Kosambi strings together in advancing his 'Theory' when, in his essay on the scripture, he writes,

> Thus, the *Gita* was a logical performance for the early Gupta period, when expanding village settlement brought in new wealth to a powerful central government. Trade was again on the increase, and many sects could obtain economic support in plenty....
>
> To sum up, writing the *Gita* was possible only in a period when it was not absolutely necessary. [Why?] Samkara could not do without the intense polemic of theological controversy. To treat all views tolerantly and to merge them into one implies that the crisis in the means of production is not too acute. *Fusion and tolerance become impossible when the crisis deepens, when there is not enough of the surplus product to go around, and the synthetic method does not lead to increased production.* Marrying the gods to goddesses had worked earlier because the conjoint society produced much more after differences between matriarchal and patriarchal forms of property were thus reconciled. The primitive deities adopted into Siva's or Visnu's household

helped enlist food-gathering aboriginals into a much greater food-producing society. The alternative would have been extermination or enslavement, each of which entailed violence with excessive strain upon contemporary production. The vedic Aryans who tried naked force had ultimately to recombine with the autochthonous people. The *Gita* might help reconcile certain factions of the ruling class. Its inner contradictions could stimulate some exceptional reformer to make the upper classes admit a new reality by recruiting new members. But it could not possibly bring about any fundamental change in the means of production [Notice the assumption – that this was the task of the scripture – from which follows the failure!], nor could its fundamental lack of contact with reality and disdain for logical consistency promote a rational approach to the basic problems of Indian society.

However, the *Gita* did contain one innovation which precisely fitted the needs of a later period: *bhakti*, personal devotion [Note the word *'later':* thus, in this account the invention of *bhakti precedes* the development of feudalism!]. To whoever composed that document, *bhakti* was the justification, the one way of deriving all views from a single divine source. As we have seen from the demand for the quite insipid *Anu-Gita* sequel, this did not suffice in its own day. But with the end of the great centralised personal empires in sight, Harsa's being the last – the new state had to be feudal from top to bottom. The essence of fully developed feudalism is the chain of personal loyalty which binds retainer to chief, tenant to lord, and baron to king or emperor. Not loyalty in the abstract but with a secure foundation in the means and relations of production: land ownership, military service, tax-collection and the conversion of local produce into commodities through the magnates. This system was certainly not possible before the end of the 6th century AD.... The further development of feudalism 'from below' meant a class of people at the village level who had special rights over the land (whether of cultivation, occupation, or hereditary ownership) and performed special armed service as well as service in tax-collection. To hold this type of society and its state together,

> the best religion is one which emphasises the role *of bhakti*, personal faith, even though the object of devotion may have clearly visible flaws.[3]

The sequence is exactly the one noticed earlier. It is assumed that everything, including scriptures setting out different paths into inner realization, is the product of the pattern of ownership of the means of production, and this pattern in turn has its roots in the stage that technology has reached. From these two assumptions, it is 'proved' that a particular scripture, or a particular notion in that particular scripture, serves the purpose of a particular arrangement! How fragile this method of reasoning is will be evident from considering the very example that Kosambi gives, and Jha repeats. Bhakti is just one of the paths in the Gita. What about the *Gyan marga?* That is as central to the Gita as bhakti: does the Gyan marga also serve the needs of the feudal lord and his feudatories? What about the emphasis in the Gita on karma, on doing things oneself, on the assurance that no effort shall be wasted, the insistence that one must fight wrong and injustice – which of these would be comforting to a feudal order?

Consider bhakti itself. Jha says that it was characteristic of Mahayana Buddhism also. That branch flourished most and lasted longest in Tibet: was the economic, social and political order of Tibet also feudal? Had the means of production and the pattern of their ownership in Tibet remained the same till the 1950s as they were in India during the Gupta period?

Consider the great revival of bhakti during the period of Islamic rule in India – the revival that occurred because of Chaitanya Mahaprabhu, of Surdas, of Kabir, of Nanak, of Tulsidas. Did this occur also because the arrangements were feudal and the Islamic rulers wanted to buttress these

[3] D.D. Kosambi, *Myth and Reality*, Popular Prakashan, Bombay, 1962, 1983 reprint, pp. 29–32.

arrangements by coming to some further 'mephistophelian bargains' with these seers? Or was it the other way round – that, seeing the onslaught of Islam and the pace at which the population was succumbing to force and thereby getting converted to Islam, these seers, by emphasizing devotion to a personal god, stemmed the tide of Islam in India?

And what about the reformers and leaders who stood India on its feet in the second half of the nineteenth and first half of the twentieth century? What were, say, Aurobindo, Tilak, Gandhi doing when they attached such pivotal importance to the Gita? Were they also buttressing feudalism?

Indeed, Islam demands devotion to the Prophet much more emphatically than does the *Bhakti marga* to any personal god. Is one to conclude from this that the set-up in the seventh-century Arabia was similar to the 'feudalism' of the Gupta period in India, and that the insistence of Islam that followers be totally devoted to the Prophet was also in aid of some feudal design?

The effect on the reader and student of the assertion-dressed-up-as-proposition is predictable, especially in an educational system such as ours which places total store on 'learning' by rote. Having come across the same assertion in book after book, in chapter after chapter of a book, by the time he graduates the student has internalized the notion. The next time he encounters it, he does not ask for proof. He takes the assertion to be a proposition, and the proposition to be a self-evident truth, a truth which has been proven for ages.

This helps perpetuate that proposition, and the theory which strings such propositions together. But it is fatal for scholarship. To start with, there is the theory as revealed to Marx and Engels. All that Kosambi has to do is to locate some Indian examples which fit into that theory – and as we are talking of thousands of years ago, no comprehensive proof is required – a bit here, a scrap there will do: that only a handful of coins of the period have been discovered, a designation of an office of state which had not been encountered in some earlier text, a verse or two in a text containing hundreds and hundreds of other verses. Kosambi has just to point to these and the theory is once again validated, and Kosambi's repute as a leading theoretician and historian is established. And all that the latterly eminent Jha has to do is to repeat what Kosambi said.

For each of the scholars to do this much is necessary of course, but it is also sufficient. And that is why Indian historical scholarship, like its counterpart in, say, Marxist economic writing in our universities has been going round and round in the same groove for decades.

In a word, the theory is programmed to self-destruct: that is a reason for hope. But in the meanwhile it will smother creativity, it will, as we have seen from the example of our eminent historians, shield charlatanry: reasons enough, as Lenin might have said, for giving history a helping hand!

20

The pattern of consequences

These eminent historians are but an example. But their line is the general line, the one which the entire lot of progressives has been insinuating into our discourse.

That line has had disastrous consequences. Seldom has our society been in as confused a condition as it is today. The whole – India – has been called so much in question, every objective has been exalted so much to be at par with every other objective – the human rights of the terrorist with the survival of the country – that often even those who man offices of the state are not sure that they would be right to save the whole.

Four features of the discourse these worthies have spawned are particularly injurious, and therefore ones which we must urgently reverse.

'Rights talk' is all we hear: education, employment, houses, old-age pensions for agricultural workers, separate personal laws in perpetuity, food at subsidised prices, uneconomically low bus fares, water and electricity rates, privacy, homosexuality, promiscuity.... have all by now been claimed and promised as rights. The list gets longer by the day, and *inevitably* so: on the one hand, the person who is aiming to set himself up as a leader of a section must conjure up something that he can demand as a right for the group; on the other, the party or leader wanting to garner the support or votes of that group must promise to make good that claim.

Moreover, as Amitai Etzioni and others have emphasized,[1] the claim having been put forth as a right, all argument and reasoning is automatically ruled out: anyone who questions the claim, anyone who even says that, while the claim is good in the abstract, society cannot afford to concede it at the moment – anyone who says, for instance, that, while the poor certainly need rice at prices they can afford, giving it today at subsidised prices will bankrupt the state – becomes by definition *against the poor;* he becomes one who is *refusing to recognize their right to life.* Next, as the claim is a right of the group or person, it follows that it is legitimate to bend the state or the rest of society *by all possible means* into conceding it. In India this has graduated over the years into the premise that if the right is not conceded immediately, the group has a right to bring the system to a halt – to jam the *chakka*s, to disrupt classes, to prevent the legislature from proceeding with the listed business…

The assertion of the right then impinges not just on the rights of others, it disables the system itself which must function well for any of the rights to be fulfilled. There are consequences for the particular right itself, as well as for the group in whose name that right was pushed. All too often, what starts as a demand for rectifying a wrong ends up disrupting what is irreplaceable: the right to a quick divorce in the West started as a device to enable women to liberate themselves from unworkable marriages; it has become one of the factors responsible for undermining the institution of the family itself. The same holds for groups: the 'rights' wrested in the name of Muslims, of Yadavs have ignited a mighty reaction.

The consequences are compounded, Etzioni and others point out, by the fact that rights talk is invariably accompanied by 'wronged-talk', by talk of the wrongs to which the group

[1] Etzioni's book is indeed apposite for Indians. Amitai Etzioni, *The Spirit of Community: Rights, Responsibilities and the Communitarian Idea,* Fontana, 1995.

has been subjected. Indeed, persons who are trying to work up a group find that instilling in its members the notion that it has been wronged is much more potent, and therefore far more useful than persuading them that there are rights which are their due. Here too the same lengthening of the list is inevitable. Among the persons who are trying to get the group behind them a competition ensues to discover wrongs, it soon leads to their exaggerating such wrongs as exist, soon to inventing wrongs. Recall the sequence through which the rhetoric of the competing Akali politicians passed during the 1960s and '70s, and the climax in which it ultimately ended: of Bhindranwale insisting that the Sikhs had been reduced to being slaves in India, and declaring that anyone who did not see that this was so was by definition anti-Sikh.

The entire politics of that group comes to revolve around this competitive grievance-mongering. It becomes not just a right to hate, an author correctly observes, it becomes *right* to hate. The degree to which one has worked up in oneself hatred towards others, the certainty with which one has convinced oneself that the system is not just crushing one's group, but that it is going to go on doing so forever, becomes the measure of one's fidelity to the cause. Eventually the sequence recoils on the group itself: it warps the self-image and psychology of the group on the one hand, and on the other it poisons relations of the group with the rest of society – recall where Muslims have been led by this kind of talk over the last one hundred years. In his important study, *Indian Muslims, Need for a Positive Outlook,* Maulana Wahiduddin shows, how, worked up and eventually caught up in these notions, Indian Muslims have become in the eyes of others 'a problem group', 'a nuisance group'. In turn this perception handicaps the group in all subsequent dealings.[2] Just as important, that kind of mindset leads the group to sink into the notion that its condition has been caused by the eternal

[2] Al-Risala Books, New Delhi, 1993.

hostility of *others* rather than by the fact that *it* is not putting in the requisite effort to rise to a higher level: Muslims do not see that the factor which most accounts for the disadvantaged condition of which they complain is their having listened to leaders who kept them away from acquiring the education and skills which modern occupations require. At first this is a comforting alibi, in the end it proves fatal.

Society too is disrupted and set back, and not just by these two facts – that a large group sinks into a self-satisfied sulk and thereby stops exerting to improve its position, and the fact that inter-group relations in society are poisoned. Groups develop a vested interest in insisting that they are being done in – look at the insistence of the champions of the disadvantaged castes that they be called '*Dalits*', look at the insistence of even dominant castes – Yadavs, Jats, Vokkaligas, Lingayats – that they be declared to be '*Backward* Castes'. This insistence, which starts as a device to fill others with guilt, soon engenders in the rest, not guilt and therefore a sense of responsibility, but resentment.

On the other side, once it has internalized the notion that it is being done down by the perfidy of others, the group proceeds to the premise that it has a right to behave in any way it likes. The apologists – the 'progressives' – fortify the group in this belief. Look at the way the aggressiveness of Mulayam Singh, the boorishness of Laloo Yadav, the opportunism of Kanshi Ram are all sought to be explained away as being the natural, indeed legitimate expression of groups 'which have been long suppressed and are at last coming into their own'.

In the beginning this sort of conduct is limited to specifics, as is its rationalization. But soon it translates into a pervasive debasement – for the process does not stop at questioning some particular standard, and demanding, for instance, that it be made less culture- or class-specific. The notion of standards itself, of norms is soon denounced as being nothing but a device which the advantaged have forged to perpetuate their hegemony: recall the denunciation, indeed the repudiation of the very notion of 'merit' during and as a result of the debate on reservations. This is ruinous in itself: for no society can survive without adhering to norms and standards. Worse, the process does not stop at this either. Soon the system of which the notion of standards and norms is a part is itself denounced and repudiated: V.P. Singh panics as Devi Lal calls a rally; to pre-empt the rally, he announces reservations; when the question of merit is raised, he declares, 'But where is the merit in the system itself which keeps millions down?' The words are ruinous enough when used by a demagogue such as him, but, such is the power of populist sloganeering that soon enough judges of the Supreme Court deciding the reservation cases quote those catastrophic words with approbation…

The abandonment of standards in one sphere swiftly spreads to affairs of the society in general. The malignancy which was introduced by rights talk becomes final and fatal. Recall that, because the demand was posited as a right, it was put beyond reason, beyond a calculus of the costs of meeting it. Now that the claim to that right has been fortified by the notion that the group has been wronged, that the system is such and the perfidy of the advantaged is such that the group can never expect to secure 'justice', the group feels free to use all means. Intimidation? Allying with and deploying criminals? Violence? The group can deploy each of them. Orderly conduct of affairs of state and society, indeed orderly life itself is the casualty.

Consequences such as these plague us at every turn today, and each of them brings home the lessons which Gandhiji laboured to teach us. We need changes in structure of course, so that conduct more conducive to the general goodwill become natural, that it will be rewarded and its reverse penalized. But in addition, in fact to enable the changes in structure to be brought about, we need to change the balance of discourse.

After fifty years of rights talk and of trying to meet the claims of all groups – of protecting small industries one year, of channelling funds to backward districts the next, of extending reservations to this group today and that one tomorrow – several lessons are evident. First, in a sense every right is legitimate, but in a society at a particular time only a few of these can be met, and that too only to a limited extent. It can be argued that each of us in India is entitled to the standard of living and social security net which the Swedes have: but our country, placed as it is today, just cannot afford to provide these.

Second, times change, and the extent to which a right is conceded has to be calibrated accordingly, often because of the tendencies which conceding that right has itself set in motion: decades ago it was generally felt that trade unions did not have opportunity enough to get employers heed the rights of workers; laws upon laws were passed and enforced so that the conditions in which workers had to labour would be hygienic, so that workers would have some protection against the whims and arbitrariness of employers; but several controllers of labour turned trade unions into instruments of blackmail, into instruments for aggrandizing their personal power rather than for furthering the interests of their members; security of tenure has also been pushed to such extremes that it has become impossible to halt disruptive conduct. Therefore, the point is not that the unions should never have been given any quarter, nor that workers should be left completely to the whim of employers, but that the balance having tilted too far in one direction, a few weights need to be added now to the other side of the scales.

Third, conceding a right has consequences beyond that right: a series of judgments and laws recognized and enforced a particular right of workers in public sector enterprises, the right to be secure in their jobs. The effect of these rulings extended far beyond this right – they have been among the principal contributors to the general inefficiencies which hobble those enterprises, and have therefore set the country back. Fourth, societies invariably grow unevenly: at every stage some individuals, some groups, some regions leap ahead, others are left behind; in fact, many are not able to get what they most manifestly deserve, even need in their lifetime. Fifth, attempts to hasten the process beyond a point invariably recoil on society, even on the group; and anyone – Lenin, Stalin, Mao, to say nothing of our pretenders here – who promises either that he will ensure all things, or even the basic things to everyone equally, or in a hurry is just using the slogans to acquire power, and he will in the end inflict unimagined costs on society – Lenin and Stalin with their millions killed, Mao with his millions killed.

Finally, while every society has on occasion to concede the demand of a group because it has acquired muscle, each time it concedes a demand on this calculation, it is teaching other groups to acquire muscle, and adopt the same intimidatory strategies. Soon enough it will either have to dig in its heels and reverse what in its weakness it has made the norm – and the longer it has been bending to such groups, the greater the force which halting further concessions will require; or the society will plunge itself into bankruptcy and breakdown: bending before every union of municipal staff and turning a blind eye as they neglect their tasks leads soon enough to epidemics as residents of Delhi are learning today; the landslides upon landslides which have followed each Pay Commission…

The moral is plain: We must tilt away from rights talk towards the responsibilities we have to discharge. Each claim must be set against the effects it will have on the rights of others – before conceding the 'right' to a group to blare away over loudspeakers on the claim that these are days of one of its religious festivals, one must set this against the fact that the blaring assaults others who may be, say, wanting to meditate at that time. Even more important, the demand for a right must be set against the effects it will have on the ability of the whole to continue to function – on occasion a demand may have to be conceded and its consequences mopped up subsequently just to keep a group from repudiating the whole, at other times granting it may well trigger the disintegration of the whole. The means which a group uses to wrest its demands must certainly be put to this evaluation: anyone who takes a gun in his hand must be reckoned to have forfeited the protection of law, he must be dealt with by the rules of war; correspondingly, anyone who commences a satyagraha must be held to Gandhiji's conditions for *satyagrahi*s.

Leaders of the group are quick to enumerate the benefits which will accrue to it by wresting the concession, and how the group can no longer do without the benefits. Even where the assertions of the leaders in this regard are valid, the benefits must also be scrutinized to discern the effects that conceding the 'right' will have on the willingness and ability of this particular group to exert in ways which the efficient functioning of the whole requires: when you give persons the feeling that a particular job and promotions in it are their right and not things for which they must strive and excel, you knock out an important impetus for them to put in their best.

Discourse has to shift from what society owes us to the responsibilities we must discharge. The frequency with which epidemics are breaking out reminds us that each individual must discharge these responsibilities whether others are discharging them or not – each must deposit the garbage from his house in the designated place, he must rid his own surroundings of stagnant water whether others are doing so or not. While one of the responsibilities the individual must discharge is to help goad and nudge the whole to perform its functions better, the responsibilities that fall to a person's lot have to be discharged whether or not his doing so will induce or impel the whole – in this case the municipality – to function better: for there is no level of efficiency at which the municipalities can function and rid the city of epidemics if individuals in it are going to continue with their unhygienic ways.

This was one of the principal teachings of Gandhiji: from clamouring for rights – which are a demand on *the other* – personified in the ultimate analysis by the state – we must shift to *making demands on ourselves:* instead of focussing on what others must do to end the discrimination of Harijans, he taught that the Harijans – in particular, their leaders – must focus on what the Harijans must do to lift themselves; correspondingly, the advantaged, instead of focussing on the many ways in which the Harijans – by addiction of the menfolk to liquor, by not exerting to educate their children – are contributing to their condition, must focus on what the advantaged have to do to create the conditions which will enable the Harijans to raise themselves.

Just as vital are two other types of talk of which we have seen such surfeit in our progressives, and which also need to be stood on their head.

Caste is real. The working class is real. Being a Naga is real. But 'India is just a geographical expression!' Similarly, being a Muslim of course is real – Islam must be seen and talked of as one block of granite – no matter that Shias and Sunnis the world over, Barelvis and Deobandis in UP, Punjabis and Bengalis in erstwhile Pakistan, and Mohajirs, Sindhis and Punjabis in Pakistan today are at each others' throats. But Hinduism? Why, there is no such thing: it is just an aggregation, a pile of assorted beliefs and practices – see, some of them put a vertical mark on their foreheads, others, a horizontal one. And anyone who maintains anything to the contrary is a fascist out to insinuate a unity, indeed to impose a uniformity, where there has been none. That is what our progressive ideologues declaim, as we have seen. In a word, the parts alone are real. The whole is just a construct. India has never been one, these ideologues insist – disparate peoples and regions were knocked together by the Aryans, by the Mughals, by the British for purposes of empire. Anyone who wants to use that construct – India – as the benchmark for determining the sort of structure under which we should live has a secret agenda – of enforcing Hindu hegemony.

This is the continuance of, in a sense the culmination of, the Macaulay-Missionary technique. The British calculated that to subjugate India and hold it, they must undermine the essence of the people: this was Hinduism, and everything which flowed from it. Hence the doggedness with which they set about to undermine the faith and regard of the people for five entities: the gods and goddesses the Hindus revered; the temples and idols in which they were enshrined; the texts they held sacred; the language in which those texts and everything sacred in that tradition was enshrined and which was even in mid-nineteenth-century the lingua franca – that is, Sanskrit; and the group whose special duty it had been over aeons to preserve that way of life – the Brahmins. The other component of the same exercise was to prop up the parts – the non-Hindus, the regional languages, the castes and groups which they calculated would be the most accessible to the missionaries and the empire – the innocent tribals, the untouchables.[3]

Marxists were in the same business – of conversion. For their outlandish dreams to be realized it was just as essential that the people lose faith in, and regard for, that they cut themselves off from their roots. Having swallowed the denunciatory writings of Marx and Lenin, having convinced themselves that the vehemence with which one abused one's people, their past, their ways was the measure of the extent to which one had liberated oneself, that it was the measure of one's commitment to the cause, these progressives did not just carry forward the denunciations which the missionaries had set afoot, they did so with redoubled vehemence. And there was also the alluring prospect of garnering followers once sections could be worked up to feel that they were the exploited ones. Each 'minority'

[3] For illustrative texts, see my *Missionaries in India,* ASA, 1994, and HarperCollins, 1997.

was a natural for this propaganda. No wonder the communists were so ready to 'see justice' in the demand for Pakistan.

Two sets perpetuated and completed the task: the socialists and the secularists. The former were not being able to get a toehold in or against the Congress, in part because it had long since stolen their slogans. Their theoreticians saw that their only hope lay in casteism – but to base oneself on this, manifestly regressive platform, required some elaborate camouflage. They found a truly Goebbelsian cover – they declared that they were mobilizing castes to destroy casteism! The secularists were doubly goaded to continue the same focus on parts. For one thing, it was the best way to garner votes: in each part of the country, and in the country as a whole, work up fears in the minorities – the non-Assamese in the North-East, the Muslims in India as a whole – and then present yourselves as the only available saviours. For another, the leaders, as well as the intellectual class which became dominant because of their patronage, were truly the products of Trevelyan and Macaulay – they had been wholly cut off from the tradition, they had internalized every canard which the missionaries had sought to plant, they were outsiders.

These are the groups which have determined the tenor and content of discourse: the essence of which is to deny the whole and insist that only the parts are real. But as this talk is accompanied by rights talk and the insistence that the part has been wronged, on the ground that the whole is not fulfilling the claim which that particular group is espousing, each group denounces the whole, it is taught to do so by its leaders. Just recall the rhetoric of the various groups of activists today: because Naxalites are not being left free to kill and intimidate others, because the demand on Narmada is not being conceded…, the entire system of governance, indeed India as we know it is unjust, it is irremediably unjust, and therefore illegitimate. As such it has no locus to claim anything from us. That is the reasoning.

This delegitimization, and ultimate repudiation itself becomes the pattern: it comes to affect all aggregates, all levels. Etzioni and others set out the sequence which has already disrupted the West. The community is not legitimate, the family is. The family is not legitimate, only the individual is – the family is declared to be an instrument of decentralized authoritarianism, the obligations it entails, of parents towards children, of the latter to look after their ageing parents, of spouses towards each other, are now declared to be shackles which prevent the individual from 'realising his full potential'. Soon enough, and predictably so, the individual himself is dismissed as an abstraction – the only thing real is his impulse, his desire of the moment. Instant gratification, self-indulgence are taken to be, they are aggressively proclaimed to be, self-actualization, first as being necessary for creativity and soon as creativity itself.

This is the dominant ideology for many in the West, and its consequences – in the breakdown of family life, in the inability of society to find an argument against even the most extreme indulgence, for instance the unlimited access to guns – are well known. But this is exactly the world view which so many of our newer publications in India embody, which so many of our celebrities revel in flaunting: 'Couples that are faithful to each other,' one of the most widely read authors told my wife and me the other day, 'are so *boring.*'

The whole has been completely decompounded, and therefore no obligation it entails remains worth a second thought. No society, certainly not one as hard-pressed as ours can survive a hollowing-out of this sort.

The balance of discourse must shift back towards the whole. Whatever we do as individuals, our survival, certainly our fulfilment requires the proper functioning of the whole – of the system of governance, of interpersonal and social relations. Accordingly, the obligations which the proper functioning of the whole entails are to be viewed not as intrusions or shackles, but as duties that are vital for the survival and flowering of the individual himself, much as banks are what enable a river to flow. The prevalent fashion of each part denouncing the whole because the latter is not able at that moment to fulfil some particular claim of that group must be replaced by the realization that the country has an existence, a validity independent of each part; that the health and efficient functioning of the whole are necessary for the well-being of each component; that, as not just I but others also suffer when I neglect to clear stagnant water in and around my house, everyone else has a right to demand that I fulfil the responsibilities which the health of the whole requires.

A particular responsibility which each of us owes to the whole is to regulate our conduct in ways which the proper functioning of institutions requires. The last fifty years teach us that we cannot proceed on the assumption that each of us, being so minuscule a part of the whole, can leave the care of the institutions to others and do as we will, or must – we cannot proceed on the premise that institutions will remain honest or that others will keep them honest even as we as individuals continue to pay and receive the bribes that we do, or have to. Institutions, no less than our bodies and minds, have to be nourished and attended to – every day, forever: 'one by one, little by little, again and again'.

Accordingly, the least each of us has to do, as the *Dhammapada* would put it, is to 'Desist from evil, learn to do good', at the least to desist from transgressing laws and doing what is manifestly wrong. How many of our problems would be lessened if as individuals we did no more than adhere to the law. Recently I had to rush to and from a hospital in the evenings as a relative, dear to all of us, lay ill. On three successive evenings the cars were backed up over half a kilometre. Each time the cause was the same: even though vehicles would be lined up to the edge of the intersection, someone would decide to wade into the intersection; the traffic signals would change before he had been able to clear the intersection; vehicles would pour in from the perpendicular road; and everyone would be in everyone's way; tempers would rise, someone would try to make a break and hurl his vehicle in the lane coming towards one on the right; and then there would be place neither to go ahead nor to reverse.... We blame governments and judges for the interminable delays in courts; but is it not a fact that in every case it is one side which deliberately delays matters – because it knows that it is in the wrong, because it expects to wear the adversary down? But how will these modes of conduct change if, from Class III onwards the child is taught that laws and institutions are just devices which 'the vested interests' have forged to perpetuate their hegemony?

The rule implies more: that each of us must see himself first as a part of the whole: a journalist is first and last a citizen; the publication is just an instrument to which he has access at the moment to help ensure that the whole advances. Similarly, the norms of each profession must be assessed in the light of their effects on the whole: 'I am bound to defend anyone who approaches me for assistance,' says the lawyer to justify shielding a crook or smuggler; but when the skills of the best legal brains in the country are going to be available to crooks and smugglers on this rationalization and the prosecution is to be led by ill-paid, ill-equipped counterparts, how can we expect the whole to survive?

Even doing that much – desisting from evil, abiding by laws – will take care of so many of the problems we create for each other. But it will not be enough: in addition we must spare time and skill to rehabilitate some one institution. Those who have the wherewithal and skills must put them to work on behalf of the institution – and so must the ones who are directly affected by its malfunctioning, that is the victims. Gandhiji made this specific: he taught that the best thing the ones with the necessary wherewithal and skills could do was to enable and equip the victims to set right the particular thing which was holding them down.

In view of what we have been seeing in the last fifty years three things specially need to be done. The essential strategy of politics in the last years has been to string together and work up components, 'minorities', to overwhelm the whole, the 'majority'. At each level, on every issue politics needs to aim at mobilizing the 'majority' – the largest number must be got to vote, the silent majority must be mobilized to register their say on Narmada.

Second, when a group claims to be disadvantaged, persecuted, 'backward', it must be held to specifying the particular disability by which it is handicapped. And the remedy should be addressed to alleviating that specific disability. The group which, because of some specific disability, begins denouncing the whole – the complex of arrangements which enables it to demand and secure redress in the first place – must be looked upon with the same wariness as the group which resorts to unconstitutional means. While the rest of society should shore up that particular deficiency, the group and its leaders must be required to conform to norms, they must meet the standards which the task requires, the standards up to which others are being asked to perform.

Third, while there is no doubt that even the effort of a solitary individual will be a force for the good, given the way the whole has been delegitimized, as the communitarians in the US have been urging, it is essential that we engage in tasks which are best done *with* others. Every day we read of some elderly couple being clubbed to death: if the youth of the neighbourhood would make it their business to visit the elderly couples of the colony, help them assess their security devices and help them obtain better ones, they would be solving a specific problem – in this case, literally saving lives – and they would simultaneously be helping restore what was so marked a feature of our society: the sense of community and neighbourhood. Ever so many times it has turned out that terrorists who planted bombs and killed scores had but recently rented a flat in some colony. Ever so often we read that the elderly couple were killed by the servant they had hired a few days earlier. Were the youth of the colony to help register all new tenants and all servants with the neighbourhood police thana, they would be saving lives, they would be restoring that sense of community, they would be restoring the sense of possibilities – that, yes, even today a handful can make a difference.

To restore the primacy of the whole, to have us adhere to rules and norms, enforcement by external agencies is of course a must – as in India today the custodians of law have made a business of fattening themselves by violating it, almost the first thing that needs to be done is for others to enforce the law on them. But an entire society cannot be policed, for, when repudiation of values becomes as pervasive as it has in India, the enforcers will themselves require to be watched. The society can function only if for the overwhelming proportion of people abiding by rules becomes an internal impulse. The progressive integration of the economy, our being packed tighter and tighter in cities will ultimately provide a new basis for adhering to rules, for keeping our word. They will provide a new basis for ethics, new pressures for doing our duty: neglect by one will injure larger and larger numbers, so they will step in and insist that each discharges his responsibility; if a person – the supplier of components, say – does not keep to the agreed date, the producer will switch to some other supplier. There are correctives afoot, therefore. But as the problems which bedevil Western societies show, these auto-correctives do not prove sufficient to, the utilitarian calculus by itself fails to ensure either social cohesion or individual fulfilment.

That internal impulse to subserve to the whole, to abide by what is in the larger good has to be rooted in the traditions which have grown up in a particular society over aeons. In the religions of the people, in the example of the lives of its great figures. We, in India, have been singularly fortunate in this regard: here alone the traditions have roots going back thousands of years, absolutely no other country has had so many luminescent figures as we have had in the last one hundred and fifty years. Their lives embody the values on which that sense of the whole can be rebuilt. But these are the traditions, these are the very persons – Ramakrishna Paramahamsa, Swami Dayananda, Swami Vivekananda, Sri Aurobindo, Lokmanya Tilak, Gandhiji, Ramana Maharshi, the Paramacharya, Narayan Guru – whom, as we have seen, our Macaulay-Missionary-Marx lot has had us repudiate.

The beginning of reconstruction, therefore, the sine qua non for it is to overturn the intellectual fashions set by these intellectuals, and defeat their verbal terrorism.

21

The changing balance

It happened for the third time – exactly as it had on the two previous occasions. First at a university in Delhi. Then at a lecture in Hyderabad. And this time at a public discussion in Calcutta. An academic of the Left got up and hurled the usual epithets at me: 'Distortion', 'Idiotic', 'Ridiculous'. And then, as befitted his profession, he dropped a name, so to say. Few in the audience would have heard of it – that is why it was the name to drop. But I could swear that as he lashed around, I was telling myself, 'Why doesn't he hurry up and get to "postmodernism"?' And sure enough within minutes he was fuming, 'As has been pointed out in postmodernist literature, there is a distinction between "faith" and "belief"...' What the distinction between the two words had to do with what I had said was not evident from his remarks. In any case what he said about the distinction would have been obvious to anyone who knew ordinary English and did not require the heavy artillery of 'postmodernist literature'. But 'postmodernism' it was. Exactly as it had been in Delhi and at Hyderabad.

'It is their latest device for reducing facts to non-facts,' explained another academic from Calcutta University at dinner that evening. I had been struck by the other feature of the invoking – what was being hurled and invoked was just the latest intellectual fad from somewhere else.

But there has been great progress over the years. They used

to hurl Marx. And then Lenin. And then Stalin – yes, Stalin: two-and-a-half sentences from an essay of his written in 1912 had been 'the theoretical basis' for the communists to embrace the demand for Pakistan. And then it was Mao. And then Lin Piao. And then Ho Chi Minh. And then Pol Pot. There was even a lot who would deem a point established once they had quoted Enver Hoxha of Albania. The names have changed over the years, but the habit has remained: just that the only *brahmastra* they can now think of is 'postmodernism'!

It is a habit that has affected the entire intellectual class in India, and no one more than the ones who have set the fashions for it – namely, the intellectuals of the Left. As I sat listening to the professor – and he was the head of an important social science department at the university, we had been told – I was reminded of what their god of once upon a time, Mao had said of their kind: 'they who with pitiful industry have picked up scraps from the dung-heap of textbooks written abroad…'

And, mind you, the ones who have been most cravenly licking that dung heap, the leftists that is, have been the ones who have always been denouncing everyone else for being a cog of the 'comprador culture', if not the actual agent of a foreign intelligence agency. That habit of dependence has till recently been fortified by a false confidence: the fact that they had been able to browbeat others into silence through their verbal terrorism had given them that confidence. Both the habit and the confidence have now recoiled. They had 'living' proof, they had been shouting for seventy years, they had the one proof which mattered, that of 'practice': the decisive 'reason' on account of which India must go Left was there for everyone to see: the great achievements of the Soviet Union – Unemployment? Abolished; Poverty? Abolished; Unhappy marriages? Abolished; Alcoholism? Abolished; Justice? Within reach of all, and purged of all class bias – the technological excellence of Czechoslovakia, the miracle that Ceausescu had wrought – 'The only debt-free country in the world'. In a word, the decisive reason in their favour, they insisted, was that Paradise had indeed been created *elsewhere,* and would just as certainly be created here in India if only India would follow the path that 'The Only Fatherland' had blazed. But those claims, that *reason* – 'The paradise *there*' reason – had been blown on the very test these great 'theoreticians' had said was the decisive test, the only test that mattered – the test of 'practice'.

Worse, the great theory which was their pride, of which they said these achievements were a vindication, the great theory which enabled them to have what no one else had – the soothsaying power, as well as the answer for everything – that is now nowhere. Even that loss need not have disabled them, but it has: having got so completely in the habit of relying on that 'dung heap of textbooks written abroad', these stalwarts and theoreticians have completely lost the faculty to think for themselves. So they have to wait for someone to show them the direction in which to look next. But no new prophet has arisen to take the place of the ones whom events have cast on the very same 'dung heap of history' onto which they were forever throwing everyone else. Nor is it just that no new prophet is in sight abroad who will tell them where they should proceed, the domestic messiahs they had rallied to have become millstones: the casteism that V.P. Singh inflamed, the casteism and corruption of Laloo Yadav's regime, the casteism, communalism and four-foot lathis of Mulayam Singh – it is becoming more and more embarassing to hold these persons up as exemplars of 'social revolution'.

The intellectuals thus have no option but to fall back on one of three things.

Just looking the other way: they just do not talk about the facts which have since come to be known about the Soviet Union, about the realities of Mao's rule, about the economic stagnation and the environmental destruction in eastern Europe. They talk even less than nothing about the reams and reams they were pouring out about these 'glorious achievements of socialism' till just a few years ago. They do not talk, true. But the people notice that they no longer talk about those things, that when they now hurl some esoteric text at you it is 'postmodernist literature', not Lenin or Stalin or Mao.

Second, they rely on going on repeating the fabrication. 'But Mr Shourie has completely ignored the violence the Hindus perpetrated on the Buddhists, the Hindus destroyed Buddhist viharas', postmodernist declaimed in Calcutta. But there is an advantage. As their verbal terrorism had always worked in the past, they have not bothered to keep up with the results of modern scholarship. In Calcutta I drew attention to what I have recalled above – to what had happened when the indefatigable Sita Ram Goel had written to several Marxist historians to lead him to the evidence on which they were basing their assertion about Hindus having destroyed Buddhist viharas: the 'historians' had been unable to produce a shred of evidence; what they had listed in their publications pointed the other way.

Just a few months earlier exactly the same assertion had been put forth by a leading Marxist theoretician during a public discussion in Hyderabad. I am not on the merits of the case at the moment, but on the fact that, when I had recalled these exchanges of Sita Ram Goel and the Marxist historians, neither the Marxist theoretician in Hyderabad nor the Marxist postmodernist in Calcutta had an answer. It is, of course, a comment on the state of affairs that such fabrications continue to remain the stock-in-trade of public discussion in India, but the advantage is just as apparent: these theoreticians and professors have not bothered to keep up with scholarly work on the subjects on which they declaim. They have, therefore, only to be confronted with the facts and their assertions fall.

The second device is the half-truth. At a public discussion in Hyderabad, in a hall packed to bursting, a progressive Muslim intellectual was trying to put the gloss of tolerance on Islam. The Quran recognizes two classes of people, he told the audience: the ones who had not received the Revelation, and the *ahl-i-kitab,* the People of the Book, the ones to whom the Message had been revealed in a Book. It recognizes the Jews, Christians and Muslims as being the ahl-i-kitab, he said. It is just that the Hindus were not known in Arabia at the time, he said, otherwise they too would have certainly been enumerated among the ahl-i-kitab, for they also have the Revealed Book in the Vedas. The Quran recognizes a long succession of prophets – from Abraham to Moses to Jesus to Muhammad, he said. It is just that the Buddha and Mahavir and other Indian saints were not known in Arabia at the time, otherwise there is no doubt that they too would have been listed as being among the prophets Allah had sent with the Message, he told the audience. As would Guru Nanak and the other Sikh gurus.

It sounds good, does it not? But just see what it implies. How does the fact that Hindus were not known in Arabia, or that Buddha and Mahavir were not known there come into the picture? I asked. After all, the Quran is not supposed to have been written by some Arab, it is said to be the Word of Allah. The ordinary Arab may not have known about the Hindus, about the Buddha and Mahavir, but surely Allah did. And so, when He chose to enumerate only the Jews, Christians and Muslims as being the ahl-i-kitab and enjoined on the faithful eternal hostility towards the non-believers, surely that fact cannot be got around just by saying, 'If Hindus, the Buddha, Mahavir had been known in Arabia…'

And about the Quran recognizing a long line of prophets: but the same Quran states most emphatically, indeed this is its cardinal message that Muhammad was the Seal of the Prophets. He was the Seal not just in the sense that he was the culmination in terms of excellence, he was the Seal in the sense that he was the final one. He had perfected the Message, he had delivered it in its final and unalterable form. The Buddha and Mahavir and Nanak are admissible only to the extent that what they said conforms to what Prophet Muhammad said. To allow even that much is to be too generous: to the extent that they merely repeated what Muhammad said, they are redundant; to the extent that they said something different, they are to be spurned for they are distorting Allah's word. Exactly as, and for the same reason as, Jews and Christians are to be shunned!

Surely, that is obvious. It would be obvious to the progressives too. Yet they put out the half-truth. Again the remedy is the same, and it is just as easy: we just have to know the facts in full, and point them out.

The situation thus is as follows: the ones who have dominated and controlled and terrorised public discourse for half a century in India are now bereft of facts, of arguments. The evidence is available to anyone who has access to their internal 'dialogues' – they are talking to narrower and narrower circles; and in these ever-shrinking circles, they are just repeating the old cliches, there is not a new idea, there is not a new fact. And that is predictable, as we have seen: regurgitating those nostrums of the theory is not just necessary, it is sufficient.

There is evidence to the same effect in the public domain also. Till just five to ten years ago, seminars and public meetings of intellectuals used to be the forte of the progressives, of the Marxists in particular. Today they are just not in a position to hold such meetings – not in Andhra, not in Kerala, not even in Calcutta. On the other hand, meetings of those who have liberated themselves from this point of view are jam-packed. When some progressive does come to one of these meetings, he cuts a sorry figure. He just reads out a speech which has been prepared and typed in advance, irrespective of what has been said by speakers before him, often irrespective of the topic itself; on other occasions he just lets fly: those allusions to the esoteric – 'postmodernist literature' – accompanied by strong and minatory words – 'idiotic', 'ridiculous'. And thereby lives up to the description given by the prophet prior to Mao – that is,

Lenin – of a person 'trying to cover inconvenient facts beneath a shroud of angry words'.

Thus, the balance of argument, of evidence, and most significantly of the public mood has shifted. Now is the time to seal it. For that, several steps ought to be taken.

First, in mapping change, in organizing movements one must pay due attention to the importance of ideas and evidence. After all, as communists, etc., were able to secure such success with the aid of wrong, unsubstantiated ideas, with falsehoods, will it not be possible to do some good with better ideas backed by evidence?

Second, it is a complete error to lull oneself with the argument that 'the people' do not need, they do not care for evidence and ideas. The claim that they had the great theory in their possession, that all the evidence was on their side was an important element in the domination that these progressives were able to secure in public discourse, for instance. Ever so often, what grab the people are crude notions, true; but they are the crude versions of these ideas – and the claim that behind those simplified notions lies an entire theory is a vital element in the success those crude notions secure. In any case, while the great avalanches of history may be affected by the people at large, decisions and discourse from month to month are in the hands of just a few thousand persons. These latter certainly are influenced by argument, reason, evidence. Therefore, work out the ideas, garner the relevant evidence to the last detail. And reach them at least to 'the influentials'.

The negative side of this task is as important. Just because 'The Only Fatherland' of these theoreticians has collapsed, just because that collapse has taken the theory down with it does not mean that they have been rendered harmless. Their claims are hollowed, they have nothing to say, but they still control large parts of our academia and a very large part of the media, certainly the media in English. Therefore, at every opportunity they must be confronted with what has become known about the regimes they had held up to us as exemplars. They must be confronted with and requested to explain what they were writing till just six years ago. The lie that they repeat should not be shrugged off just because it is the same old lie: it must be nailed with evidence – each time, and as many times as it is repeated. As must every half-truth by which they seek to once again inveigle us into looking away.

Third, the factor which has enabled them to broadcast their concoctions, as we have seen through the example of the ICHR, has been their control of institutions. They have not used these institutions for the country. They have used these institutions to promote each other, to have a comfortable time. But that has been just a misdemeanour compared to their real crime: they have used these institutions to sow in the minds of our people the seeds of self-hatred. This hold has to be countered.

To do so we should change our laws and our pattern of incentives so that private individuals and groups get enthused to set up a multitude of foundations and institutions; the changes which are required are marginal, they are obvious – all that is required is faith in others: that we step out of the hangover of the socialist days and have faith that those outside the state apparatus too are anxious to do good by the country. Second, we should loosen the hold over existing institutions of eminences of the kind we have surveyed here: and for this all that is necessary is to awaken people to what they have done with these institutions over the last twenty years.

Once again, the negative side of this lesson is just as important. If after purging these institutions of such entrepreneurs, some new group stuffs them with the same sort, if it sets about to put the institutions to the same sort of use, it will inflict the same injury on the institutions, on scholarly work, and eventually on the cause it set out to advance. That is a warning for enthusiasts – and it is a reassurance for the rest of us: the hijacked institution swiftly loses its credibility, and with that its ability to do harm!

Even so a problem remains. For the first time after thirty to forty years scholarly work is again being done which brings out facts as they are. But it is not being allowed to reach large numbers. The reason is simple: much of the media, many universities, most of the controlling bodies remain in the hands of the same progressives, defunct though they be. That is a legacy of fifty years of perverted discourse and politics, of tenures, of their placing each other in positions of authority, of their speciality – networking. Even here the breach is of course evident: many in these institutions speak the truth in private, what they do not have as yet is the courage to speak it in the company of others. This cowardice will break one day all of a sudden: when the numbers have reached a critical mass, when some random event shows the persons how many they actually are. But for the time being the hold of the old intellectual terrorists remains an obstacle to the dissemination of new research.

This is where a marriage of many skills, of diverse resources is required. Resources to establish new research institutions which would be beyond the stranglehold of the progressives. Resources to start new publications which would not be held back by that intellectual cowardice. New, modern marketing methods by which the new publications can be reached to a wider circle of readers.

This is the next step we need: this gelling of diverse talents, of resources of different kinds.

22

The insidious, the false

'The mine of learning, honoured Nalanda' – that is how the sixteenth-seventeenth century Tibetan historian, Taranath, referred to the university at Nalanda. Said to have been set up in a grove in which the Buddha himself had spent some time, in the birthplace of one of his greatest disciples, Sariputta, the university was enlarged by successive rulers. Harshvardhana assigned the revenue of a hundred villages for its expenses. By the time I-tsing studied at it (AD 675–685), the number of villages whose revenue had been endowed to the university had risen to 201. The university was a beacon for all. 'In the 7th century of the Christian era,' Vincent Smith wrote, 'the Nalanda establishment undoubtedly was the most important and splendid of its kind in India, or, in fact, the world. It was the principal centre of Buddhist learning, and was crowded with students from every quarter. It was truly a great university…'[1]

Scholars who had passed its rigorous programme were honoured throughout the Buddhist world. Yuan Chwang's – Hieun Tsang's – telling expression gives a glimpse: '…Hence foreign students came to the establishment to put an end to their doubts and then became celebrated, and those who stole the name (of Nalanda Brother) were all treated with respect

[1] James Hastings, ed., *Encyclopedia of Religion and Ethics*, Volume IX, T&T Clark, Edinburgh, 1908, Reprint, Charles Scribner's Sons, 1926, New York, pp. 126–27.

wherever they went....'[2] The great Guru Padmasambhava who took Buddhism to Tibet, and who is revered there next only to the Buddha himself, was from the university. Dharmakirti, one of the deepest of scholars, and a founder of philosophical logic, taught there. Hieun Tsang spent five years there (AD 640–645). I-tsing – he came to Nalanda thirty years after Hieun Tsang – spent ten (AD 675–685). Of the sixty monks who visited India during the Tang dynasty and whose account I-tsing wrote, thirteen spent time in Nalanda.

The highest standards were maintained – right from the examination for entering the university. Hieun Tsang recorded that out of every ten who sought to enter it, only two or three eventually were able to do so. Discipline was very strict, the rules and regulations were austere as can be. The university was the centre of Mahayana learning, of course – so much so that, reviewing its significance, Vincent Smith observed, 'A detailed history of Nalanda would be a history of Mahayanist Buddhism, from the time of Nagarjuna in the 2nd cent A.D. (?), or possibly even from an earlier date, until the Muhammadan conquest of Bihar in A.D. 1197 – a period well over a millennium. All the most noted doctors of the Mahayana seem to have studied at Nalanda...'[3]

Nor were the courses confined to Buddhist subjects. In addition, they covered Vedic texts, non-Buddhist philosophical schools, grammar, medicine, practical sciences, fine arts and much else. Hieun Tsang was especially struck by the fact that the university actively brought together adherents and scholars of different sects and creeds. Debates among these diverse scholars were detailed and extensive, and one of the principal modes of learning.

At the time I-tsing was at the university, there were 3,700 monks. The total complex had around 10,000 residents...

[2] Thomas Waters, *On Yuan Chwang's Travels in India*, Royal Asiatic Society, London, 1905, p. 165.

[3] *Encyclopedia of Religion and Ethics*, op. cit., pp. 126–27.

And yet, the university was run more democratically than we can even imagine an institution being run today. 'If the monks had some business,' I-tsing recorded, 'they would assemble to discuss the matter.'

> Then they ordered the officer, Viharpala, to circulate and report the matter to the resident monks one by one with folded hands. With the objection of a single monk, it would not pass. There was no such use of beating or thumping to announce his case. In case a monk did something without the consent of all the other residents, he would be forced to leave the monastery. If there was difference of opinion on certain issue, they would give reason to convince (the other group). No force or coercion was used to convince. There were some monks who were in charge of the treasury of the monastery. Even if there were two or three resident monks, the officer (in charge of the monastery) would send monks of lower rank with folded hands to ask their permission for spending money. With their unanimous consent, they would be allowed to spend. Without the consent of all resident monks, nobody could decide the affairs of the monastery. If anyone used the money without giving explanation, even if it were a quantity of rice in husks, that person would be expelled from the monastic life.
>
> ...The decision taken by anyone without the consent of others was regarded as a sin against one's religion. This [the decision] may be for the welfare of the monastery but it was finally considered as committing a grave sin. A wise monk would never do such things.[4]

The structures housing the university were as splendid and as extensive as the learning they housed. When excavations began, the principal mound alone was about 1,400 feet by 400 feet. Hieun Tsang recounts at least seven monasteries and

[4] I-ching, *Chinese Monks in India, Biography of eminent monks who went to the Western world in search of the Law during the Great T'ang Dysnasty,* Latika Lahiri (trans.), Motilal Banarsidas, Delhi, 1986, p. 55.

eight halls. The monasteries were of several storeys, we are told, whose 'upper rooms tower above the clouds. Their richly adorned towers and fairy like turrets resembled pointed hilltops. The observatories were lost in the morning mists. From the windows one may see how the winds and clouds produce new forms, and from the soaring eaves the sun set splendorous and moon lit glories.'

> Down below, the grounds were variegated by deep translucent ponds bearing on their bosom the blue lotus intermingled with Kanaka flower of deep red colour, while at intervals the Amra groves spread all their shade. The massive external grandeur of the buildings contrasted with the delicate artistic beauty of their interior.
>
> All outside courts, in which are the priests' chambers, are of four stages. The stages have dragon projections and coloured eaves, pearl red pillars, carved and ornamented, richly adorned balustrades, while the roofs are covered with tiles that reflect light in a thousand shades. These things add to the beauty of the scene. The *sangharamas* in India are counted by myriads but that is most remarkable for grandeur and height… In this establishment, the work of a succession of sovereigns, the sculpture was perfect and really beautiful.[5]

A figure of the standing Buddha made of copper – 80 feet high, presented to the monastery by King Purnavarma of Kanauj…

A library complex of three buildings – one of them nine storeys high…

'This marvellous building,' I-tsing informs us while writing about the main, three-storeyed building, 'surpassed all the buildings in grandeur and artistic workmanship. It was one of the most splendid ones in India. It is pretty difficult to describe the artistic skill and beauty of this temple…' Halls. Rooms

[5] Cited in *Encyclopedia of Buddhism*, W.G. Weeraratne, (Editor-in-Chief), Volume VII, Fascicle I, p. 108.

for monks. 'This imposing monastery had a thirty or forty feet high enclosing wall with rows of well-modelled stucco figures.' Courtyards. Open spaces. Stupas – 'about a hundred in number'. Eight temples. Fourteen big and eighty-four smaller monasteries. '…It was difficult for the author to recollect the vast number of sacred relics over there. These were erected over different sacred vestiges and adorned with gold and priceless lustrous stones…' There were seven monasteries of very similar appearance and layout. 'Hundred paces to the south was a stupa more than hundred feet high … The ornamentation of the stupa was delicate and superb. The seat in the hall with mosaic floor was made of gold and was studded with jewels…' I-tsing gave a detailed account of the successive steps by which the courtyard was polished with paste of powdered lime, earth, jute-fibres, oil and jute-fluff: '…Finally, it was rubbed with oil, which gave to the brickwork the look of a mirror. The flights of stairs of the hall were also polished like this…'[6]

The Fatal Blow

For a variety of reasons, Buddhism faded from India – among these were the intellectual challenge posed by Adi Shankaracharya and others; the fact that the religion had become too heavily oriented towards and dependent on monks; corruption in the order of monks; the receding of patronage. The importance and upkeep of Nalanda too would have declined. But it remained a living and vital centre. As the Islamic invaders advanced through Afghanistan and north-western India, they exterminated Buddhist clergy, they pillaged and pulverized every Buddhist structure – the very word '*but*', the idols they so feverishly destroyed, was derived from 'Buddha'. Nalanda escaped their attention for a while – in part because it was not on the main routes. But soon enough, the marauders arrived, and struck the fatal blow. The

[6] I-ching, *Chinese Monks in India*, op. cit., pp. 51–54.

ransacking is described in the contemporary *Tabakat-i-Nasiri* by Maulana Minhaj-ud-din.

Minhaj-ud-din rose under successive rulers. He received several honours and grants – among other things, a village was assigned to him by Balban. Minhaj-ud-din was appointed to important offices: 'law-officer, and director of the preaching, and of all religious, moral and judicial affairs' of Gwalior, the qazi of the city, the principal of a college of learning, and so on. His account is highly regarded for its detail, its accuracy and the absence of embellishment.[7]

In the course of his narrative, Minhaj-ud-din turns to the achievements of Malik-ul-Ghazi, Ikhtiyar-ud-din, Muhammad, son of Bakhtiyar Khalji. Muhammad Ikhityar-ud-din, he writes, 'was a man impetuous, enterprising, intrepid, bold, sagacious, and expert'. He rose and came to the notice of the rulers of the time – Kutb-ud-din Aibak and others – because of his raids and depredations, and because of the enormous booty he gathered, booty sufficient for him to set himself up as a plunderer in his own right. 'His reputation reached Sultan (Malik) Kutb-ud-din, who despatched a robe of distinction to him, and showed him honour,' the historian writes. With its high wall, its large buildings, Nalanda seemed like a well-endowed fortress to Ikhtiyar-ud-din and his force. He advanced upon it with two hundred horsemen 'and suddenly attacked the place'. Minhaj-ud-din continues,

[7] In Elliot and Dowson, for instance, we learn, '*The Tabakat-i-Nasiri* is held in high esteem both in India and Europe. Firishta and others refer to it as an excellent work of high authority; Anquetil du Perron calls it a "precious work", and Elphinstone mentions it as a work of the highest celebrity. Stewart in his *History of Bengal* follows it very closely, and considers it "a very valuable book"... H.M. Elliot and John Dowson, *The History of India as told by its own historians, The Muhammadan period*, Volume II, Trubner & Co., London, 1867–77, Reprint, Kitab Mahal, Allahabad, [no date], pp. 259–65.

> The greater number of inhabitants of that place were Brahmans, and the whole of those Brahmans had their heads shaven,[8] and they were all slain. There were a great number of books there; and when all these books came under the observation of the Musalmans, they summoned a number of Hindus that they might give them information respecting the import of those books; but the whole of the Hindus had been killed. On being acquainted (with the contents of the books), it was found that the whole of that fortress and city was a college, and in the Hindu tongue, they call a college, Bihar [*vihara*].[9]

'When that victory was effected,' Minhaj-ud-din reports, 'Muhammad-i-Bakhtiyar returned with great booty, and came to the presence of the beneficent Sultan, Kutb-ud-din I-bak, and received great honour and distinction…' – so much so that other nobles at the court became jealous. All this happened around the year 1197 A.D.

The Aftermath

The Tibetan monk Dharmaswamin came to India in AD 1234, that is, within forty years of the destruction and plunder of Nalanda. He stayed in Magadha for about two and half years, and spent about six months in Nalanda itself. People lived and hid in dread of the marauding Muslim rulers: '… he [Dharmaswamin] and his hosts were always in apprehension of a Muslim attack any time,' Dr. A.S. Altekar informs

[8] This is the usual description of Buddhist monks among Muslim historians of the period.

[9] Maulana Minhaj-ud-din, *Tabakat-i-Nasiri*, H.G Raverty [trans.], Volume I, Asiatic Society of Bengal, 1881, reprinted by Oriental Books Reprint Corporation, Delhi, 1970, pp. 548–53. Minhaj-ud-din recorded that the account of the assault was given to him by Sam-sam-ud-din, one of the two brothers, 'men of learning', who 'were soldiers among that band of holy warriors when they reached the gateway of the fortress and began the attack…' Ibid, p. 552.

us while introducing the *Biography*. Altekar summarizes Dharmaswamin's account:

> When Dharmaswmin reached Vaisali on his way to Bodh Gaya, the town was all deserted on account of the apprehended arrival of a Muslim force. People used to desert their houses by day and come back to them at night. Vikramsila had been completely destroyed before 1206 A.D. and its foundation stones had been hurled into the Ganga. The Bodh Gaya establishment had been deserted by all except four monks. The ancient image had been walled up by a brick wall and a new one had been put in the ante-chamber. The old image had, however, been already despoiled of its emerald eyes earlier. The king of Bodh Gaya had fled to the forest. Dharmaswamin himself had to flee away for seventeen days...[10]

Dharmaswamin found Nalanda to be a ghost of what it had been. Of the eight temples and the fourteen large and eighty-four smaller monasteries, only two viharas were in serviceable condition. There was 'absolutely no one to look after them or make offerings,' Dharmaswami noted. Of the great multitude of monks and teachers that had been there, only one ninety-year-old teacher, Rahulasribhadra, four pandits, and seventy monks were left. All lived in dread. While Dharmaswamin was at Nalanda, Muslim soldiery reached the sister monastery, the vihara of Odantapuri. They sent for two lay followers of Rahulasribhadra, and put them in chains. The two sent a message through a traveller to Rahulasribhadra: flee, as the invaders will surely kill you and the followers. In spite of

[10] *Biography of Dharmaswamin, (Chag lo tsa-ba Chos-rje-dpal)*, original Tibetan text deciphered and translated by George Roerich, reprinted by K.P. Jayaswal Research Institute, Patna, 1959, p. xix. As this book is about our Marxist historians, I should note that at the time George Roerich was the professor and head of the Department of Philosophy at the Institute of Oriental Studies of the Academy of Sciences, Moscow, USSR.

entreaties by his followers, Rahulasribhadra decided to stay. 'You flee,' he told the others, including Dharmaswamin. 'I am more than ninety years old. It does not make any difference whether I shall escape, or not, whether I shall go or not.'

As messages to the same effect kept coming, the followers fled. Dharmaswamin refused to leave with the rest, and chose to stay with the guru. Eventually, there was no alternative for them also but to leave the place. Dharmaswamin carried the guru on his shoulders, and they took refuge in a shrine dedicated to a protecting deity. It had survived because of what the invaders believed had happened on an earlier occasion. The Muslim invaders had carried away the stones of this shrine, and smeared the idol with filth and mud. 'A man who had participated (in this work),' Dharmaswamin recorded, 'died the same evening ... Next morning the image was found undamaged, so it was said. Since then the Turushka-heretics [the Muslim invaders] did not dare to approach it and cross the threshold.'

Soon enough, a posse of 300 Muslim soldiers appeared, 'armed and ready for battle'. Had the guru and Dharmaswamin been found, the latter noted, they would surely have been killed. But the soldiers did not find them, and went away. The two lay supporters of the guru were kept in irons for several days, but eventually set free...[11]

And that is how the great, luminous light of learning, one of the most influential in the history of religions anywhere, was extinguished.

The Marxist Account

We have already encountered D.N. Jha, and seen how he concocts 'evidence' and distorts sources in his textbook on ancient India. Professor of History at the Delhi University at present, in 2004 he was the president of the Indian History Congress. In the presidential address he delivered – one to

[11] Ibid., pp. 90–95.

which we shall turn as an example of Marxist 'scholarship' – this is the account he gives of the destruction of Buddhist viharas, and of Nalanda in particular:

> A Tibetan tradition has it that the Kalacuri King Karna (eleventh century) destroyed many Buddhist temples and monasteries in Magadha, and the Tibetan text *Pag Sam Jon Zang* refers to the burning of the library of Nalanda by some 'Hindu fanatics'.[12]

'*Hindu fanatics*'? The expression struck me as odd. A Tibetan text of the eighteenth century using so current an expression as '*Hindu fanatics*'? Especially so because, on Jha's own reckoning, as we shall soon see, Hinduism is an invention of the British in the late nineteenth century?

So, what is this 'Tibetan text'? What does it say? Had Jha looked it up?

Pag Sam Jon Zang was written by Sumpa Khan-Po Yece Pal Jor. The author lived in 1704-1788: that is, five hundred years after the destruction of Nalanda. That is the first thing that strikes one: our historian disregards the contemporaneous account, *Tabakat-i-Nasiri*, and opts for a text written five hundred years after the event.

But had he read the text at all? Could a self-respecting Marxist have at all believed what is written in it?

This is how Sarat Chandra Das, the translator and editor of *Pag Sam Jon Zang*, sets out the account of the destruction of Nalanda as given in this text:

> While a religious sermon was being delivered in the temple that he (Kakuta Sidha, a minister of a king of Magadha) had erected at Nalanda, a few young monks threw washing water

[12] Dwijendra Narayan Jha, 'Looking for a Hindu identity,' presidential address to the Indian History Congress, 2004. Accessed at http://www.sacw.net/India_History/dnj_Jan06.pdf

> at two Tirthika[13] beggars. The beggars being angry, set fire on the three shrines of *dharma ganja*, the Buddhist university of Nalanda – viz. *Ratna Sagara, Ratna Ranjaka* including the nine-storey building called *Ratnadadhi* which contained the library of sacred books. (p. 92.)[14]

Two beggars could go from building to building of that huge campus and, with all the monks present, burn down the entire, huge, scattered complex?

And, the account of the relevant passage reproduced above is the one set out by Sarat Chandra Das in his *Index*. That is, it is just a summary of the actual passage – in an index, it scarcely could be more. What does the relevant section, and in particular the passage about the burning down of the library, say?

The author is giving an account of how Dharma has survived three rounds of destructive attempts.[15] One round was occasioned by the fluctuating relations between Khunimamasta, a king of Taksig (Turkistan?), and Dhrama Chandra, a king of Nyi-og in the east. The latter sends gifts. The former thinks these are part of black magic. He, therefore, swoops down from 'dhurukha' and destroys 'the three bases' of Magadha – monasteries, scriptures and stupas. Khunimamasta drives out and exiles the monks. Dharma Chandra's uncle sends many scholars to China to spread the teaching. He receives gold as thanksgiving. He uses this and other gifts to appease rulers of smaller kingdoms to join the fight against the king of Taksig (Turkistan?). The uncle thereafter revives 'the three bases'.

[13] The term that Buddhists used to designate Hindus at the time.

[14] Sumpa Khan-po Yece Pal Jor, *Pag Sam Jon Zang, History of the Rise, Progress and Downfall of Buddhism in India*, Part I, Sarat Chandra Das, (ed.), The Presidency Jail Press, 1908, Index.

[15] I am grateful to Geshe Dorji Damdul, the director of Tibet House in Delhi, for the translation, and for instructing me about the meaning of the text, as well as the personages and places involved.

Almost all the shrines are restored and eighty-four new ones are built. And so, the dharma survives.

In the next round, 'the teacher who taught *prajnaparamita* for twenty years is assassinated by burglars from dhurukha. His blood turned into milk and many flowers emerged from his body. (Thus) he flew into the sky.'

We now come to the crucial passage, the one that Jha has ostensibly invoked. I reproduce the translation of it by Geshe Dorji Damdul in full:

> Again at that time, there was a scholar by the name Mutita Bhadra, who was greatly involved in renovating and building stupas. Eventually he had a vision of Bodhisattva Samantabhadra. He flew to Liyul by holding the garment (of Bodhisattva Samantabhadra) and there he made great contributions to the welfare of sentient beings and the Dharma. Reviving the Dharma that way, the Dharma flourished for forty years in the Central Land (Magadha?). At that time, during the celebration over the construction of a shrine in Nalanda by Kakutasita, a minister of the king, some naughty novice monks splashed (dish) washing water on two non-Buddhist beggars and also pressed (the two) in-between the door and (the door frame.) Angry over these gestures, one (beggar) served as the attendant to the other who sat in a deep pit for twelve years to gain the *sidhi* of the Sun. Having achieved the *sidhi*, they threw ashes of a fire *puja* (*havan*) they did, on eighty-four Buddhist shrines. They were all burned. Particularly, when the three *dharma ganja* of Nalanda – the shrines which sheltered the scriptures – as well got consumed in fire, streams of water ran down from the scriptures of *Guhyasamaja* and *Prajnaparamita* which were housed in the ninth storey of the *Ratnadhati* shrine. This saved many scriptures. Later, fearing penalty from the king, the two (beggars) escaped to Hasama in the north. However, the two died due to immolation, which happened on its own.

Surely, no self-respecting Marxist could have made his account rest on not just one miracle – acquiring *sidhis* and raining fire on to the structures – but two, for we also have the streams of water running down from the scriptures.

Marxist Originality

But we strain unnecessarily. There is a clue in Jha's lecture itself. He doesn't cite the Tibetan text, he does what Marxists do: he cites another Marxist citing the Tibetan text!

To see what he does, you must read the lines carefully. This is what we saw Jha saying:

> A Tibetan tradition has it that the Kalacuri King Karna (eleventh century) destroyed many Buddhist temples and monasteries in Magadha, and the Tibetan text *Pag-Sam-Jon-Zang* refers to the burning of the library of Nalanda by some 'Hindu fanatics'.

As his authority, Jha cites a book by B.N.S. Yadava, *Society and Culture in Northern India in the Twelfth Century*. What did Yadava himself write? Here it is: 'Further, the Tibetan tradition informs us that Kalacuri Karna (11th century) destroyed many Buddhist temples and monasteries in Magadha.'

Jha has clearly lifted what Yadava wrote word for word – at least he has been faithful to his source. But in the very next sentence, Yadava had gone on to say: '*It is very difficult to say anything as to how far this account may be correct*.'

Words that Jha conveniently left out!

Yadava had continued, 'However, we get some other references to persecution.'

He cited two inscriptions and a *Puranic* reference. And then came to the Tibetan text. Recall what Jha wrote about this text: '…and the Tibetan text *Pag-Sam-Jon-Zang* refers to the burning of the library of Nalanda by some 'Hindu fanatics'.

And now turn to what Yadava wrote about this very text: 'The Tibetan text *Pag-Sam-Jon-Zang* contains a [I am leaving out a word] tradition of the burning of the library of Nalanda by some Hindu fanatics.'

Close enough to pass for plagiarism? But wait, there is originality! Notice, first, that two Hindu *beggars* have become 'Hindu *fanatics*'. Notice, next, that the words 'Hindu fanatics' that Jha had put in quotation marks as if they were the words that the author of the Tibetan text had used to describe the arsonists, were actually the words of his fellow Marxist, Yadava. But the best clue is the word that I omitted from what Yadava had actually written. Yadava's full sentence was as follows: 'The Tibetan text *Pag-Sam-Jon-Zang* contains a *doubtful* tradition of the burning of the library of Nalanda by some Hindu fanatics.'

Just as he had left out the words, '*It is very difficult to say anything as to how far this account may be correct*,' Jha now leaves out the word '*doubtful*'. And all this in the presidential address to the Indian History Congress.

In a word,

- There is a Tibetan text written five hundred years after the destruction of Nalanda
- Sarat Chandra Das annotates it, and includes in his Index a summary in English of a passage in the text – the summary naturally leaves out telling components of the original passage
- Yadava looks only at the summary in the Index – 'non-Buddhist beggars' becomes 'Hindu fanatics'
- Yadava notes that the account is based on a 'doubtful tradition'
- Jha omits the word 'doubtful'
- And we have a presidential address to the Indian History Congress!

Given what we have seen of Marxist historians even in this brief book, the brazen-faced distortions – to the point of falsehood – do not surprise me. What *does* surprise me is that no one looked up either the source that Jha had cited or the text.

Indeed, in concluding his section, Yadava had stated,

> A great blow to Buddhism was, no doubt, rendered by the Turkish invasions, leading to the destruction and desertion of the celebrated Buddhist monasteries of Magadha and Bengal. Many Buddhist scholars fled to Tibet and Nepal.[16]

Their Inventiveness

How do these progressive historians deal with contemporary accounts like the *Tabakat-i-Nasiri* that we encountered above? Accounts that celebrate the destruction of viharas and temples, that celebrate the slaughter of Buddhist, Hindu and Jain monks and other infidels? Accounts that enumerate these deeds at length and in gory detail to show how faithful the rulers were to Islam, to establish their piety, to record for Allah and all believers how much the rulers did to exterminate other religions and establish Islam – how do our progressives deal with them?

After all, one cannot get away from the fact that such accounts are legion. Inscriptions on the Islamic buildings themselves proclaim that they have been constructed on the site of Buddhist, Jain and Hindu temples. Annual reports of the Archaeological Survey of India contain reproductions after reproductions of these inscriptions – inscriptions from Rajasthan, from Uttar Pradesh, from Bihar, from Bengal, from Madhya Pradesh, from Karnataka. Accounts – scores of them, written at the very time that the structures were being pulverized and the kafirs were being butchered – record in detail how a temple was reduced to rubble, and how the material was

[16] On the preceding quotations from B.N.S. Yadava, see his, *Society and Culture in Northern India in the Twelfth Century*, Central Book Depot, Allahabad, 1973, pp. 346–47.

used to construct the tomb, the palace, the mosque in question. Muslim rulers experienced a special elation in using the material for tombs and for mosques. A much-favoured stratagem was to break up the idols and put the fragments under the steps leading up to the mosque or tomb so that the faithful would tread upon the broken idols as they came for prayers. Another frequent device of putting down the devotees of our religions was to turn the idols around, and put them into the walls so that the faces of the deities would be turned into and towards the rubble with which the wall was made.

To appreciate the theories that our progressives construct to explain away the contemporary texts, to appreciate the inventiveness of the 'explanations' that they devise, you must first read a sample or two of what the texts record. So as not to lose the thread of the argument, we will have to make do with just one typical account.

The *Maasir-i-Alamgiri* of Saqi Mustad Khan is the best-known account of Aurangzeb's reign.[17] As Jadunath Sarkar explains in his introductory remarks to the volume, starting with Akbar, the Mughal rulers appointed officers in each province to send regular reports of every event of significance happening in their jurisdiction. These were collated at the court. In addition, a newsletter was prepared every day about happenings at the court. And a person who had a flair for writing was appointed to prepare an overall account of events on the basis of these sets of reports – emanating from each province as well as from the court. The first ten years of Aurangzeb's reign were recorded in this fashion by Mirza Muhammad Kazim. By that time Aurangzeb had become preoccupied with a host of tasks and problems. At the urging of the 'last secretary and favourite disciple in State policy and religiosity' of Aurangzeb, as Jadunath Sarkar informs us, the thread was

[17] Saqi Mustad Khan, *Maasir-i-Alamgiri*, translated and annotated by Jadunath Sarkar, Royal Asiatic Society of Bengal, Calcutta, 1947, reprinted by Oriental Books Reprint Corporation, Delhi, 1986.

taken up by Mustad Khan and completed three years after Aurangzeb's death. The account was scrupulously based on the daily, weekly and fortnightly reports – so much so that where an error had occurred in recording a date, for instance, because of an oversight of the copyist, Jadunath Sarkar, as he records, was able to correct it.[18]

Here are a few passages from this, absolutely contemporary account. Do read them for only then will you be able to appreciate the inventiveness of our progressives, and also their dedication to their line:

> *13 May* 1669: Saf Shikan Khan, was appointed *faujdar* of Mathura *vice* Abdun Nabi Khan and Dilir Himmat, son of Bahadur Ruhila, that of Nadarbar. Brahma Deo Sisodia was appointed to accompany Saf Shikan Khan, Sayyid 'Abdul Wahhab, messenger of the King of Machin, had audience. Salih Bahadur, macebearer, was sent to demolish the temple of Malarna.
>
> *2 September* 1669: It was reported that, according to the Emperor's command, his officers had demolished the temple of Viswanath at Kashi.
>
> *27 January 1670*: During this month of Ramzan abounding in miracles, the Emperor as the promoter of justice and overthrower of mischief, as a knower of truth and destroyer of oppression, as the zephyr of the garden of victory and the reviver of the faith of the Prophet, issued orders for the demolition of the temple situated in Mathura, famous as the *Dehra* of Kesho Rai. In a short time by the great exertions of his officers, the destruction of this strong foundation of infidelity was accomplished, and on its site a lofty mosque was built at the expenditure of a large sum. This temple of folly was built by that gross idiot Birsingh Deo Bundela. Before his accession to the throne, the Emperor Jahangir was displeased with Shaikh Abul Fazl. This infidel [Birsingh] became a royal

[18] Ibid. Jadunath Sarkar, Translator's Preface, pp. iii–v. All dates have been changed from the *Hijera* to the Christian calendar.

favourite by slaying him [Abul Fazl], and after Jahangir's accession was rewarded for this service with the permission to build the temple, which he did at an expense of thirty-three lakhs of rupees.

Praised be the august God of the faith of Islam, that in the auspicious reign of this destroyer of infidelity and turbulence [Aurangzeb], such a wonderful and seemingly impossible work was successfully accomplished. On seeing this instance of the strength of the Emperor's faith and the grandeur of his devotion to God, the proud Rajas were stifled, and in amazement they stood like facing the wall. The idols, large and small, set with costly jewels, which had been set up in the temple, were brought to Agra, and buried under the steps of the mosque of the Begam Sahib, in order to be continually trodden upon. The name of Mathura was changed to Islamabad.

16 October 1678: Abul Muhammad Khan Bijapuri became *faujdar* of Oudh *vice* Tahawwar Khan; Darab Khan was sent with a strong force to chastise the Rajputs of Khandela and demolish the great temple of the place.

2 April 1679: As all the aims of the religious Emperor were directed to the spreading of the law of Islam and the overthrow of the practices of the infidels, he issued orders to the high *diwani* officers that from Wednesday, the 2nd April, 1679/1st Rabi A., in obedience to the Quranic injunction 'till they pay commutation money (*jazia*) with the hand of humility' and in agreement with canonical traditions, *jazia* should be collected from the infidels (*zimmies*) of the capital and the provinces.

25 May 1679: On Sunday, the 25th May/24th Rabi, S. Khan Jahan Bahadur came from Jodhpur, after demolishing the temples and bringing with himself some cart-load of idols, and had audience of the Emperor, who highly praised him and ordered that the idols, which were mostly jewelled, golden, silvery, bronze, copper or stone, should be cast in the yard (*jilaukhanah*) of the Court and under the steps of the Jam'a mosque, to be trodden on. They remained so for some time and at last their very names were lost.

17 December 1679: Hafiz Muhammad Amin Khan reported that some of his servants had ascended the hill and found the other side of the pass also deserted; (evidently) the Rana had evacuated Udaipur and fled. On the 4th January/12th Zil. H., the Emperor encamped in the pass. Hasan 'Ali Khan was sent in pursuit of the infidel. Prince Muhammad 'Azam and Khan Jahan Bahadur were permitted to view Udaipur. Ruhullah Khan and Ekkataz Khan went to demolish the great temple in front of the Rana's palace, which was one of the rarest buildings of the age and the chief cause of the destruction of life and property of the despised worshippers. Twenty *machator* Rajputs[19] [who] were sitting in the temple, vowed to give up their lives; first one of them came out to fight, killed some and was then himself slain, then came out another and so on, until every one of the twenty perished, after killing a large number of the imperialists including the trusted slave, Ikhlas. The temple was found empty. The hewers broke the images.

24 January 1680: On Saturday, the 24th January, 1680/2nd Muharram, the Emperor went to view lake Udaisagar, constructed by the Rana, and ordered all the three temples on its banks to be demolished.

News came that Hasan 'Ali Khan having crossed the pass on Wednesday, the 21st January/9th Zil. H. had attacked the Rana, who had fled leaving his camp and property behind. In this expedition much grain was captured by the soldiers and it led to cheapness.

On the 29th January [1680]/7th Muharram, Hassan 'Ali Khan brought to the Emperor twenty camel-loads of tents and other things captured from the Rana's palace and reported that one hundred and seventy-two other temples in the environs of Udaipur had been destroyed. The Khan received the title of Bahadur 'Alamgirshahi.

On Monday, the 22nd February [1680]/1st Safar the Emperor went to view Chitor; by his order sixty-three temples of the place were destroyed.

Abu Turab, who had been sent to demolish the temples of Amber, returned to Court on Tuesday, the 10th August

[19] 'Opium-bemused Rajputs "who never rise from their beds, but to go to war".'

> [1680]/24th Rajab, and reported that he had pulled down sixty-six temples...[20]

Reports of this kind can be multiplied by the score. And there are the buildings, starting with the Quwwat-ul-Islam mosque in Delhi – the mosque celebrating the Might of Islam – and the Qutab Minar, celebrating victory over the infidels. The inscriptions on the buildings proclaim that they have been built by destroying temples (twenty-seven in the case of the Quwwat-ul-Islam mosque says the inscription at this mosque). Even to this day, the materials testify to the fact that they were of Hindu temples.

How do our progressives get around these inscriptions and the materials in the buildings? How do they talk away the contemporary accounts?[21]

[20] For the preceding extracts, ibid., pp. 53, 55, 60, 106, 108–09, 114–15, 116–17, 120.

[21] An entire volume can be filled with the apologia and rationalizations that our progressives advance. I will confine myself to just an example or two as they will suffice to illustrate the kinds of theories that these progressives spin. The following two articles on Islamic monuments and on Aurangzeb are taken from *Mythifying History, Seminar*, Number 364, December 1989. This issue had contributions by Romila Thapar, Nasir Tyabji, Michael W. Meister, R. Nath, Satish Chandra, Gyanendra Pandey, and by 'some members of the Centre for Historical Studies at the Jawaharlal Nehru University'. The last was a contribution, 'The political abuse of history,' issued by twenty-five leftist historians. It asserted that there was no evidence that Ayodhya was the birthplace of Ram; that the present Ayodhya was the Ayodhya referred to in the Ramayana; that the Babri mosque was constructed on the site that had earlier been occupied by a temple; that Muslims were invariably opposed to Hindus or Hindu temples; that, in fact, Ayodhya had been sacred to many religions. Among the signatories were the usual eminences: Romila Thapar, Sarvepalli Gopal, Bipan Chandra, Harbans Mukhia, K.N. Panikkar, B.D. Chattopadhyay, Muzzafar Alam. In a word, it was an issue having the usual constructions put forward by the usual eminences.

Humans come to regard certain sites as sacred, we are instructed. Sites that were regarded as sacred by followers of a religion are often taken over by followers of another religion and come to be regarded as sacred by the latter, we are instructed. So, there is nothing special about mosques having been built on the sites of temples. Buildings themselves come to be used for different purposes: 'Viable reuse can be part of social growth,' we are instructed. 'Lutyens's Viceregal palace appropriately has become the President's House...'[22] Is the destruction of temples as recorded in contemporary accounts, in the inscriptions on the very buildings, akin to the viceregal palace being rechristened Rashtrapati Bhavan?

Furthermore, we are instructed, when we do come across instances of temple destruction, as in the case of Aurangzeb, we have to be circumspect in inferring what has happened and why. As 'the destruction of young students and their "Goddess of Democracy" statue in [the Tiananmen Square of] China' reminds us, we 'must understand that assertion of authority and the expression of an ideology need only slightly overlap'.[23] In the case of Aurangzeb in particular, his 'reputation for politically desecrating monuments (as opposed to Islam's canonical iconoclasm) rests more on his selective use of retribution against insubordinate populations through the destruction of shrines than on evidence of a general public-works programme in his period to dismantle monuments'.[24]

Third, the early monuments – like the Quwwat-ul-Islam mosque in Delhi – had to be built in 'great haste', we are instructed. And so available construction materials were used. 'Finished building materials have economic value in every

---

On the evasions and concoctions of this lot, see, Meenakshi Jain, *Rama and Ayodhya*, Aryan Books International, New Delhi, 2003.

[22] Michael W. Meister, 'Mystifying monuments', *Seminar*, Number 364, December 1989, p. 27.

[23] Ibid., p. 27.

[24] Ibid., p. 25.

tradition,' we are instructed, 'and in all pre-industrial societies it was a common practice to reuse materials as a matter of simple efficiency and practicality … Economy and availability, not religious or political sentiments, in most cases govern such use' – notice the escape clause that has been slipped in, '…in most cases'. In any case, there is no doubt in regard to the Might of Islam mosque: 'The Qutb mosque in Delhi was built in great haste … The proclamation of political power, as well as the need to meet immediate physical expediency, was undoubtedly part of its programme. Available materials assembled and incorporated into the first phase of this hypostyle building clearly came from Hindu sources…'[25]

Proclamation of *political* power, alone! And what about the religion which insists that religious faith is all, that the political *cannot* be separated from the religious? And the name: the Quwwat-ul-Islam mosque, the Might of Islam mosque? Of course, that must be taken to be mere genuflection! And notice: '*available* materials were assembled and incorporated', they 'clearly came from Hindu sources' – may be the materials were just lying about; may be the temples had crumbled on their own earlier; may be the Hindus voluntarily broke their temples and donated the materials? No? After all, there is no proof they didn't! And so, the word 'plundered' is repeatedly put within quotation marks!

In fact, there is more. The use of such materials – from Hindu temples – for constructing Islamic mosques is part of 'a process of architectural definition and accommodation by local workmen essential to the further development of a South Asian architecture for Islamic use'. The primary responsibility thus becomes that of those 'local workmen' and their 'accommodation'. Hence, features in the Qutb complex come to 'demonstrate a creative response by architects and carvers to a new programme'. A mosque that has clearly used materials, including pillars, from Hindu temples, in which undeniably

[25] Ibid., p. 25.

'in the fabric of the central dome, a lintel carved with Hindu deities has been turned around so that its images face into the rubble wall' comes '*not* to fix the rule'. 'Rather, it stands in contrast to the rapid exploration of collaborative and creative possibilities – architectural, decorative, and synthetic – found in less fortified contexts.' Conclusions to the contrary have been 'misevaluations'. We are making the error of 'seeing salvaged pieces' – what a good word that, '*salvaged*': the pieces were not obtained by breaking down temples; they were lying as rubble and would inevitably have disintegrated with the passage of time; instead they were '*salvaged*', and given the honour of becoming part of new, pious buildings – 'seeing salvaged pieces where healthy collaborative creativity was producing new forms'.

But what about the inscriptions? What about the ayats from the Quran that were carved into the walls, over the doorways, into the lintels – exhorting the faithful to, as they would say in government, 'do the needful'? 'Only Islamic believers could read the Koranic inscriptions on such monuments, and understand them as instructions to maintain the pure faith,' we are instructed – the implication being that the rulers, etc., were being so considerate as not to cause non-believers to feel guilty at not abiding by the instruction to live up to the Islamic faith. Surely, that only Muslims could read the instructions would have the opposite effect – the faithful would be charged up to do the needful, and the infidels would remain unaware of what was coming! The rationalization becomes comic: 'It is interesting to note the apparent programmes of these inscriptions, for they speak most often of earthly rewards as a prelude to paradise, and give "fervent warnings to disbelievers and deniers of the Revelation" ... Such proclamations, however, were not directed toward the local population. Like warnings in the *Shilpa Shastras* that tell workmen that a breach in measurement will bring them barren spouses, so these excoriate the Islamic faithful.'[26] Either the man is a fool – in that he does not know what the faithful are exhorted to do vis-à-vis the 'disbelievers and deniers of the Revelation' – or a knave, in that he knows, and is knowingly equating that to measuring doorways and arches incorrectly.

And then comes the crowning bit of creativity. After all, one just cannot deny that contemporary records celebrate the destruction of temples, that they celebrate the number of infidels who were put to the sword. No problem. Our authority has advice: '... broad rhetorical claims in some Muslim sources' – pause right there for a moment. '*Broad rhetorical claims*'? The claims are specific as can be: the campaign, the date of the massacre or destruction of the sacred structure, the number killed... 'In *some* Muslim sources'? But these are in *most* Muslim sources. However, to proceed: we have the crowning rationalization: '... broad rhetorical claims in some Muslim sources that temples had been levelled and idol-worshippers punished *should be read with a sensitivity to the value of verbal virtue*.'[27]

That is, the chroniclers were just proclaiming all this without it having been done. Pray, why? Simple: destroying temples, slaughtering infidels is what was expected of the faithful; they were acquiring 'verbal virtue' without adhering to the mandate.

Naturally, the next historian takes this one step further. In a book decorated with convoluted 'reasoning', jargon and long words – I occasion one! '[R.S.] Sharma's remarks nevertheless construed – indeed, they still are, if one considers the severe animadversions passed upon his work by Arun Shourie...' – Vinay Lal, cites this passage of Meister approvingly and builds on it. Where Meister had talked away the contemporary descriptions of destruction by saying that the authors and their patrons had put in these passages merely to acquire 'verbal virtue', Lal says that the very fact that Muslim sources

[26] Ibid., p. 26.
[27] Ibid, p. 27.

proclaimed that the rulers had carried out the destruction and killing may precisely be what *proves* that Muslim rulers had *not* indulged in destruction and killing. This 'great leap' is worth reading in the original:

> An inscription in Delhi's 'Might of Islam' mosque records the 'fact' that it was built with the remains of 27 temples, but as Meister notes, the number 27, which reflects the 27 *Nakshatras* (asterisms) of India's lunar calendar, may have been chosen for its 'symbolic value'.

A moment's pause: assume that the number twenty-seven was, in fact, chosen for its 'symbolic value'. How does that prove that, contrary to what the inscription itself says, the material was *not* from twenty-seven temples? How does the choice of the number prove that twenty-seven temples were *not* destroyed for the purpose? Could one not argue the *opposite*? That precisely twenty-seven temples were chosen to be destroyed because the Hindus thought this number to be auspicious and potent?

But to continue with our eminent historian:

> He [Meister] suggests that broad (and loud) claims in Muslim sources about the levelling of temples and the punishment of idolaters 'should be read with sensitivity to the value of verbal virtue', *to which one might add that the rhetorical claims may have been all the more exaggerated to disguise the degree to which Muslim rulers desisted from the destruction and plunder of Hindu temples.*[28]

The ludicrous nature of such assertions apart, two points are worthy of note.

First, how do these progressives infer from *Manusmriti* what they do? Namely, that the text proves that Brahmins had special

[28] Vinay Lal, *The History of History, Politics and Scholarship in Modern India*, Oxford University Press, Delhi, 2003, p. 116.

privileges, that the other castes were kept down, that large sections of the population were cast out as untouchables. As my friend, Arvind Sharma once wrote, on a parity of reasoning should one not conclude the *opposite*? Namely, that the text was written and insertions to it were made by Brahmins who did *not* have those privileges, and merely *wished* that society would grant them those privileges.

Second, this historian is telling us that precisely because the inscription records that materials obtained from twenty-seven temples were used to construct the mosque, they were *not* so obtained. Just a little later, he proclaims precisely the opposite. The fact that the inscription over the Babri Masjid did not mention that it had been constructed by bringing down a temple, proves that it was *not* built by destroying a temple! Unbelievable? Here is what he says in this regard on the Babri masjid: 'If the Muslim is enjoined, as Hindus are asked to believe, to celebrate the defeat of the infidel and the destruction of idolatry...'

Pause: the 'if' and the 'as Hindus are asked to believe' insinuate that there really is no such mandate in Islam. Are historians completely exempt from reading the Quran, the hadis, and the canonical books on Islamic law? Are they completely exempt from reading centuries of Islamic history? Perhaps it is not that they are exempted from reading these, but that they are confident that no one else has read these – *that* is why they can continue to peddle their theories.

But to continue:

> If the Muslim is enjoined, as Hindus are asked to believe, to celebrate the defeat of the infidel and the destruction of idolatry, why did not Mir Baqi, whom [sic.] the inscription states as having built the mosque, mention the destruction of the temple, a deed for which he would have acquired merit?[29]

[29] Ibid., p. 150.

Hence, temples were *not* destroyed because a contemporary history – *Maasir-i-Alamgir,* say – records that they *were* destroyed. And the Ram temple was not destroyed because the inscription on the mosque does *not* say that it was destroyed! QED!!

In any case, if there is incontrovertible proof that the temples *were* indeed destroyed, that cannot be taken as evidence of any animosity that the Islamic invaders bore towards Hindus and Hinduism. The destruction 'might be better understood within a framework of the politics of conquest', the historian instructs us. Vinay Lal quotes with approval the authors of 'Black Sunday', a pamphlet that was issued by one of those organizations that spring up and go away, the Sampradayikta Virodhi Andolan, 'a small organization comprised mainly of left-wing activists, historians and other scholars.' This is how Vinay Lal reports what these activists had declared:

> ... They [the activists] are absolutely right to point out that, even if it were established that a temple was torn down to make way for the Babri Masjid, the destruction of the mosque could not be justified. A historical wrong which can be laid at the foot of a conqueror is scarcely corrected by demolishing, some 500 years later, a religious edifice at which prayers were still offered by members of the community. 'The destruction of places of worship in medieval and ancient times,' note the authors of 'Black Sunday', was 'an integral part of political power'; those who wielded temporal power also exercised religious control, and had a temple been destroyed to make way for the mosque (a proposition in itself difficult to substantiate), one is to infer from it nothing more than the fact that in 'medieval' times the destruction of religious edifices signified not necessarily the animosity between adherents of different faiths but rather an essential aspect of political authority and the whims of the conquerors.
>
> The authors of 'Black Sunday' are entirely right in insisting that the actions of warriors, leaders, and invaders in the pre-modern period might be better understood within a framework of the politics of conquest, and that is also the productive path

> pursued by Romila Thapar in her interpretation of Mahmud of Ghazni's raid in 1026 of the fabled Hindu temple at Somnath...[30]

The double standards are visible from a mile. What do these historians infer after alleging that, in the wake of a victory, Hindus destroyed Jain temples in Karnataka? That the destruction *proves* that intolerance is germane to Hinduism. And here? That the destruction of temples by Muslim invaders was just part of 'the politics of conquest'!

The Touchstone

Before we move on, it will pay us to spend a moment more with Aurangzeb and his chronicler, Mustad Khan's *Maasir-i-Alamgiri*, for the touchstone of secularism in India is whether one is prepared to stand up for Aurangzeb or not.

And for this we do not have to travel far. We can go back to that issue of *Seminar*, with all its eminences. Satish Chandra contributes an essay, 'Reassessing Aurangzeb'.[31] The thesis is that Aurangzeb was not propelled by religious zeal, but by the compulsions imposed on him by a complex situation. Satish Chandra recalls the various 'theories' that have been advanced by the progressives: the contention with the Rajputs; the recalcitrance of the Marathas; the deep problems presented by the Deccan; the need to control the Europeans who were exploiting the weaknesses of the southern states to extend their sway. And then concludes:

> Anyhow, in none of these speculations does religion or Aurangzeb's orthodoxy figure anywhere. Thus, emphasis on Aurangzeb's religious policy is slowly giving place to a deeper

[30] Vinay Lal, op. cit., pp. 162–63.

[31] Satish Chandra, 'Reassessing Aurangzeb,' *Seminar*, Number 364, December 1989, pp. 35–43.

> study of socio-economic, intellectual, cultural, geographic (regional) and political factors. These studies tend to show neither a hero nor a villain, but a somewhat rigid and unimaginative politician who failed to understand the societal problems at work in the country, and often took recourse to religious slogans in order to meet complex socio-economic and political problems.[32]

Better that he is a failure, an unimaginative politician than what his chronicler recorded and what to this day his votaries in Pakistan think he was: a religiously driven person!

So, what about those temples that Mustad Khan recorded as having been destroyed by the order of the emperor, Aurangzeb? The argument that they were destroyed in pursuance of a general order by Aurangzeb has not been accepted, Satish Chandra says, 'because no copy of any such order has been found' – has any copy of a general order by Hitler decreeing the extermination of Jews in gas chambers been found? – 'and has been referred to by no contemporary observer except Sagi [sic.] Mustad Khan who wrote half a dozen years *after* Aurangzeb's death'.[33]

That no one other than the person who was charged with drawing up the chronicle of the reign of Aurangzeb referred to the order is proof that the order was not issued! And that bit about the chronicle having been written six years after the death of Aurangzeb – I won't quarrel about three years having become six. Recall instead the case with which we started: the destruction of Nalanda. How many years after the destruction of Nalanda had that Tibetan text on which D.N. Jha relied been written: *five hundred years*! That is a worthy foundation on which to build a theory. One written three or six years after Aurangzeb's death is not.

Our progressives are not done. Satish Chandra, Vinay Lal, and others make it a point to recall that 'Aurangzeb continued

[32] Ibid., p. 38.
[33] Ibid., p. 36.

to grant land and other favours to non-Muslim places of worship (for instance, the famous temples of Vrindavan, the Sikh shrine at Dehra Dun'.[34] These grants prove that he was not a religious zealot. The motivation that our historians detect here is a *religious* one; not a political one: it is not the case that Aurangzeb gave these grants to secure political and military support of some local groups against others. On the other hand, where temples were destroyed, they were destroyed for *political* and not religious reasons. Thus, Satish Chandra's somewhat convoluted apologia:

> On the other hand, it does appear that Aurangzeb had begun to look upon the *preservation of prominent temples* as a kind of guarantee of good conduct on the part of the Hindus of the area. Thus, places of worship began to be treated as fit objects of reprisal in case of misconduct or rebellion. This was applied to the case of Bir Singh Deo Bundel's temple at Mathura when the Jats of the area rose in rebellion, and in Marwar when there was conflict following the death of Maharaja Jaswant Singh. But this policy seems to have been modified after the conquest of Bijapur and Golkonda in 1687. Hardly any Hindu conflicts [sic.] were broken in the south despite continued conflicts with the Marathas.[35]

It is not all together evident what the historian means by the later avtaar of the policy – the policy after 'modification' – but the tenor is that the general policy was to preserve 'prominent temples' and to have them destroyed only as 'reprisal in case of misconduct or rebellion'. Don't miss that escape clause: '*prominent* temples'. That leaves us free to disregard the scores of temples that Mustad Khan records as having been destroyed; they were just not prominent enough to be counted!

And Vinay Lal:

[34] Satish Chandra, op. cit., p 36. Vinay Lal, op. cit., p. 103.
[35] Satish Chandra, op. cit., p. 36.

> ... They [studies by progressive historians that he finds authoritative] suggest, moreover, that Aurangzeb did not indiscriminately destroy Hindu temples, as he is commonly believed to have done, and that he directed the destruction of temples only when faced with insurgency. This was almost certainly the case with the Keshava Rai temple in the Mathura region, where the Jats rose in rebellion; and yet even this policy of reprisal may have been modified, as Hindu temples in the Deccan were seldom destroyed. The image of Aurangzeb as an idol-breaker may not withstand scrutiny, since there is evidence to show that, like his predecessors, he continued to confer land grants (*jagirs*) upon Hindu temples, such as the Someshwar Nath Mahadev temple at Allahabad, Jangum Badi Shiva temple in Banaras, Umanand temple in Gauhati, and numerous others.[36]

Much can be said about the 'evidence'. Vinay Lal cites Richard Eaton in the fortnightly news-and-views magazine, *Frontline*, M. Athar Ali, and the article of Satish Chandra in *Seminar* that we have been discussing! But there is the even more telling point that we have encountered earlier. When Aurangzeb makes a grant to a non-Muslim place of worship, it has a *religious* motivation: he is, if not tolerant of other religions, at the least not intolerant of them. The motivation is *not* political; he is not giving these grants to get some local group or chieftain to his side. When he orders the destruction of a temple, his motivation is *not* religious. It is political: he is just punishing people for their 'misconduct or rebellion'!

In a word, irrespective of what the chronicler of the time, Mustad Khan says, Aurangzeb did not act out of Islamic zeal. *Pari passu*, irrespective of what Guru Ramdas may have taught him; irrespective of what he himself may have said or believed; irrespective of the fact that in those faraway days, he organized a naval force; irrespective of the fact what in his coronation itself, Shivaji proclaimed himself to be founding, irrespective

[36] Vinay Lal, op. cit., p. 103.

of the fact that he and his associates made clear that they were striving to free the country from the tyranny of Mughals, he was acting out of completely different, almost secular, certainly base motives! Here is Vinay Lal: 'It was to mark his independence from the Mughals, and to repudiate his formal relation to them of a feudatory, that Shivaji had himself crowned, but that very gesture of defiance points to the fact that he recognized the overwhelming power of the Mughals.'

How does recognizing that at the time Mughals had overwhelmingly greater power detract from the cause Shivaji stood up to champion? On the contrary, does the fact that, even as he realized that the Mughals had overwhelming power, he resolved to fight them, not testify to his dedication to the cause? But to continue, for the next proposition of this progressive historian is breathtaking: 'Moreover, as a lower-caste person, Shivaji had perforce to enact some ceremony by means of which he could be raised to the status of a *kshatriya* or traditional ruler: thus, in every respect his coronation pointed to his anxieties about his origins and subservience.'[37]

How much more perverse can one get? At the least, is the fact that a 'lower-caste person' came to be and continues to be embraced as a national hero and symbol not call into question the claptrap that the progressives have been purveying about the rigidities of the caste system, about the immobility it enforced, and the attitudes it has drilled into us?

And yet, none of this is accidental. As we have seen in the texts that we have surveyed in this book, it is all part of a line. India turns out to be a recent construct. It turns out to be neither a country nor a nation. Hinduism turns out to be an invention – surprised at the word? You won't be a few pages hence – of the British in the late nineteenth century. Simultaneously, it has always been inherently intolerant. Pre-Islamic India was a den of iniquity, of oppression. Islamic rule liberated the oppressed. It was in this period that the Ganga-

[37] Vinay Lal, op. cit., p. 105.

Jamuna culture, the 'composite culture' of India was formed, with Amir Khusro as the great exponent of it, and the Sufi savants as the founts. The sense of nationhood did not develop even in that period. It developed only in response to British rule, and because of ideas that came to us from the West. But even this – the sense of being a country, of being a nation, such as it was – remained confined to the upper crust of Indians. It is the communists who awakened the masses to awareness and spread these ideas among them.

In a word, India is not real – only the parts are real. Class is real. Religion is real – not the threads in it that are common and special to our religions but the aspects of religion that divide us, and thus ensure that we are *not* a nation, a country, those elements are real. Caste is real. Region is real. Language is real – actually, that is wrong: the line is that languages *other* than Sanskrit are real; Sanskrit is dead and gone; in any case, it was not, the averments in the great scholar, Horace Wilson to the House of Commons Select Committee notwithstanding, that it was the very basis, the *living* basis of other languages of the country;[38] rather, it was the preserve of the upper layer, the instrument of domination and oppression; one of the vehicles of perpetuating false consciousness among the hapless masses.

Scores of publications advancing these 'theses' can be adduced. But it will be enough to glance at one, and then return to the presidential address with which we started – for that piles up all this drivel in one place. But before we do that, another eminence.

Scholars 'Who with Pitiful Industry...'

By the mid-1980s, Marxism had come under severe strain. Reality was proving increasingly obdurate. Things were

[38] *Select Committee on Indian Territories*, Minutes of Evidence taken on 18 July 1853. For a summary of the relevant remarks, see my *Missionaries in India*, ASA, New Delhi, 1994, pp. 172–75.

galloping in directions that were the direct opposite of what, on the basis of their much-vaunted theory, Marxists had been proclaiming they would take. Facts about Stalin's period – a period lauded to the skies in India – could no longer be denied. Far from creating the New Man, the Soviet system, wherever it had been institutionalized, had ended up creating fiefdoms for the *nomenklatura*. The loud trumpets that had been blaring away in our Left journals – *Mainstream* and the rest – about the industrial excellence of East European communist countries were getting muted as the true state of those economies had become apparent. China and the Soviet Union had split. Their invective against each other had all the epithets that communists had perfected while abusing others. Capitalism had not been overtaken – indeed, that the Soviet Union as well as East Europe were stagnating was evident. Within India, workers and peasants had not risen to overturn the order. Quite the contrary: the communist parties were not being able to extend their reach. True, Marxists were repeating the well-practiced phrases and 'theses' – but mechanically. And to ever-shrinking circles.

Irfan Habib had been, and remains one of the dons among Marxist historians and ideologues in India. He sought to allow reality to intrude, a bit, into the master theory. In an important essay, 'Problems of Marxist historiography', he set out, point-by-point, where, in view of what was happening all round, Marxist theory, diagnoses and prognoses, all needed to be reformulated.[39]

The essay illustrates both – how much of the theory, on the basis of which our history had been distorted by these worthies, had been thrown into question even by then; as well as how fatiguing it always is for the faithful to acknowledge that they have been living and proclaiming an untruth. And there is another feature that the essay illustrates about these scholars: they cannot acknowledge a fact even as large as a hill until they

[39] Irfan Habib, 'Problems of Marxist historiography,' *Social Scientist*, Volume 16, Number 12, December 1988, pp. 3–13.

can invoke some fragment of some sentence written by some foreign authority: even to acknowledge a simple fact, even to urge the mildest reappraisal, Irfan Habib feels compelled to invoke Marx and Mao, or at the least Althusser or Gramsci or Rosa Luxemburg! How well Mao's description fits these personages: 'scholars who, with pitiful industry, have picked up scraps from the dung-heap of textbooks written abroad'!

Information accrues, Irfan Habib notes. Marx could not have had the information about Indian conditions that has become available since he wrote: 'Without undue modesty, we can say we know more about India's past than Marx did.' Events do not always transpire as had been forecast. Therefore, we need to look at Marxist construction of Indian history again, Irfan Habib acknowledges.

But this is of the very essence of Marxism, he quickly adds! 'Marxism sees an innate unity between perception of the past and present practice,' he says. 'This unity implies continued interaction: as time passes and history (human experience) lengthens, we draw greater lessons from it for the present; and as our present experience tells us more about the possibilities and limitations of social action, we turn to the past and obtain new comprehensions of it'[40] – one way to acknowledge how completely wrong one has been and must start again! And all this Marx himself prescribed, says Irfan Habib. Did Marx not say, 'Philosophers have so far interpreted the world. The point is to change it.' How this maxim foretells the need for reappraisals is left to the reader as an exercise: had the interpretations that the Marxist Masters been advancing not been advanced to change the world? 'It is inherent in the unity of past and present that Marxist historiography must continuously turn to fresh aspects to explore and re-explore and fresh questions to answer,' he writes – of course, anyone who demurs at the formulation that the worthies have finalized at a particular moment – why, he is a renegade, he is one who has 'crossed the barricades'.

[40] Ibid., p. 3.

Irfan Habib then adds a curious, practical consideration: merely dismissing and ignoring the interpretation of others as 'bourgeois' doesn't carry conviction, he says, because they do not accept the basic class-approach in any case. We have to answer them with detailed arguments, Habib says, and doing so requires 'constant preparation and self-examination: the refining and extension of Marxist positions'. 'This examination must cover everything from general principles to specific facts, because both are all the time being brought into question by others. We have to answer them not by denunciation – always a bad counsellor – but careful scrutiny and investigation.'[41] This after a century in which intimidation and abuse have been the bludgeons of choice! Ghalib had the measure of such repentants:

> *Kee merey katl ke baad usney jafaa sey taubhaa*
> *Hai, us zood pashemaan kaa pashemaan honaa . . .*
>
> How she foreswore cruelty the moment she had beheaded me
> Ah, the repentance of one who is so promptly repentant…

Of course, what Irfan Habib is urging is the opposite of Lenin's prescription.

For those uninitiated, it will be worthwhile to recount an interaction between Lenin and Valentinov. Valentinov recalled what happened when he told Lenin about his encounter with Plekhanov, someone who at that stage Lenin regarded as the greatest exponent of Marxism since Engels, and whom, of course, Lenin was soon to pillory and denounce as worthless. Articles that Valentinov had written had been referred to Plekhanov to ascertain that there were no ideological deviations in them. Upon meeting Plekhanov, Valentinov got into an argument with him about the soundness of two philosophers.

[41] Ibid, p. 4.

Plekhanov declared that he had not read them, and had no time now to read them, but that he knew they were wholly wrong. Valentinov reported all that transpired to Lenin. Lenin reprimanded him for seeing merit in the writings of those two philosophers, tainted as their thinking was with bourgeois notions, and for being alarmed at Plekhanov's denouncing them without having read anything they had written. And then laid down the operating principle that our Marxists have followed with such fidelity! Scolding him, Lenin told Valentinov,

> ...Today we know perfectly well where attempts to link Marx with theories alien to his spirit can lead. Bernstein is an object lesson in this; and in Russia we have Struve and Bulgakov. Struve soon went on from 'modified' Marxism to the most vulgar, stinking liberalism, and Bulgakov is sinking into an even nastier morass. Marxism is a monolithic conception of the world, it does not tolerate dilution or vulgarization by means of various insertions and additions. Plekhanov once said to me about a critic of Marxism (I've forgotten his name): '*First let's stick the convict's badge on him, and then after that we'll examine his case.*' And I think we must 'stick the convict's badge' on anyone and everyone who tries to undermine Marxism, even if we do not go on to examine his case. That's how every sound revolutionary should react. When you see a stinking heap on the road you don't have to poke around in it to see what it is. Your nose tells you it's shit, and you give it a wide berth.[42]

'Lenin's words took my breath away,' Valentinov recalled.

Accordingly, Lenin used to routinely denounce others as 'curs', 'swine', 'scoundrels', 'brigands', 'rascals', 'lick-spittle', 'absolute ignoramuses'. And so, to urge even that little bit – 'We have to answer them not by denunciation – always a bad counsellor – but careful scrutiny and investigation' – Habib has to invoke the shastras! 'Gramsci, in criticizing Bukharin's *ABC*

[42] Nikolay Valentinov, *Encounters With Lenin,* Oxford University Press, London, 1968, p. 182. Italics in the original.

of Communism said that in the war of ideas, unlike ordinary war, you have to attack the enemy's strongest, and not weakest points,' this eminent historian reminds us.

But, we will soon see, as we revert to that example of the genre, the Presidential Address to the Indian History Congress, that our committed historians have ignored Irfan Habib's counsel, and remained true to Lenin!

'Finally, I believe,' the historian tells us, 'that Scientific Socialism requires constant debate within itself, without need for polemics from outside' – nor is the shastra lacking for that. 'Long before the current recognition of the virtues of "plurality",' Irfan Habib says, 'Mao Tse-tung had urged that truth could belong to a minority, and all truths are first espoused only by a minority. This applies to a revolutionary party as well as society at large'[43] – as Mao, no doubt, demonstrated by the way he crushed underfoot the hundred flowers that had bloomed in response to his call!

The case for reappraisal, for 'the close interaction between the past and present', having been made, in what particulars does Marxist history-writing need to be modified? First and foremost, Irfan Habib says, we must realize that, contrary to what may be inferred from Stalin's essay, 'Dialectical and Historical Materialism', Marxist theory is not deterministic. It is very difficult to substantiate that a particular ideology – Marxism – 'inevitably or automatically' arose from, say, capitalism, and no other ideology could have risen from it. All one can say is that capitalism set the context for that ideology to arise – not its structure.

Ideas and perceptions have a potency of their own, especially as, under capitalism, workers come to see ever more clearly the reality in which they are cabined, and as they come to realize their own revolutionary potential – 'blind struggles have been replaced by sighted ones'. And for this too, there is the canonical scripture! 'When he [Marx] spoke of the future as one where

[43] Ibid, p. 4.

mankind marched "from the realm of necessity to the realm of freedom", I feel convinced (in spite of Engels's unfortunate gloss of "freedom" as the "recognition of necessity"),' Irfan Habib makes bold to say, 'that Marx looked forward to ideas at last gaining ascendancy over matter, not by any spiritualist exercise, but by the abundance of material wealth which Communism would ultimately produce' – within the year, for the lecture was delivered in 1988, the Soviet Union had disintegrated, and 'the abundance of material wealth which Communism would ultimately produce' had been shown up for the chimera it had always been.

As determinism was not valid, and as it had never been so conceived by the prophets, '...today liberation from the textbook "inevitability" theory, erroneously ascribed to Marxism' – by no one more fervently than Marxists – 'is a major necessity'. A nod to reality – 'Capitalism and other exploitative systems are not going to break down by their own weight or by the "General Crisis of Capitalism"' – and then the call to go on doing what committed intellectuals like him have been doing: 'There is no alternative to entering the battle of ideas; economic action, on behalf of toilers to teachers, is a help, but it is no substitute for class consciousness.'[44]

Next, to study class struggles, classes have to be defined. New information has shown that the traditional categorizations were inadequate. We must pay greater attention to the role that exploitation of colonies by the imperialist powers played – a point that had been stressed by nationalist commentators since Dadabhai Naoroji. A diversion to point out the inadequacies of a new 'school' of history that had arisen, 'subaltern studies', a 'school' to whose fate we shall turn soon, and which 'by the way,' Irfan Habib noted, drawing the line, 'treat[s] the Left also as part of the elite leadership'.

And then the partial, self-righteous acknowledgement of the need to revisit the abuse that they had hurled at leaders like

[44] Ibid., p. 6.

Gandhiji, and to revise the Marxist assessment of the national freedom movement – 'however, this need not mean that the Communists or the other Left groups were incorrect in all the basic positions they took, for example in 1942.'[45] The new line is that the national freedom movement should be treated 'as a common heritage', one to which the Left made singular contributions; the movement directed by the nationalist leaders was only 'partial', it is the Left which mobilized the masses. 'An overwhelming preoccupation with the "errors" of the Left,' Irfan Habib writes – collaborating with the British; submitting reports to them about the sterling work communists were doing to sabotage the Quit India Movement; insisting that the freedom movement be subordinated to the interests of the Soviet Union; supporting the Muslim League in its demand that the country be partitioned: just errors, and that too within quotation marks – 'as in the volume edited by Professor Bipan Chandra, is unfortunate, since by this very preoccupation, it belittles the achievements of the Left during the National Movement and its contributions to it. After all, the creation of the organized Kisan Movement and the trade unions was mainly the handiwork of the Communists and their allies; and that cannot be forgotten.'[46]

Even the 'bourgeois-democratic values' of the national movement – 'such as secularism, women's rights, national unity, freedom of the press, and parliamentary democracy' – can be put to good use today, Irfan Habib points out. 'These can form the initial points for a people's front, in which all classes may be united as can carry forward the cause of democracy and socialism. Such a front could be a worthy successor to our

[45] For both – the vile abuse they hurled at leaders like Gandhiji, and the assistance they rendered to the British to sabotage the Quit India Movement of 1942 – see the companion volume, *'The Only Fatherland', Communists, 'Quit India' and the Soviet Union*, ASA, New Delhi, 1991, HarperCollins, New Delhi, 2014.

[46] Irfan Habib, 'Problems of Marxist Historiography,' op. cit., p. 10.

National Movement' – that elusive hope, 'a people's front', and don't miss that '*our*' in 'our National Movement'! And, it goes without saying, that those 'values' are just 'bourgeois-democratic' ones, mere instruments that the Left is to use at a particular stage, values that have no place in a socialist/communist state.

And, finally, the climactic call: 'one of the admitted weaknesses of Marxist historiography lies in the limitations of its analysis of the history of socialist societies, whose existence began with the Russian Revolution of 1917,' Irfan Habib writes. Marx had not provided for such a history. Only in 1952 did we get 'an authoritative exposition of some of the elementary questions relating to socialist economy'. In what? In Stalin's pamphlet, *Economic Problems of the Socialism in the USSR*, our historian instructs us! But unfortunately, he too had 'left many important problems unresolved,' Habib notes, 'or omitted them altogether'. Mao's *On Contradiction* registered 'a breakthrough' on them. And this essay has been commended by Oskar Lange and Althusser, our historian emphasizes. Mao developed his views further in *Correctly Handling Contradictions Among the People* and *Ten Great Relationships*. 'But unluckily, by the mid-1960s he seems to have altered his views so as to hold that the contradictions of socialism were being transformed in China into contradictions *between* socialism and capitalism; and he thereupon initiated and led the Cultural Revolution, which our Chinese friends now hold to have been an error.'[47]

How many errors make a wrong?

'For the second stage in which the USSR and China now are, two basic contradictions may be defined,' Irfan Habib continues. And how may this be done? '…by looking at the goals which Marx in his *Critique of the Gotha Programme* set for "the higher stage of Communism" towards which socialist societies would evolve' – that 'pitiful industry' again.

These are the contradictions between 'mental and physical labour' and between 'town and country'. Then there is the

[47] Ibid., p. 11.

contradiction between the ruling party apparatus and leadership and the working class, a contradiction 'which cannot be glossed over by a mere designation of the party as a Working Class Party'. And, of course, 'national contradictions' are bound to arise. Mind you, not because there has been anything wrong with the concept of the communist utopia, certainly not because there has been anything wrong with the way its votaries have chosen to march towards it, but because of the circumstances in which the utopia is being constructed! The national contradictions are bound to arise, not because of the way the Soviets crushed the smaller nationalities – hadn't Stalin solved the nationalities question? – not because of the Han racialism that the Chinese communists have always fanned; not because the Soviet Union and Communist China, for all their proclamations of internationalism, remained intensely nationalist states, but because 'Socialism has come about in a system of nation states'.[48] The fault, dear Brutus, is once again in the stars!

In the event, we need to work out the historiography of socialist societies: 'With socialism a reality for the last seventy years,' Irfan Habib concludes, 'the people's choice for it cannot be invoked on the basis of the inequities of capitalism alone. It is surely obligatory on us to frame our own independent analysis of the history of socialist societies in order to define the contours of the socialism that we aspire to build in India.'[49]

The lecture was delivered in September 1988 and printed in December that year. Within the year, the need for working out the history of socialist states had become even more pressing. The Soviet Union as well as the communist states of Eastern Europe had become history. China had regressed from socialism to state capitalism.

[48] Ibid., p. 12.
[49] Ibid., p. 13.

The Insidious Version

So, reappraisal it had to be. But there is an unvarying trajectory of Marxist reappraisals. As reality diverges more and more from what the theory had forecast, calls are made for reappraisal – these calls establish how open-minded the faithful are, and how there is no need for outsiders to poke their nose. In turn, the reappraisal invariably leads to the conclusion that the original scriptures were absolutely correct, that the seers had actually anticipated exactly what has transpired, and, so, the reappraisal reconfirms the original line!

In line with this Iron Law of Reappraisals, Soviet Union or no Soviet Union, a China hurtling towards state capitalism or not, an Eastern Europe that has bolted or not, Irfan Habib recovered his authoritative airs, and was soon pressing the standard line. It will be sufficient to recall just one of his essays, a typical one, 'The formation of India: Notes on the history of an idea'.[50] He obliquely scoffs at those who believe that Aryans were native to India. There always is a subterranean insinuation under such scoffing: that evidence to the contrary is a fabrication, that it has been conjured up by non-historians, that it is nothing more than a manifestation of jingoism – of the impulse to claim that our ancient texts and cultures did not come from outside the geographical contours of present-day India. Incidentally, I have never, but never seen any of these scholars detect, and of course never insinuate anything remotely similar in the determination of Chinese scholars to establish that the Han Chinese did *not* descend from any African ancestor – human or ape; that, instead, as fragments of the Peking Man, of the Yuanmou Man, and now of the Xuchang Man – the county in Henan – show, the Han are descended from a *native* ape. Nor have I seen one of them

[50] Irfan Habib, 'The formation of India: Notes on the history of an idea', *Social Scientist*, Volume 25, Numbers 7/8, July–August 1997, pp. 3–10.

note that the very word 'Han' was an invention of a Chinese nationalist writer of the late nineteenth century.[51] Perhaps that is because examining Chinese claims to this effect would take our Marxist scholars too far afield from their history-ordained responsibility here in India of awakening us to the non-reality of India!

To proceed: Irfan Habib cites a few statements from assorted texts and concludes, 'Such statements show that the perception of India as a country marked by certain social and religious institutions begins to be present only by the time of the Mauryan Empire (c. 320-185 B.C.) was established.'[52]

Pause right there and reflect. First, 'c. 320-185 B.C.' is quite a while ago. What would the corresponding dates be for Saudi Arabia, Iraq, Jordan – countries that were created in the inter-war years; some indeed, that were created, as Churchill said, on the beach one afternoon with nothing more than a piece of paper and a red pencil. What of the United States or countries in South America? The late-lamented Soviet Union? 'c. 320-185 B.C.'? What about what we know as 'China' today? The original 'China' was no more than a third of the China of today.

The second point that springs from Irfan Habib's conclusion is, '... the perception of India as a country *marked by certain social and religious institutions.*' You choose some criteria; you say these are what defines a 'country'; and pronounce, 'And so, India was not a country till...' Here the criteria chosen are 'certain social and religious *institutions*'. To gauge the artificiality

[51] It can't be that in all these decades our Marxist writers have not been able to access accounts of African and other students of the extreme racialism that they experienced while in China or studies of scholars such as Frank Dikotter and Steven Harrell who have written extensively on the subject. For an easily accessible volume, see Martin Jacques, *When China Rules the World, The end of the western world and the birth of a new global order*, Penguin, London, 2012, pp. 297, 308–41.

[52] Irfan Habib, op. cit., pp. 5–6.

of this, suppose we say, 'A religion is one that has one Book, and an organized church headed by a supreme authority.' Only a few – Roman Catholicism, Eastern Orthodoxy – would qualify as 'religions'. If we dropped 'a supreme authority', the Protestants also would qualify. If we substituted 'an organized church headed by a supreme authority' by 'a Prophet', Islam would qualify but the others would be left out. Not really: for all Middle Eastern religions – Judaism, Christianity, Islam – have numerous prophets. If, however, we replaced '*a* Prophet' with '*the* Prophet' or better still with 'the Seal of Prophets', Islam alone would qualify as a religion!

Why only religious *institutions*? Why not, say, religious *practices*? Why not religious *practices and rituals*? You would have to push the date back to the Vedic Age, no? But they have a stock answer: 'The rituals you are thinking of were performed only by the upper crust, the high castes, in particular Brahmins. So, Brahmanism may have been a religion but not Hinduism.'

What about gods? 'But in what we know as India today, different groups, people living in different regions worshipped *different* gods. So, the moment you introduce "gods", you are actually proving that there was no single religion.' But what if *believing in a multiplicity of gods* is one of the foundational beliefs of the religion? To explain the difference this makes, Arvind Sharma draws attention to a telling study. He points to the returns on religion filed in Japan in 1985. The total population of Japan at the time was 121 million persons. When asked about their religion, 92 million said they were Buddhists; 115 million said they were Shinto; 1 million said they were Christians; and 14 million said they believed in the New Religions. As you would have noticed, that makes a total of 222 million – as against a total population of 121 million. Those who had said they were Buddhists constituted *seventy-six per cent* of the total population of Japan. Those who had said they believed in Shintoism constituted *ninety-five per cent* of the total population of Japan.[53] Going by the West's 'either/or' categories, this is just not conceivable: you can *either* be a Buddhist *or* a Shinto-believer. But for us, it is entirely natural to believe in elements of both.

You can see what is happening. These eminences just define 'nation', 'country', 'religion' in one way – a very Western way, even as they denounce the West (excluding the late-lamented Soviet Union, of course) – and *on that basis* pronounce India not to have been a 'country', Indians not to have been a 'nation', and Hinduism not to be a 'religion' till, in this case, the Mauryan period, or, as we shall soon see, till the late nineteenth century!

And there is a further twist in this selection of criteria. For the one religion, the generic religion of India, Hinduism, one that permeates all others, the one that most suffuses our consciousness is one that, as we shall soon see, these authorities proclaim just isn't there!

Irfan Habib continues, 'That empire [the Mauryan empire] embracing most of India, doubtless reinforced the process of cultural integration at least in the upper strata of the country.'[54]

Bear in mind, first, that we are dealing with a landmass that is truly continental; we are dealing with periods in which the means of transport were elementary as were the means of communication; we are dealing with periods in which the density of population was meagre, with small groups of people living at vast distances from each other. To insist that evidence be produced that shows that the degree of integration, of commonality of practices, etc., we notice today prevailed in those remote times, is to work to a design.

Moreover, from where does the assertion at the end of the

[53] Ian Reader, *Religion in Contemporary Japan*, Macmillan, London, 1991, p. 6. I am grateful to Arvind Sharma for drawing my attention to this study.

[54] Irfan Habib, op. cit., pp. 5–6.

sentence come, namely, that the process of 'cultural integration' was reinforced 'at least in the upper strata of the country'? What is the evidence that the 'lower strata' was excluded from this 'process'? Consider pilgrimages. To this day, the overwhelming proportion of pilgrims are *not* from the 'upper strata' – you just have to look out of your window at the kawadiyas; you just have to look at the streams of humanity from all over Maharashtra who converge on the samadhi of Sri Jnaneshwar in Alandi or the Vithal temple in Pandharpur. Look at the Buddhist pilgrims who proceed, strenuous prostration by strenuous prostration, to Lhasa or Bodh Gaya. Any of them from the 'upper strata'? But you exclude pilgrimages from 'cultural integration', and assert that the 'process' was 'reinforced at least in the upper strata of the country.'[55]

Our historian isn't done. He has had to concede that at least a limited process of integration had begun; he quickly recovers, and points to its dark side! 'The recognition of the 'foreigner' in friendly terms in Asoka, and hostile in the Manu, was a necessary complement of this vision.'[56] Even the most elementary reflection will show that the moment a child becomes conscious of herself as a person in her own right, she distances herself from the rest; the moment a group identifies itself as a group, it necessarily defines itself as being *not* one with the rest. And whether she or the group will come to look upon others 'in friendly terms' or with hostility, depends on the experience they shall have of the others. Indeed, the mere identification of oneself with one group entails a preference for fellow-members of *that* group. Experiment upon experiment has shown how, even children, divided into two groups at random – say, by the toss of a coin – treat members of their 'own' group much better

[55] For an evocative account, one that sets out how the pilgrimages and the places to which the pilgrims throng permeate the lives of our people, Diana Eck, *India: A sacred geography*, Crown Publishing, New York, 2012.

[56] Ibid., p. 5.

than they treat members of the 'other' group. This discrimination happens just as emphatically when they do not even know who are members of 'their' group and who are members of the 'other' group. These basic considerations apart, could there not be a historical explanation, my friend Arvind Sharma asks, for that change from regarding foreigners in friendly terms at Ashoka's time and in hostile terms by the time the *Manusmriti* came to be written? Ashoka's reign is said to have ended around 232 BC. The *Manusmriti* is usually placed around second century AD. In the period that intervened, north India was overrun by foreigners. It has been characterized as the 'Age of Invasions'.[57] Could the experience that Indians had at the hands of these foreigners not have been such as to trigger a change in the attitude towards foreigners?

But how can we expect our eminences to spare a thought for studies that would disable them from hurling their charges? How can we expect them to reflect on the verse – not from Manu but from the Quran – 'Muhammad is the Messenger of Allah. *Those who follow him are firm and unyielding towards unbelievers, yet full of mercy towards one another*'?[58]

And there is the further point in the case of our historians: they damn us either way. When doing so is convenient, they stress that the Hindus had no awareness of themselves as distinct from others – a frequent charge when our eminences want to assert that Hinduism was not a religion till recently, that it is an invention of the British in the late nineteenth century. On the other hand, when faced with evidence that the Hindus were in fact thinking of themselves as different, they charge that the religion is exclusivist, that it looks down upon others: as I mentioned, I have never but never heard them say a word about the extreme and all-pervasive racialism of, say, the Han Chinese.

[57] A.L. Basham, *The Wonder That Was India*, London: Picador, 1954, pp. 57–61.

[58] Quran, 48.29.

'To achieve such a vision on the part of its own inhabitants (or the upper part of them) was an important achievement in itself,' Irfan Habib concedes, only to add, 'For India was not naturally a country from "times immemorial"; it evolved by cultural and social developments, and closer interaction among its inhabitants, in which geographical configuration helped, but was not necessarily decisive.'[59] Which country was 'naturally' a country? Which has not been affected by interaction among its inhabitants? The Soviet Union? China?

The way that our historian deals with the blood-drenching assaults of Mahmud Ghazni and others is as typical as it is dainty:

> Even when Alberuni was writing his book a new wave of cultural diffusion into India was under way. *It had its violent side,* which the scientist recognized as he spoke of 'the wonderful exploits' of Mahmud of Ghazni [1000-30] 'by which the Hindus became like atoms of dust scattered in all directions and like the tale of old in the mouth of the people'. *But the expansion of knowledge proceeded.* Alberuni goes on to tell us that when at Lahore, in his conversations with Hindu scholars, he himself began to expound the principles of science and logic (derived from the Hellenistic-Arabic tradition) 'they flocked together round me from all parts, wondering and most eager to learn from me.'[60]

The depredations of Mahmud Ghazni and others are just 'a violent side'. And there is the 'expansion of knowledge' that took place as a result of the Muslim invaders. Not one word, now or later, about the centres of learning that these invaders pulverized. Not one word, now or later, of the legions of monks and scholars that they butchered. And do make a note of the use of the word 'Hindu' by Alberuni – for we shall soon see how our progressives deal with this inconvenience.

[59] Irfan Habib, op. cit., pp. 5–6.
[60] Ibid., p. 6.

The 'composite culture' is born. The word 'Hindu' becomes a territorial signification, not a religious one – a slip there; we will soon see that, according to other eminences, the word *never* had a religious connotation at all till the missionary-type pasted that connotation on it in the nineteenth century! Hindi and Hindustani emerge. Amir Khusro becomes the harbinger and symbol of this 'composite culture'. 'We see here a conception, perhaps, for the first time, so explicitly propounded of a composite culture being the distinguishing feature of India,' Irfan Habib writes. 'That religious barriers continued to exist is hardly to be contested: all cultures in the world have had internal tensions.'[61] Just 'internal tensions'? The pulverization of every sacred place; the massacre of hundreds of thousands; the extreme disabilities placed upon non-Muslim populations? Just 'internal tensions' that are common to all cultures of the world?

'Yet Kabir, the Muslim weaver (c. 1510),' Irfan Habib reminds us, 'was allowed his strongly monotheistic verses to condemn both Hinduism and Islam and their sacred ritual in the sharpest terms; and Nanak, his younger contemporary, allowed to form a religion independent of both Hinduism and Islam. These are facts surely indicative of conditions in which religious freedom too was seen as part of the cultural milieu of India.'[62]

Is it possible that our Marxists have never read or even heard of what Guru Nanak himself had to say about Muslim invasions and Muslim rule?

> *Khuraasaan khasmaanaa kiyaa Hindustaan daraayaa*
> Having subjugated Khuraasaan, Babar terrified Hindustaan
>
> *Aapai dos na deyee kartaa jam kar Mughal chadaayaa*
> So that blame does not come on Him, the Creator has sent the Mughal as the messenger of death

[61] Ibid., p. 7.
[62] Ibid., p. 7.

Aitee maar payee karlaane tain kee darad na aayaa
So great was the slaughter, such the agony of the people, even then You felt no compassion, Lord?

Kartaa toon sabhnaa kaa soyee
O Lord, You are the Master of all

Je saktaa sakte kao maarey taa man ros na hoyee
If some powerful man strikes another, one feels no grief

Saktaa seehu maarey pai vagai khasmai saa pursaayee
But when a powerful tiger slaughters a flock of helpless sheep, its master must answer

Ratan vigaar vigoe kutee muiaa saar na kaayee . . .
This jewel of a country has been laid waste and defiled by dogs, so much so that no one pays heed even to the dead…

Guru Nanak proceeds to describe how the oppressors shaved off the maidens, their 'heads with braided hair, with vermillion marks in the parting'; how 'their throats were choked with dust'; how they were cast out of their palatial homes, unable now to sit even in the neighbourhood of their homes; how those who had come to the homes of their husbands in palanquins, decorated with ivory, who lived in the lap of luxury, had been tied with ropes around their necks; how their pearl strings had been shattered; how the very beauty that was their jewel had now become their enemy – ordered to dishonour them, the soldiers had carried them off. 'Since Babar's rule has been proclaimed,' Guru Nanak wrote, 'even the princes have no food to eat.' Their sacred squares shattered, where will the Hindu women bathe, how will they worship? the Guru lamented. Dishonoured, how may they now apply the tilak on their foreheads? Some return home to inquire about the safety of their loved ones. Others are cursed to sit and cry out in pain. The invaders were, of course, to blame for what had befallen the people, the Guru said, but not only them: the rulers had lost themselves in luxury; the people had forgotten the Creator: *Raam na kabhoo chetio hun kahan na milai khudaae* – They never remembered their Ram, and now they cannot even chant *Khudaae*...[63]

'Composite culture'? Mere 'internal tensions'? 'Religious freedom'?

Irfan Habib then posits two prerequisites of nationhood. One, on the authority of Stalin, and the other on the authority of John Stuart Mill! Stalin, he reminds us, 'had once described the national question essentially as a "peasant question", which implied a mass diffusion of the sense of belonging to one's country, pervasive over other loyalties'. And Mill had placed his emphasis on 'the existence of a feeling widely shared that the country must be governed by those belonging to it'. Using these two criteria, Irfan Habib concludes, 'What perception existed of India as a country, a cultural and political unit, until the 19th century was one largely confined to the upper strata, the townsmen, traders, scholars and the like. It did not, moreover, override parochial identities. With his great insight, Ram Mohun Roy noted in a letter in 1830 that India could not yet be called a nation, because its people were "divided among castes". From the outside too, Karl Marx in 1853 identified castes as "those decisive impediments to Indian progress and Indian power".'[64]

Now, I detest caste. I entirely agree that it is an impediment to Indian progress and power – as are, say, corruption, mal-governance, venal leaders, and the rest. But do these features make India less of a nation? Or consider the programme of Marxists, the fervent internationalists: to awaken workers to their identity as workers, and nothing but workers. On Stalin's criterion, did the success of that programme in the Soviet Union preclude it from being a nation or a country? Similarly, what is

[63] *Guru Granth Sahib*. I leave out the precise identification of the verses in the hope that our historians will read the *Granth Sahib* – to locate the verses, if for no other reason. Why not imbibe a little 'false consciousness'?

[64] Ibid., p. 8.

the evidence that the consciousness of India being a country or of our being a nation was confined to 'the upper strata'?

As for the feeling that the country should be ruled by its own people, there is a circular subterfuge. The evidence of resistance – ever so often, violent resistance – is determinedly driven out of court by these historians on the ground that those episodes were merely resistance to local tyrannies, in particular of local landlords or chieftains; that the impulse behind them was revolt against economic exploitation.[65] There was no national sentiment behind them. By what evidence have they reached conclusions about what was in the mind of the resistors? By what evidence have they concluded that when the Islamic invaders slaughtered and looted, the non-Muslims did not chaff, that they did not feel that the country 'must be governed by those belonging to it'?

The same thing holds for the assertion that such awareness and sense of belonging as there was, was confined to the upper strata. Quite the contrary. The participation in pilgrimages, to recall an example we encountered earlier, the immersion in religious beliefs and practices, the veneration of particular saints and savants, the adoption of indigenous systems of medicine, of disciplines like yoga and meditation, the prevalence of common systems of music among the ordinary folk across vast distances, the celebration of common festivals in distant parts of the subcontinent – a host of such indices suggest that the sense of belongingness was much, much greater among the 'lower strata' of our people than in the 'upper strata'.

[65] Irfan Habib's major work was devoted to showing that the uprisings that occurred from the later part of Aurangzeb's rule – uprisings of Jats, Satnamis, Sikhs – were triggered by excessive taxation; that these were led by local zamindars and manned by the peasantry; the fact that the peasants joined hands with their local masters because of economic exploitation from above showed that class consciousness had arisen among the peasants, that they were not captives to mere caste consciousness. The thesis has been called into question by others who have argued that the uprisings were triggered by multiple causes.

In any event, on our historian's reckoning, India did not have those two ingredients of nationhood – the 'consciousness of identity widely shared' and the feeling, again widely shared, that the country must be governed by those belonging to it. It was only as a reaction to British rule that it acquired these: 'It was this that the national movement was about.' India's opening to the rest of the world and 'the diffusion of modern ideas and social values among wider and wider sections of the people' went hand in hand – through 'Gandhi's rurally oriented constructive programme' and 'the Kisan Movement led by the Left (where Marxism provided the impulse).'[66] Gandhiji and the Marxists at par!

The standard Marxist line. Soon, though, circumstances led our historian to urge his comrades to rethink Marxist historiography. But first back to that other representative of the genre – the Presidential Address to the Indian History Congress that we encountered earlier.

Inventions of the Nineteenth Century

D.N. Jha devotes his Presidential Address to uprooting what he calls the 'virulent version of Hindu cultural chauvinism', to battling 'xenophones and communalists', to exposing those 'guilty of fakes and frauds', to showing up the 'hollowness of the ideas which have been the staple diet of the monster of Hindu cultural nationalism in recent years'. With becoming modesty, he sees his own role in this great war as heroic: 'I accept the honour conferred on me [the Presidentship of the Indian History Congress] but, conscious as I am of my limitations, I treat it as encouragement to one who has been involved in the ongoing battle against jingoist, communal and obscurantist perceptions of India's past...'[67] Committed objectivity!

[66] Ibid., p. 9.

[67] Dwijendra Narayan Jha, 'Looking for a Hindu identity,' Presidential Address to the Indian History Congress, 2004. Accessed at http://www.sacw.net/India_History/dnj_Jan06.pdf, pp. 1-3.

His basic 'theses' are as follows:

- 'Hinduism is the youngest of all religions, a nineteenth century neologism popularized by the British. That it has come to stay, despite the endless ambiguities of connotation in it, is a different matter.'[68] Hindu groups, and lamentably some progressive scholars too 'not only ignore the plurality of religious beliefs and practices covered by the umbrella term "Hinduism", invented in the colonial period, but ... also deny the centuries-long process of their evolution'.[69] 'Several scholars have argued that Hinduism is a colonial construct which finally took shape when the imperial administration engaged in the classification into categories of the Indian people through the mechanism of the census.'[70]
- Nor did any '*sanatanadharma*' exist, it 'had to wait for its first codification by the Englishwoman, Annie Besant who, in collaboration with Indian scholars like Bhagwan Das, drew up a textbook on *sanatanadharma* for use at the Central Hindu College, Benaras, whose establishment in 1898 owed much to her initiative'.[71]
- That Hinduism did not exist as a religion is evident from the fact that the Vedas were not accepted universally as the final authority.[72]
- '...India as a country evolved over a long period ... the formation of its identity had much to do with the perceptions of the people who migrated into the subcontinent at different times, and Indian nationalism developed mostly as a response to Western imperialism'[73] – Irfan Habib reinforced!

[68] Ibid., p. 18.
[69] Ibid., p. 27.
[70] Ibid., p. 17.
[71] Ibid., pp. 20–21.
[72] Ibid., p. 21 onwards.
[73] Ibid., p. 3.

- Even though appellations like 'Bharat' and 'Aryavrata' were used, they denoted varying geographical spans: 'It was only from the 1860s that the name Bharatvarsa, in the sense of the whole subcontinent, found its way into popular vocabulary. Its visual evocation came perhaps not earlier than 1905 in a painting by Abanindranath Tagore, who conceived of the image as one of Bangamata but later, 'almost as an act of generosity towards the larger cause of Indian nationalism, decided to title it "Bharatmata".'[74]
- '...The word [Hindu] retained its territorial connotation for a long time and did not acquire any religious dimension. According to one scholar [Arvind Sharma], the earliest use of the word "Hindu" in a religious sense is found in the account of Hsuan Tsang, who tells us that the bright light of "holy men and sages, guiding the world as the shining of the moon, has made this country eminent and so it is called *In-tu*" (the Chinese name for India being *Indu*, moon). But the religious affiliation, if any, of these "holy men and sages" remains unknown, which hardly supports the view that Hsuan Tsang used the word *In-tu* (Hindu) in a specifically religious sense: indeed, the later Chinese pilgrim I-tsing questioned the veracity of the statement that it was a common name for the country.'[75] 'It was not before the first half of the nineteenth century that the word "Hindu" begins to appear in the Sanskrit texts produced as a result of Christianity's encounters with Brahmanical religions.'[76]
- True, there are instances such as Muhammad ibn Qasim appointing his adversary Dahir's minister as his own advisor after the latter had accepted Islam, and of the Brahmin princes of Sind converting to Islam 'at the invitation of the Caliph Umar b. Abd al-Aziz,' 'but mere

[74] Ibid., p. 6.
[75] Ibid., pp. 10–11.
[76] Ibid., p. 14.

acceptance of Islam by certain Sindhis does not justify a reified perception of Hinduism as early as the eighth century.'[77]

- True, Alberuni referred to the Hindu religion, but this reference 'just as the sack of Somnatha by Mahmud, has been blown out of proportion by some scholars, e.g., Arvind Sharma…'[78]
- 'Another myth which, through repetition, has been made to stick to the artifact called Hinduism is that it is a tolerant religion.'[79]

It really will be a waste of time to do excavatory work of the kind we did on Jha's basing his assertion about the destruction of Nalanda and other viharas on the 'Tibetan tradition' and the 'Tibetan text'. The same sort of conclusions will emerge. In the interests of economy, I will just recall the kind of arguments he uses to advance his 'theses'.

Let us start with Alberuni. Recall that Irfan Habib did not cavil at the use of the word 'Hindu' by Alberuni – of how Hindus had been blown off like atoms of dust by Mahmud Ghazni, of how Hindu scholars had flocked to him, Alberuni, when he began expounding the learning that he had brought with him, 'derived from the Hellenistic-Arabic tradition', Irfan Habib was careful to note! In any case, no quarrel about Alberuni's use of the word 'Hindu', at least not in the essay we were dealing with. And now Jha. Having dismissed the use of the word by Hsuan Tsang, Jha informs us, 'The first use of "Hindu" in the religious sense is found in *Kitabu-ul-Hind* of Alberuni (A.D. 1030), who at one place distinguishes Hindus from Buddhists but at another holds the distinction to be between *sramans* (Buddhists) and brahmans. He states that "they (Hindus) totally differ from us in religion". *Alberuni's understanding was*

[77] Ibid., p. 5.
[78] Ibid., p. 11.
[79] Ibid., p. 27.

limited to Brahmanical religious beliefs and practices, and his use of the word "Hindu" was far from clear and coherent. It is therefore not possible to credit him with any definite and essentialist view of a Hindu religion, much less treat his perception of one as a landmark in the development of Hindu religious identity.' The ambivalence continued. Three centuries later, Ziauddin Barani used the term sometimes as a religious category, sometimes as a political one, and sometimes as both.[80]

Notice, first, the sleight of pen: when one cannot deny that a reference is to a religion, the religion becomes merely 'Brahamanical'. Notice, second, that when the visitor concerned uses the term to identify both a religious and a territorial entity, that is taken as ambiguity rather than as evidence of the fact that the two categories were in fact one, that they were coterminous.

Next comes Ibn Battutah, a contemporary of Barani. He, Jha maintains, 'interpreted the name *Hindukush* as "Hindu killer" because Indian slaves passing through its mountainous terrain perished in the snows...' only to add 'Ibn Battutah's derivation of the word, however, *may have been based* on folk etymology, and the name Hindukush *probably* originated from the Arabic *Hindu koh,* meaning "mountains of India".'[81]

'May have been based,' 'probably' and the great leap forward to a definite conclusion! And notice that the word 'India' – as in 'mountains of *India*' – had occurred to Ibn Battutah and the folk etymologists but not the word they actually used, 'Hindu'!

Jha next disposes of the fact that successive Muslim travellers and historians continued to use the word 'Hindu'. He says that their use of the word varied – sometimes it included Jains and other non-Islamic groups, and sometimes not; furthermore, that their understanding of what constituted the religion was marked by 'vagueness'.[82]

[80] Ibid., pp. 10–12.
[81] Ibid., p. 12.
[82] Ibid., pp. 12–13.

Does the fact that the understanding of these travellers was marked by 'vagueness' establish that their understanding was vague or that the religion was so 'vague' as not to exist at all? There is the even more telling point: that visitors at times saw Jains and Buddhists as being the same as Hindus and at times not, goes *against* the thesis of Jha – often times the travellers and historians did not see the religions as being different precisely because in their eyes the differences were in the second order of smalls. A Hindu from India or a Christian from Europe may go to Iran and talk of 'Islam' and 'Muslims'. He may go to Iraq or Pakistan or Saudi Arabia and similarly talk of 'Islam' and 'Muslims'. To him they would seem as one, when, in fact Shias and Sunnis are blowing each other up all across the Islamic world. Does the fact that some visitors to these countries would write separately about Shias and Sunnis and some would write of 'Islam' and 'Muslims' mean that Islam as a religion does not exist?

Suddenly, a 'Religion'!

Jha is even more ingenious! Hinduism did not exist – not till the British invented this 'neologism' in the nineteenth century. But when it comes to finding the cause of, when it comes to locating the root of inequity, of the oppression of millions, Jha declares that it is Hinduism which is the root and cause, and Hinduism *as a religion*, no less!

'Hinduism is the youngest of all religions,' Jha says, 'a nineteenth century neologism popularized by the British.' Hinduism is just a term 'invented during the colonial period,' he says. He speaks with scorn of 'the artifact called Hinduism'.[83]

And now see to what he attributes intolerance. But first the 'evidence' he adduces to establish that Hinduism was intolerant, indeed that it is *inherently* intolerant.

He has to begin with a concession: 'It is true that religious

[83] Jha, op. cit, pp. 18, 27.

sects showed a certain degree of mutual accommodation so that the Buddha as well as the first Jain Tirthankara Adinath (Rsabha), both associated with heretic religions, were accepted as incarnations of Vishnu, and sacrifice to the former was recommended for worshippers desirous of beauty.'[84] But he swiftly recovers: 'But it is forgotten that Siva is believed to have appeared on earth in the form of Sankara to combat a Buddha *avtara* and that his followers "opposed and persecuted the Vaishnava philosopher Madhu/Madhava".'[85] Two things strike one at once. One, that a Marxist will believe *anything* if it serves his line – here that Shiva took birth as Adi Sankara to combat an avatara of Buddha! Second, that the authority he quotes for the latter part of his sentence is not some haloed text but Wendy Doniger O. Flaherty!

Next, another inconvenient fact – but all one needs to get over it is to replace one word. Jha notes that the Vedantist Madhava Acharya showed 'exemplary tolerance' towards the points of view to which he was opposed – so much so that he, Madhava Acharya, presented them fairly and in detail in his own work. 'What, however, is missed,' declares Jha, 'is that this was in keeping with the traditional *Indian* practice of presenting the opponents' view before seeking to refute it.'[86]

Not the 'traditional *Hindu* practice', Shiva forbid. The 'traditional *Indian* practice'. Islamic too? That of the Christian missionaries too? Beheading was the 'traditional practice' in one case, and calumny and distortion in the other. Either of these religions showed that 'exemplary tolerance'? But suddenly 'Indian' it is.

In any case, Jha continues, 'a *religion* with caste and untouchability as characteristic features was and is inherently incapable of promoting tolerance...'[87] Suddenly – when one

[84] Ibid., p. 28–29.
[85] Ibid., p. 29.
[86] Ibid., p. 29.
[87] Ibid., p. 29.

is to lay the blame for caste and untouchability – Hinduism becomes a *religion*!

Evidence!

The 'evidence' that Jha cites to establish that Hinduism – the *religion* Hinduism – was and is inherently intolerant is laughable. He says that the 'antipathy' of Hinduism towards and persecution by it of Jains was 'much more' than towards the Buddhists. To substantiate this, he cites a text that refers to Jain monks as ones who 'hated others', who were 'shameless', 'naked', 'wicked', 'weak and filthy', 'mad', as ones who 'wear mats and pluck their hair and eat their food standing'. This 'intolerance' is at par with pulverizing the places of worship of other religions, of burying their sacred objects under steps so that when the faithful come for prayers, they tread on them? Using such epithets is at par with beheading hundreds of thousands, and celebrating that in court histories as emblems of fidelity?

Jha then cites a text that describes the encounter of two Nayannar saints with Jains and remarks, 'The most important and well-known part of his [Sekkilar's] narrative relates to how Sambandar defeated the Jains in all contests and succeeded in converting the Pandian king of Madura from Jainism to Saivism, *leading eventually to the impalement of eight thousand Jain monks*.'

Strong evidence, won't you admit? Till you see the next few words: '*although there is no record of such a massacre*'. But our eminence does not give up: 'Saiva intolerance of Jains is corroborated by several *legends* found in the *Sthalpurana* of Madura...'[88]

Hence,

- 'although there is no record of such a massacre'
- what we have are 'several legends'
- and the intolerance is proven!

[88] Ibid., p. 36.

There is the even more telling point, one that we have glimpsed earlier, one that runs as a thread throughout Jha's Presidential Address, and one that strikes a reader even if his words are taken at face value. Throughout his exposition, Jha cites animosities between sects such as Saivites and Vaishnavites as evidence to prove that no entity that may be called 'Hinduism' existed. But here he cites the 'intolerance' of Saivites to establish that the religion Hinduism has been, and, therefore, is inherently intolerant! As we shall soon see, Jha argues at length that the fact that sects like the Lingayats did not accept the authority of the Vedas establishes that there was no such thing as Hinduism with the Vedas as their foundation. But now he cites the 'slaughter of Jains' by the 'militant Saivite Lingayat sect' as proof to establish that intolerance and violence are inherent in the religion.[89]

Next, Jha states that monks of some 'Brahmanical sects' were given military training, and that thereafter they performed a military role. 'The militarization of military sects and the growth of temple militias,' he writes, 'created conditions for violent conflicts between arms-bearing Brahmans and the votaries of non-Brahmanical sects.'[90] He cites no instance of these violent clashes, and, of course, even assuming that he is correct in his assertion about the Brahmans of some sects being given 'military training', he does not tell us what proportion of those sects got this training or became parts of 'temple militias' – a figure that would be necessary for us to assess his assertion regarding 'the militarization of Brahmanical sects'. You would have noticed how he evades the responsibility of adducing evidence that shows that the specific violent clashes were caused by the 'militarization' of the Brahmans – he carefully avoids linking specific conflicts to this 'militarization'; after all, all that he has said is that the military training and the creation

[89] Ibid., p. 37.
[90] Ibid., p. 38.

of 'temple militias' '*created conditions for* violent conflicts'; he is not obliged to prove that such violent conflicts actually took place or that they were caused by the 'militarization'!

And so, his conclusion: 'There is little doubt that Brahmanism was inherently intolerant as all religions are, and that its intolerance, often expressed through violence, *may have* received much sustenance from the martial brahmans.'[91] Notice the rigour of his logic:

- Brahmanism is a religion
- As all religions are inherently intolerant, so Brahmanism is inherently intolerant
- This intolerance was 'often expressed through violence' – as the pervasive reach of this violence is self-evident, no evidence need be given
- This violence '*may have* received sustenance from the martial brahmans'
- QED!

Resolute Ignorance

One of the assertions by which Jha argues that Hinduism was not a religion at all till it was created by the British in the nineteenth century is that the Vedas 'were not accepted universally' as the final authority. 'Universally' is a very useful word in this context! For if you can show even one clutch that did not accept the Vedas as the final authority, you have proven your case!

First, what if in the eyes of the religion the final arbiter is your personal, direct experience, darshan, and not what some passage in some book says? That it is your own inner experience, not what some fragment of the teaching of even the greatest prophet or master or seer or avatara says?

That certainly is the case in Hinduism and Buddhism. Of

[91] Ibid., pp. 38–39.

what weight is Jha's 'evidence' then that the authority of the Vedas was not universally accepted?

In any case, what is the 'evidence' that Jha, with all his diligence, is able to marshal?

Once again, he is compelled to start with a concession! For the fact, as he acknowledges, is that texts and schools and teachers did try to establish their authority by claiming 'Vedic status' or, at least, Vedic genealogy. 'Many religious teachers holding different opinions,' Jha says, 'sought to legitimize their teachings with reference to the Vedas during the medieval period.' 'Acceptance of the authority of the Vedas,' he continues, 'is in fact an important feature even of modern Hindu revivalist movements like the Arya Samaj of Dayananda, who is sometimes called the Luther of India.' Why would these teachers and authors of texts have strained across centuries to do so unless the Vedas did have preeminent position in the minds of the people?

Jha is not deterred, however. He proceeds: 'But all this cannot be construed to mean that Hinduism acquired a monolithic character: for it has rightly been pointed out that the allegiance to the Vedas was very often a fiction, nothing more than a mere "raising of the hat, in passing, to an idol by which one no longer intends to be encumbered later on"'[92] – that attractive phrase, as you would expect, is from a foreigner! But two things. First, is 'allegiance' to the Bible or the Quran of either lay Christians and lay Muslims or of the different sects of Christianity and Islam anything more than 'a mere "raising of the hat, in passing, to an idol by which one no longer intends to be encumbered later on"'? It most certainly is no more than that if you ask any sect about the depth of the allegiance of members of the other sects. It certainly can't be more if you ask the Taliban about the allegiance of 'moderate Muslims' to the Quran, or vice versa. The second point is even more important: what is so special about a religion having a 'monolithic character'? What

[92] Ibid., p. 21.

is wrong if it has *pluralism* as a central feature of its thought and belief systems?[93]

The same question arises when Jha points to some texts – some Puranas, some Upanishads, the Mahabharata – which, he says, put themselves at par with the Vedas, which claim that reciting them will confer unparalleled boons.[94] Does the very effort of these texts to place themselves at par with the Vedas not show the vantage point that the latter occupied among adherents? Second, Jha himself seems a bit sheepish about how much his citations have been able to establish. He says, 'All this may not amount to a repudiation of the Vedas, but it certainly indicates that all post-Vedic Brahmanical religious tradition' – how he strains to avoid using the word 'Hinduism' and letting the word 'religion' get close to it! – 'did not look to them for legitimacy.'

Next, to establish that the Vedas were not 'universally' accepted as the final authority, Jha points out that some persons scoffed at those who put faith in rituals that are prescribed in the Vedas.[95]

First, several of the statements that he cites to prove his point suggest the opposite! He cites a passage in which we are told that those who 'delight in euologistic statements of the Vedas are full of worldly desires'. Jha cites another text that warns that the 'desire-ridden followers of the Vedic sacrificial rites stagnate in hell'. In what way do these admonitions ridicule or scoff at the Vedas? On the contrary, the statements, which stand true to our day, emphasize that one cannot serve Mammon and the Vedas alike, that devotion to the Vedas entails that we adhere to their teaching and prescriptions wholeheartedly.

Second, the examples that Jha cites to prove the animosity that other sects bore towards each other are mild as can be! Jha cites

[93] Cf, Arvind Sharma, 'Hinduism,' in *Our Religions*, Arvind Sharma (ed.), Harper, San Francisco, 1993, pp. 56–60.

[94] Ibid., pp. 25–26.

[95] Ibid., pp. 23–27.

a text that he says 'speaks of a Vedantist who was humiliated by Basava at the court of Bijjala'. He cites another text that 'narrates how a Vedic scholar was ridiculed by the Lingayats, who had the Vedas recited by dogs'.[96] Two examples in all! Thousands of years of history at his command, and all that our committed historian can come up with are two examples. Second, I would certainly like to meet the dogs who could recite the Vedas. Given the devotional streak in our people for the Vedas and other sacred texts, were some dogs to acquire the ability to recite the Vedas, far from that fact bringing down the Vedas in the esteem of the people, the people would start venerating the dogs! Jha points with some satisfaction to the fact that one sect rejected the Vedas, and 'composed a Veda of their own'. But that also shows that the Vedas were the gold standard!

Saints such as Kabir and Tukaram rejected the Vedas, Jha says.[97] Did they scoff at empty recitation of the Vedas and the mechanical performance of rituals prescribed in the texts, or did they repudiate the texts themselves? Assume that some text asks us to turn beads in prayer. And Kabir extols us *mankaa mankaa chaand ke man kaa mankaa pher*? Is he condemning prayer and repudiating beads? Or is he telling us that beads and their turning are just devices, and urging us to focus on the real task – that of transforming our minds? Which ass would not know the meaning of the verse? But take Jha at face value for a moment, and assume that Kabir and Tukaram repudiated the Vedas themselves: does the fact that even so these very saints are venerated by all Hindus across the length and breadth of India not strike Jha as indicative of a very special feature of Hinduism?

Soon, Jha ascends to absurdity. Among the persons he cites as ones who ridiculed or scoffed at the Vedas is none other than Sri Ramakrishna Paramhamsa.[98] Manifestly, Marxists

[96] Ibid., p. 26.
[97] Ibid., p. 27.
[98] Ibid., p. 27.

are not obliged to know even the first letter of the nature of mysticism or the mystic experience – and how *everything* – every ritual, every text, every distinction, not just between sects and religions but in space and time – falls away from those who are immersed in that experience, how all the ladders by which one has ascended to that state automatically move away.

What can one say, what *need* one say about such resolute ignorance of these Marxists out to vanquish the 'monster of Hindu fundamentalism'?

'Not Altogether Impossible'

'There were antagonisms between the various Brahamanical sects,' Jha writes, 'as well as between Brahmanism, which accepted the authority of the Vedas, and the heterodox non-Brahamanical sects which rejected it.'[99] Much can be said about the 'evidence' he adduces as well as the authorities he cites – Wendy Doniger prominent among them! But two facts will be sufficient.

The first thing that strikes one is the mild nature of the 'antagonism'. In case after case that he cites, all that happens – and I am quoting Jha's account – is that X 'defeated' Y in debate; that X scoffed at a text; that X claimed that his object of worship, say Vishnu, was superior to Y's object of adoration, say Shiva; that X 'rejected' the arguments of Y; that X asserted that Y was 'misleading' the people; that X considered the arguments of Y so devoid of merit that he 'excludes them from consideration'; that X scoffed at a monk [at one monk!] of Y and said that he was 'naked, devoid of manliness, [with] his hair plucked out and [that he was] carrying a peacock feather in his hand'; that X 'criticized' the practices of Y.[100] Jha himself seems to be aware of the paucity as well as of the mild nature of events he has cited. And so he remarks: 'Although

[99] Ibid., pp. 29–30.
[100] Ibid., pp. 31–34.

the evidence of Buddhist and Jain antipathy towards Saivism *may not be voluminous* [!], *and needs to be investigated further* [that is, more has to be dug up somehow!], *it is not altogether impossible* that anti-Saiva literature was destroyed in the medieval period.'[101]

Notice:

- 'Although the evidence … may not be voluminous'
- 'Needs to be investigated further'
- 'It is not altogether impossible that … was destroyed…'

And if the VHP had said, 'Although the evidence that the Babri Mosque was built by destroying the Ram temple may not be voluminous, and needs to be investigated further … it is not altogether impossible that the relevant records may have been destroyed in the medieval period,' what would these historians have proclaimed in return – committed as they are to combating 'virulent version of Hindu cultural chauvinism', to battling 'xenophones and communalists', to exposing those 'guilty of fakes and frauds', to showing up the 'hollowness of the ideas which have been the staple diet of the monster of Hindu cultural nationalism in recent years', committed as they are to waging 'the ongoing battle against jingoist, communal and obscurantist perceptions of India's past'?

Response to 'Heresy'

With manifest satisfaction, Jha quotes Wendy Doniger to the effect that 'To the Hindus as a whole, Buddhists and Jains and Carvakas … are heretics. To many Vaishnavas, Saivas are heretics, and to many Saivas, Vaishnavas are heretics.'[102] Assume for a moment that 'many' are really *many*! Has Jha, or Doniger for that matter, never glanced at the Quran and Hadis, have they never been through Islamic history, are they completely

[101] Ibid., p. 34.
[102] Ibid., p. 31.

unaware of even recent documents? Consider a single example – the classic report of Justice Muhammad Munir.[103] The Commission found that none of the Islamic authorities was able to agree with any of the others on who is a Muslim. Second, each of the sects that these worthies represented had proclaimed the other sects to be kafirs, apostates and the rest. After setting out verbatim pages and pages of definitions of a 'Muslim' given by the highest religious authorities of the time in Pakistan, the Commission concluded as follows:

> Keeping in view the several definitions given by the Ulema, need we make any comment except that no two learned divines are agreed on this fundamental. If we attempt our own definition as each learned divine has done and that definition differs from that given by all others, we unanimously go out of the fold of Islam. And if we adopt the definition given by any one of the Ulema, we remain Muslims according to the view of that alim but kafirs according to the definition of every one else.[104]

Nor was this discord over the definition of a Muslim just an academic disagreement. It had an immediate and fatal

[103] In 1953, Pakistan, the Pakistani part of Punjab in particular, was rocked by riots. Clerics harangued the people about conspiracies that, they said, were being hatched by the Ahmediyas. They harangued mobs asserting that these perfidious creatures were out to destroy Islam. They demanded that the government pass laws declaring Ahmediyas to be non-Muslims. Mobs rampaged cities and villages hunting for Ahmediyas, destroying their homes, breaking down their mosques. The government set up a commission to inquire into the riots. It was headed by Justice Muhammad Munir. The report of that commission remains one of the very best reports produced in the subcontinent since the two countries became independent.

[104] *Report of the Court of Inquiry constituted under Punjab Act II of 1954 to enquire into the Punjab Disturbances of 1953,* Superintendent, Government Printing, Lahore, Punjab, 1954, p. 218.

operational consequence. For in the eye of each authority, every other authority and the sect he represented automatically became apostates. And the punishment for apostasy, the Commission emphasized, was just one – death.

> According to this doctrine, [on which, the Commission noted, there was near-unanimity among the Ulema] Chaudhri Zafarullah Khan, if he has not inherited his present religious beliefs but has voluntarily elected to be an Ahmadi, must be put to death. And the same fate should befall Deobandis and Wahabis, including Maulana Muhammad Shafi Deobandi, Member, Board of Talimat-i-Islami attached to the Constituent Assembly of Pakistan, and Maulana Daud Ghaznavi, if Maulana Abul Hasanat Sayyad Muhammad Ahmad Qadri or Mirza Raza Ahmad Khan Barelvi, or any one of the numerous Ulema who are shown perched on every leaf of a beautiful tree in the fatwa, Ex. D.E. 14, were the head of such Islamic State. And if Maulana Muhammad Shafi Deobandi were the head of the State, he would exclude those who have pronounced Deobandis as kafirs from the pale of Islam and inflict on them the death penalty if they come within the definition of murtadd, namely, if they have changed and not inherited their religious views.
>
> ...According to Shias all Sunnis are kafirs, and Ahl-i-Quran, namely persons who consider hadith to be unreliable and therefore not binding, are unanimously kafirs, and so are all independent thinkers. The net result of all this is that neither Shias nor Sunnis nor Deobandis nor Ahl-i-Hadith nor Barelvis are Muslims and any change from one view to another must be accompanied in an Islamic State with the penalty of death if the Government of the State is in the hands of the party which considers the other party to be kafirs. And it does not require much imagination to judge the consequences of this doctrine when it is remembered that no two Ulema have agreed before us as to the definition of a Muslim. If the constituents of each of the definitions given by the Ulema are given effect to, and subjected to the rule of 'combination and

> permutation' and the form of the charge in the inquisition's sentence on Galileo is adopted *mutatis mutandis* as a model, the grounds on which a person may be indicted for apostasy will be too numerous to count.[105]

Over the years, Hanafis, Ahl-i-Hadis, Deobandis, Barelvis, Shias, each of the Sufi orders – one and all – have had fatwas issued declaring them to be kafirs and apostates, *wajib-e-qatl*, putting whom to death is obligatory. And ever so many of the most honoured figures of each sect have been individually pronounced to be kafirs and apostates by the best-known and authoritative figures of other sects. From Syed Ahmed Khan to Maulana Maudoodi to Muhammad Iqbal to Muhammed Ali Jinnah, one and all have been pronounced kafirs and murtads by Islamic authorities. Remember, the punishment for apostasy in Islam is only one – death. And remember too that the believers – both Sunni and Shia – are faithfully implementing the command of Allah to this day by blowing each other up in Pakistan, and across the Middle East.

Two questions for Jha, and his authority, Doniger: (a) Anything comparable in Hinduism? (b) And yet Islam is a religion and, in view of the 'animosities' that Jha cites, and the declarations that Doniger cites, Hinduism is a neologism invented and popularized by the British in the nineteenth century?

Deliberate Conflation

Thus far, our Marxist has been trying to establish that Hinduism has been extraordinary – in that while other religions exist, Hinduism just isn't there. Now he seeks to establish that Hinduism is like any other religion! Like other religions, it indulges in conversion and reconversion. The short answer is

[105] Ibid, pp. 218–19. I have dealt with this matter in detail in *The World of Fatwas, Or the Shariah in action*, HarperCollins, 2012.

that if it is all right for other religions to convert members of our Scheduled Castes and Scheduled Tribes, why should it not be permissible for Hindus to convert them back into Hinduism? If it is all right to convert tribals by proffering rice and other 'material incentives' – to tot up the number of what Gandhiji called 'rice Christians' – why is it not permissible for Hindus to convert them back to Hinduism, or, if you insist that they were *not* Hindus in the first instance, to convert them to Hinduism?

The point is simple: all right, Hinduism is like any other religion. So? Do we now have the right to convert and reconvert?

But it will pay us to go through the 'evidence' that Jha adduces in his Presidential Address for that too shows the kind of subterfuge these eminences have perfected.

Throughout, Jha conflates ordinary conversion – using force or allurement, for instance – with, say, a spiritual master making a person go through a ritual as an aid to making the latter shed worldly concerns and goals, and devoting himself exclusively to a spiritual goal. The distinction is so obvious, and the chasm between the two so vast that confusing them or conflating them cannot but be deliberate. Jha talks at length, for instance, of the diksha ceremony as an example of conversion, even as he himself notes that this ceremony is 'generally understood in the sense of initiation (upnayana) or consecration, which 'implies death to profane existence, enables man to gain sacred knowledge and wisdom, a higher degree of existence and access to heavenly life', as 'purification'.[106]

The deliberate device apart of equating a ceremony of this kind with conversion into Christianity or Islam, there is a trick here that we encounter often in the writing of such eminences. If a text says that lower castes or tribals, say, are unfit to perform X or Y ritual – say, they are not fit to conduct a havan – that is projected as evidence of Hinduism's disdain for these groups,

[106] Jha, op. cit, pp. 39–40.

as proof of its 'inherent intolerance'. If it prescribes a ritual by participating in which individuals from these groups can become priests; or, as has indeed been done, if an organization like the RSS commences a programme to train Harijan youth into priesthood, and prescribes a simple ceremony that they should go through to commence their training, the same ceremony that all trainees have to go through; and the head of the Kanchi Math himself comes and distributes certificates of their having successfully completed the course, and are henceforth full-fledged priests, as he has done – that is projected as evidence of the boa constrictor swallowing up persons outside the pale!

This leads to laughable contradictions. On the telling of these mutually acclaimed scholars, Hinduism is exclusionary. In speaking of diksha, Jha records declarations to the effect that this ceremony is 'the most important method of attaining integral Sivahood', as it being the ritual that 'alone opens the door of Vaisnavism'. And then he says, 'of particular significance here is the fact that this route is available also to outsiders who seek admission to the fold'.[107] He cites these to establish that in Hinduism, as in other religions, there is 'the possibility of conversion'. But does that very fact – that 'the route is available also to outsiders who seek admission to the fold' – not explode much of what personages like him allege about Hinduism being exclusionary?

Jha moves on to say that Virasaiva monasteries were established in different parts of the country after the twelfth century and their objective 'was to convert non-Lingayats to Virsaivism'. From this, Jha makes a leap, indeed two: '*Tradition has it* that large-scale conversions from Jainism to Virsaivism took place in Karnataka in the wake of Ekantada Ramayya's victory over the Jains. *What could conversions in these circumstances have been if not forced?*'[108] Two leaps:

[107] Ibid., p. 40.
[108] Ibid., p. 40.

- 'Tradition has it'
- 'What could conversions in these circumstances have been if not forced?'

And if I said, 'Tradition has it that large-scale conversions from Hinduism to Islam took place across north India in the wake of the victories of Islamic conquerors over the natives. What could conversions in these circumstances have been if not forced?' – what would our eminences not hurl at me? Assuming that large-scale conversions of Jains to Virsaivism did take place at that juncture, these could not have been but by force. But the large-scale conversions that took place in the wake of the Islamic invasions, why, they were just the oppressed Dalits escaping from under the heel of Hinduism!

And what is the incident on which our historian is placing his reliance – 'the victory of Ekantada Ramayya'? Jha cites the book of P.B. Desai, *Jainism in South India*, and that book points to an inscription at Ablur. This inscription, Desai records, deals with the exploits of Ekantada Ramayya, 'the militant protagonist of the Saivite upheaval in the 12th century.'[109] The incident that the inscription sets out is as follows, and it is such that it should give a believing Marxist reason to pause!

Ekantada Ramayya got into a controversy with some local Jains – the latter were led by the village headman. Ekantada put a wager in writing: he would cut off his head, place it at the feet of Somanatha, and have it restored within seven days. If all this happened, the Jains were to give up their beliefs and the god they worshipped. The miracle transpired. The Jains refused to live up to their side of the wager. Incensed, Ekantada laid waste the shrine, and built a temple dedicated to Shiva instead. The Jains complained to the king, Bijjala. Summoned, Ekantada produced the written wager. Furthermore, he said he would do all that he had done again. The Jains did not accept going

[109] P.B. Desai, *Jainism in South India and Some Jaina Epigraphs*, Jaina Samskriti Samraksha Sangha, Sholapur, 1957, pp. 182–83.

through the contest a second time. The king gave Ekantada a document acknowledging his accomplishment, and urged the Jains to live in harmony with others. A dialectical materialist putting his faith in such a miracle?

The incident was put in perspective long ago by Professor P.V. Kane in his monumental study. While narrating and setting out the evidence of the extraordinary tolerance that was the hallmark of the Hindu rulers over two thousand years, he recalled this incident in full, and remarked, 'Nothing is gained by a total denial of even sporadic cases of religious persecution and vandalism. But such cases were very few and their very paucity emphasizes and illuminates the great religious tolerance of the Indian people for more than two thousand years.' Having set out the account of the incident, Kane observed, 'It is clear that a Jain image was overthrown and a Saiva one was substituted by Rama[yya] (leaving aside the superhuman feat ascribed to him). Rama[yya] is to be placed before 1162 A.D. There is a great difference between local brawls as in the above case and a general policy by a community or a king of wholesale persecution.'[110] Not only is such sagacity alien to our eminent historian, it is petit bourgeois anathema, for it would leave nothing to his charge!

In fact, Desai's book presents a complex picture, and that should have been apparent to Jha – even if he had read only the paragraph dealing with Ekantada. Concluding that very paragraph in which he mentioned this inscription, Desai had observed, '*In my review of Jainism in Karnataka, above, I have made passing observations on the age of decadence that saw the downfall of Jainism. The evidence adduced here lends additional strength to those observations.*'[111]

P.B. Desai's book was published by a Jain organization

[110] P.V. Kane, *History of the Dharmashastras, Ancient and Medieval Religious and Civil Law*, Volume V, Part II, Bhandarkar Oriental Research Institute, Poona, 1977, p. 1011, note 1645a.

[111] P.B. Desai, op. cit., p. 183.

based at the time in Sholapur. He used a variety of sources – inscriptions, antiquities discovered in villages, literary sources, legends, kaifiyats, the village records. Naturally, as he himself noted, greater reliance could be placed on some of the sources than on others: the village records, for instance, could not always be regarded as accurate. Similarly, on occasion Desai had to read significance into what he found, he had to connect the dots, so to say. To take just one example, Desai cited the appellations that are recorded for some persons: so and so, 'a death to the Jainas' or 'an eagle to the Jaina snake', and stated, 'This shows that hostile propaganda against the followers of the Jaina doctrine was already afoot in the country [around Annigeri] by the latter part of the 12th century…'[112] Assume, for instance, that an inscription or a kaifiyat describes a local chieftain or strongman as 'the terror of Jains', as one who 'vanquished' them, as 'a menace to the heads of Svetambara Jains'. Should one infer from a description of this kind that the person actually beheaded the Jains or that he defeated them in argumentation? Consider a current parallel. Because of his work in exhuming corruption, a journalist is described as 'the scourge of the corrupt', as a 'slayer of the mighty' – descriptions with which I am familiar! Coming across the epithets centuries later – in the case of Jainism in south India, we are trying to infer meaning a thousand years after the events – should the future historian conclude that the journalist actually beheaded the corrupt or that, because of his writings, the normal processes of an open democracy and society ensured that some corrupt rulers had to shed their office? The inference would have to depend on a host of circumstantial evidence.

In the event, P.B. Desai wrote about the 'ruthless persecution' of, about 'ruthless attacks' on the Jains in some districts and localities of Andhra, Tamil Nadu and Karnataka. He singled out three persons as ones who indulged in violence against the

[112] Ibid., p. 148. For two particularly colourful strings of epithets, see pp. 398–99.

local Jains. Ekantada was one of the three, the other two being Vira Goggideva and Viruparasa. Accept all this at face value.

The fact, as I just pointed out, is that Desai painted a complex picture. Of ebb and flow, of 'conversions and reconversions', of contestation among religions – Buddhism, Jainism, Hinduism. A place that was a 'Buddhist stronghold' in one century becomes a 'Jain stronghold' in the next, and a Hindu stronghold in the third. The Jains propagate their doctrines and try to turn the people away from Buddhism and orthodox Brahmanism. The latter wean people away from Jainism. Desai alluded to not just these pulls and pressures. He noted also the effect of Mohammadan invasions on all the indigenous religions:

> Jaina religious institutions and works of art must have also become victims of the forces of vandalism let loose in the country in the wake of foreign invasions. Revealing in this context are the incidents recorded in two inscriptions in Mulgund. One found on a pillar in the Parasvanatha temple, refers to an encounter with the Mohammadans who burnt the temple of Parasvanatha and states that the preceptor Sahasrakirti ... died in the fight. Another on a pillar in the Chandranatha Basadi states that Bandambike, wife of Nagabhupa, reconsecrated the image of Arhat Adinatha, which was polluted by the Mohammadans. The former epigraph bears no date and the latter is dated in A.D. 1675. It is not known whether the two records allude to one and the same raid by the Mohammadan aggressors or to two assaults on different occasions.[113]

On occasion, the village records, sculptures and paintings offer evidence of attacks and persecution by Hindus, Desai found. On occasion, he found that the accounts are not to be taken at face value – in regard to the *Periyapuranam*, which Jha cites in support of his argument, for instance, Desai records, 'The accounts of the persecution of the Jains given in the *Periyapuranam* and other literary works of the Brahmanical school present a highly

[113] Ibid., p. 148.

coloured and exaggerated picture of the times. Still it must be a fact that the Jains met with iniquities and maltreatment at the hands of their intolerant opponents...' – and he went on to point to sculptures and paintings in two temples.[114] In the event, on occasion conversions and reconversions could be attributed to persecution. On others, they took place without much ado. Desai wrote,

> With the ascendancy of other creeds, the influence of Jainism declined in this area [of Tamil Nadu] and its followers either migrated to other parts or passed into different folds. This happened, it seems, without much rancour, particularly in the lower layers of society. The common people, in spite of their allegiance to the new gods and goddesses, did not entertain sense of abhorrence as such towards the Jaina deities. Nay, sometimes they even offered worship to the Jaina images wittingly or unwittingly.[115]

Desai listed a number of factors that attracted people to the Jain doctrine and the Jain preceptors. The Jain monks were greatly respected, he wrote, for their vows of simplicity, for their learning. They were pragmatic and, when necessary, 'toned down' the requirements of their faith. The Yapaniya sect, for instance, declared that the followers of other doctrines could also attain salvation; that lay householders, and not just monks, could attain freedom from worldly bondage; that women and not just men could attain moksha in this very life. But then the inevitable happened, decadence took over:

> All these measures which were actuated by the best of motives and contributed to the prosperity of the Jaina religion at one time, had their perversions at a later age, when the original ideals fell into disuse and degeneration set in among the monastic orders. The degenerate practices of the monks who

[114] Ibid., p. 82.
[115] Ibid., p. 81.

> took to the life of pleasure and enjoyment, became the subject of severe condemnation by the advocates of austerity. This must be the real reason why such monks were ridiculed as pseudo-Jaina.[116]

All this is resolutely shut out by Jha. All we have is violent Hindus pouncing on hapless Jains and exterminating Jainism from the country – the Saivite Lingayats, non-Hindus when our friend is arguing that Hinduism is a nineteenth-century neologism because they do not accept the authority of the Vedas, having suddenly become Hindus as they pound the Jains. And we have a Presidential Address!

'Tall Tales' as Proof

Our Marxist presses into service as proofs the very narratives that his kind would otherwise dismiss as myths. 'Among the early *myths*, the *legend* of Daksa Prajapati ... The climax of *the story* is represented by Siva's destruction of the sacrifice performed by Daksa, followed by Daksa's realization of Siva's superiority and conversion to him,' Jha writes.[117] *Myth, legend, story* – each and every one of them suddenly worthy of being proof!

Next, our eminent Marxist yokes in a text that describes the conversion of nine Buddhists to the 'Kaula religion'. '*According to the tradition*,' Jha begins, a guru claims that he is a siddha, and has acquired divine powers. The Buddhists laugh at him, and challenge him to substantiate his claims. 'Srinath, *the story goes*,' Jha says, 'uttered the syllable HUM and all the Buddhist monasteries collapsed. The monks acknowledged his authority and later he converted them.'[118]

In the ordinary course, even a half-boiled Marxist would dismiss as supernatural nonsense the story that all Buddhist

[116] Ibid., p. 170.
[117] Ibid., pp. 40–41.
[118] Ibid., pp. 41–42.

monasteries collapsed because a syllable was uttered. But as the fable is serviceable, Jha pedals it at face value. After all, if the collapsing of the monasteries – the deus ex machina here – is a figment, what is the evidence that the rest of the story is true? But, then, for his thesis to advance, our committed historian must have it both ways. So, he cites the account to prove that there were conversions, and, at the same time, slips in phrases that would suggest that he, a committed materialist no doubt, doesn't believe such superstitious nonsense – 'tradition has it...', 'the story goes...' Notice also, the old trick: Jha uses Virsaivism, etc., to argue that these were religions in their own right, and that, therefore, there was no such thing as Hinduism; but here, Jha is arguing that as Virsaivism, etc., resorted to conversions, conversions were germane to Hinduism also and so Hinduism was and is like any other religion!

Several of these absurdities come together in one paragraph. Let us read it in full:

> Religious conversions *may have been* of central importance to the many *bhakti* saints and *gurus* on the religious scene with the development of devotional sects, especially in early medieval south India, and who were inspired by a strong missionary zeal *to convert the people to a life of spiritual surrender to the highest god.* This is corroborated by the instances of conversion recorded in the early medieval Saiva hagiographies. The twelfth-century work *Periyapuranam* of Sekkilar tells us that the Nayanar saint Appar was born in an orthodox Saiva family of the Vellala community but became a Jain monk at an early age. Agitated, his elder sister sought Siva's help. Appar was then afflicted with a serious abdominal disorder, which was cured not by the Jain physicians and their mantras but only by the grace and miracle of Siva. Repentant over his earlier conversion to Jainism, he came back to the fold of his family faith. Enraged at this, the Jains brought charges against him before the Pallava king Mahendravarman, who was a follower of Jainism. Appar, however, succeeded in convincing the king

> of the truth of Saivism, whereupon Mahendravarman himself became a Saiva. *Although various assumptions underlying this narrative, related in the Periyapuranam five centuries after the event, have been rightly questioned,* it is true that Appar and Mahendravarman changed their religions.[119]

Notice:

- 'Religious conversions *may have been* of central importance to the many *bhakti* saints and *gurus* on the religious scene…' – they may *not* have been!
- 'who were inspired by a strong missionary zeal *to convert the people to a life of spiritual surrender to the highest god…*' Notice, how Jha is conflating conversion to '*a life of spiritual surrender to the highest god*' with conversions of 'rice Christians', with the 'harvesting of souls' that the Pope urged missionaries in India to ensure, with the conversions that took place to Islam in the wake of Islamic conquests of India.
- Siva intervenes – to set right a stomach disorder!
- And then the self-exculpatory, 'Although various assumptions underlying this narrative, related in the Periyapuranam five centuries after the event, have been rightly questioned…' If the 'many assumptions underlying this narrative' are questionable, how come you are citing it as evidence?

That much done, our historian invokes for a second time the fable for which he himself has already acknowledged no evidence exists! Another 'story', he says, narrates an encounter between the Saiva saint, Sambandar and Jains. In this story, you will recall, the saint establishes his superiority through miracles and the Pandian king embraces Saivism. In the wake of this, '8,000 Jains are said to have been impaled. *Like the story of the conversion of Mahendravarman, that of the Pandian king may be*

[119] Ibid., p. 42.

a tall tale told by Sekkilar; but in neither of the two cases can the fact of conversion be questioned.'[120]

Next, this so-called historian – by now that seems to be the appropriate way of referring to the President of the Indian History Congress – turns to the fact that lands were granted to some persons, and the latter were supposed to popularize the Puranas, to teach Vedic lore, and to perform some rites and rituals. Here is a typical passage from the Presidential Address:

> An interesting eighth-century inscription from the Raipur district in Chhattisgarh mentions two Saiva ascetics, Sadyah-sivacarya and Sadasivaacarya, and records the dedication of a temple to the latter and his spiritual successors along with plots of black soil land located in different villages. It states that the ascetics, in return for the endowment, were expected to arrange free feeding house (*annasya sattaram*), a sacrificial rite (*yagya*), the exposition of the Saiva doctrine (*vyakhyah samaasya*) and the ceremony of initiation (*diksa*) into the Saiva faith which was capable of securing salvation.[121]

Now, if the inscription or a text had stated, 'tribals are not fit to hear this text' or that 'lower castes are not fit to take part in this rite', that would be flaunted as proof of the exclusionary character of Hinduism. When it states that the ascetics should initiate tribals into the rites, when it asks them to impart Vedic lore to the latter, when it asks them to arrange food for them, why, it is the old boa constrictor beguiling them into its belly! Why is the inscription not proof of the *inclusive* nature of Hinduism?

And then the leap – this time to encompass Sankara's mendicants. Once again we should read it as it contains both: the implicit acknowledgement that the evidence is not

[120] Ibid., pp. 42–43.
[121] Ibid., pp. 44–45.

sufficient to support the generalization that Jha pedals, as well as the kind of non sequitur that we have seen time and again. Here is Jha's conclusion:

> Similarly, while the monasteries and mendicant orders traditionally believed to have been established by Sankara certainly spread his ideas, *their role in converting people needs to be examined,* despite the reference to the initiation of novitiates in the *Naradaparivrajakopanisad. The number of inscriptions which provide direct evidence on the Sankarite monasteries may not be large; nor is the evidence on the Sankarite monasteries clear about their possible proselytising activities.* But to make the sweeping statement that Hinduism has been a non-proselytising religion appears unwarranted and *calls for rigorous reappraisal by historians.*[122]

The exhortation itself shows how much work remains to be done!

So much for 'the on-going battle against jingoist, communal and obscurantist perceptions of India's past'.

And yet it wanes.

[122] Ibid., p. 45.

23

A few reasons, a few lessons

The line was not going to hold for long, in any case, certainly not in regard to a land with as ancient and continuous a civilization, a land as vast and diverse as India. To explain thousands of years of history of such a vast and diverse land in terms of a single explanatory variable – say, classes – was reductionist in the extreme. Manipur, Kashmir, Gangetic plane, the South – it is not just that the changes that took place over thousands of years in these far-off regions could not be expected to be synchronous; the nature of societies and states that got established, the mores of life and thought that congealed were all different. And yet a thread – that of the foundational religion, Hinduism – ran through every part, and everything: music, dance, sculpture, painting, literature. And it required little to see that to fit those long centuries, those great diversities into a single set of explanations, these historians had, on the one hand, been cooking up 'evidence', and, on the other, they had shut their eyes to evidence that was all too visible – the findings on the Saraswati river, for example. Moreover, as Arvind Sharma points out, the basic theme around which they had built their entire narrative – that India is a land in which the majority has oppressed the minorities – is contrary to what has actually transpired: the minorities have been oppressing the majority – first the Muslims suppressing the Hindus; then the

Christians sitting on, first, both the Muslims and Hindus, and then, in collaboration with the Muslims, on Hindus.

A telling symptom of the hollowness of their theory is that for decades now, the Left parties as well as these progressive intellectuals have rationalized the worst kind of politics. In the 1940s they first clamoured for taking advantage of the bind in which the War had placed Britain; then, as the Molotov-Ribbentrop Pact fell apart, they shouted that all opposition to the British cease – they strained to help the British by sabotaging the Quit India Movement. Unable to make headway on their own, they took to espousing the cause of the Muslim League that the country be partitioned. When the country became independent, their theory led them to declare that the Independence the country had won was a sham, that India continued to be the lackey and instrument of imperialism. Soon, they launched an armed rebellion in Telangana, as the precursor of the larger revolution. From the 1950s right to this day, the progressives have advocated all sorts of Quixotic economic policies. As they remained stuck in a small part of the country, their theory helped them rationalize doing the unthinkable: they declared that in India, 'Caste is Class'. In the 1960s and 1970s, leading lights among them announced that, what with the Green Revolution making land more valuable, the 'kulaks' would be buying up the land of the poor and marginal farmers; that this would lead to 'immiserization of the masses', and thus the Green Revolution would turn Red. When Sikh militancy erupted, they saw in it a vindication of their warnings. As a consequence, they shut their eyes to the fact that Pakistan had armed, trained, financed, provided sanctuaries to the violent Khalistanis. Next, they leant a sympathetic ear to militant regional 'struggles', wherever they were occurring, on the ground that India had not solved the nationalities question. Many supported Naxalite terror on the ground that it was just a reaction to 'State terrorism'. In between, at least one-half of the official Communist Party inveigled that China is the one that was in the right in its invasion of India.

The impulse was to grab at anything that was likely to help them enlarge their 'base'. The theory provided the 'theoretical underpinning', and the 'tactical adjustments' made by Lenin, Mao and other stars, provided the Hadis-in-practice for opportunism of the crassest kind. The opportunism had the predictable consequences: on the one hand, it provided a veneer of justification to those who were working against the country; on the other, it weakened the national cause. But such opportunism is self-limiting: it sparks loathing among those who love the country; the frequent twists and turns stamp the intellectuals as rationalizers, and the line as being nothing more than an instrument of convenience. To the extent that they fall for the rationalizations, the people at large go for the real stuff – if politics of caste is right, why settle for those who are singing hosannas for casteist leaders, why not go for the real practitioners – the 'socialists', Mulayam Singh, Lalu Yadav, the woman and men 'of the people', Mayawati, to say nothing of Bhindranwale? Legitimizing the politics of these leaders has another consequence: when these leaders behave the way such leaders are bound to do – amassing wealth, bending and genuflecting to those who control the CBI, say, exercising 'vulgarity as a right', enforcing mediocrity as the norm – it is not just them but their rationalizers too who are discredited. And to top it all, the communists themselves, in the long years in which they wielded power in West Bengal and Kerala, proved to be the architects of stagnation. Finally, the skills that they had honed to do in others, they deployed against their comrades. You have just to spend a month or two in Kerala, and you see that the papers are full of the invective comrades hurl at other comrades, they are full of accounts of comrades having murdered other comrades.

That the stagnation that communist rule had inflicted on West Bengal and Kerala went unremarked for decades; that the abuse they hurl at each other, that the murders – even though routine in a state like Kerala, to say nothing of the erstwhile Soviet Union – have taken so long to be taken up by the media and our intellectuals shows how, for these long decades, the Left has set the norms of political correctness. But, the norms of political correctness apart, there is another reason on account of which the sort of falsehoods and perversities that we have sketched in this brief book could be pedalled for sixty long years: they just were not examined. And that failure is that of those who knew, or instinctively felt that the Leftists were pedalling falsehoods but did not put in the work to take the assertions and 'theses' of the latter apart.

In spite of the failure of the Right, however, it was inevitable that eventually a recoil would set in. After all, every single forecast that had been put out on the basis of that much-vaunted theory came out wrong. The revolution did not take place as the culmination of capitalist development. The New Civilization did not produce the New Man. It most emphatically did not turn out to be the workers' and peasants' paradise that had been forecast. The state, religion, nationalism, the armed forces and intelligence apparatus – none of these withered away. Capitalism also had not behaved the way it was supposed to. In accordance with the theory, it was supposed to hurtle inexorably along one set course, completely unable to learn from its mistakes. Those who had Marxist theory to guide them were supposed to be far-seeing: they were to be forever learning from the mistakes of capitalism. In the event, capitalist states had not collapsed. Quite the contrary: they had proved resilient. They had learnt from their mistakes – capitalism turned out to learn, to adapt, to correct course. The Soviet states turned out to be the ones that did not – they turned out to be rigid, and uncreative, and ultimately stagnant, no more capable of learning than a boulder. The central and incessantly repeated prophecy – the imminent collapse of capitalism – became as credible as that of the imminent end of the world. This turned out to be all the more so because it was repeated with such vigour at each crisis – WWI, 1929, WWII ... right up to the financial meltdown of 2008.

Nor could Indian devotees continue to pretend that communist states were fraternal towards other communist states, as the theory had said they would be. 'Fraternal' as the Soviet Union towards East European States? Towards China? China towards Vietnam? The theory held that communist states would be fiercely anti-imperialist. But the Soviet Union had established nothing less than an empire across Eastern Europe and Central Asia. The invasions by China of India in 1962 and then of Vietnam left our intellectuals speechless: they could not applaud these, they could not condemn these, they could not get the local populations to ignore the assaults. Nor have they been able to explain away the assistance that China has been giving to Pakistan – for developing rocketry, atomic weapons, to developing conventional weapons and bases and infrastructure in POK. The difficulty has been acute in particular because the objective of China in doing so has certainly not arisen from any ideological affinity – the objective has been only one: to keep India busy in South Asia – an objective that can be explained only in terms of China being, not a communist but a nationalist state. Today, China's grab of the minerals and oil of African states, its dumping of cheap manufactures and thereby destroying the little industry that had developed in those countries are no less predatory than the identical, exploitative practices of the old imperialist countries – practices against which every single freedom movement had struggled, practices which the theory had forecast and denounced. Similarly, our intellectuals could convince themselves that they were taking the moral high ground when they condemned the demand that Article 370 be scrapped; they could strike dramatic poses while insisting that the 'identity of the Kashmiris must never be violated'. But they had nothing to say about the systematic policy of China – a policy that goes back not just decades but centuries, if not millennia: to change the demographic balance in regions it grabbed – Mongolia, Xinjiang, Tibet – by settling Han Chinese in those regions.

All that the progressive intellectuals could do in the face of reality so recalcitrant was to advance one 'explanation', and hold out one hope. The explanation for every atrocity, for every U-turn was that socialism was being established amidst the sea of predatory capitalism and, so, 'aberrations' were inevitable. The solitary hope was that, in any case, these aberrations were transient. The 'explanation' didn't work: the oppression and stagnation were so pervasive, and so persistent that they just could not be passed off as 'aberrations'; the factors that were triggering the oppression and stagnation in the communist states were so obviously indigenous to the regimes that to attribute them to pressures or constraints imposed by the capitalism of other countries did not carry conviction. And, with each passing decade, the hope receded – especially for the unfortunate residents of the communist countries: with each passing decade, the oppression and stagnation seemed less and less 'transient'.

One after the other, these incongruities taxed the ingenuity of our progressive intellectuals. Their 'explanations' taxed credulity. And then came the final blow: their Holy Book was disowned in their Mecca – Moscow – and Medina – Beijing. The Soviet Union collapsed, and China lunged for state capitalism. East Europe bolted from under the Soviet heel. And truth about those countries and their regimes burst into the open. I remember issues of prominent Left magazines as late as 1988 – they contained adulatory articles about the superlative industrial excellence that had been achieved by Czechoslovakia, about the invincible bonds of East Germany and the great Soviet Union; an issue had an account of the wonders that had been realized in Nicolae Ceausescu's Romania – and within months the whole edifice split open: with Ceausescu's grotesque palace with its gold-taps on the one side, and, on the other, the horrible condition of the country's orphaned children and the tormented lives of its citizens in full view. The hapless citizens of those countries had seen the future, and seen too that, the Webbs notwithstanding, it didn't work. Far from being the workers' and peasants' paradise, the places had become mafia states, working solely for the aggrandizement of the *nomenklatura*.

All this stared the progressives in the face. They had lived the lie all their lives; they had paraded around the world hailing that lie; they had forced that lie down the throats of two generations of students; it is on the ladder of that lie that they had climbed, and acquired perks and prominence. They had invested all their lives into that lie. Suddenly, they could not pretend that the lie was truth. Nor could they shed it. Their solution was to look the other way. Here was a hallmark of the intellectual dishonesty that had become their genetic trait. Our progressives, so swift and thorough to build an entire thesis on every wiggle of a crisis in non-communist states, have to this date not produced one, single, solitary analysis of the facts that have surfaced about the reality of the Soviet and Chinese regimes.

Nor did any of them produce anything to account for how they had come to believe such falsehoods. Nor of how they had shut facts out. Certainly not of how they had lived the lie. An apt case for psychologists and psychiatrists: this shutting their eyes to what they had shut their eyes to, and of the inner deformities that this shutting out is bound to inflict.

Our eminences offer another theme for psychologists and psychiatrists. While they were singing halleluiahs to Marx, Lenin, Stalin, Mao, some even to Pol Pot, while they were swallowing and vomiting falsehoods on behalf of these leaders, no one had poured as much scorn on intellectuals of their kind as those very leaders. Here too is something worth analysing: what consequences form inside as one goes on adulating the very ones who are kicking one?

One trait that developed in them certainly was that the more they were flogged by the icons they worshipped, the more they yearned to flog – exactly as Paulo Freire in his *Pedagogy of the Oppressed* might have forecast they would, if only he could have included them among the oppressed.[1] A distinguished civil servant, describing a Soviet-oriented worthy we both knew, had used an apt expression – 'O, 'X'? A master of dialectics: Strong to the weak, weak to the strong.' The result was predictable. While they fawned and cringed for trips to and a pat from The Only Fatherland,[2] within the departments and institutions that they controlled, they enforced 'academic feudalism': they conducted themselves like any other set of insecure control freaks. A young journalist described what these eminent historians ensured, and how. 'A breed of cerebral czars' has ensconced themselves in positions of control, she wrote, 'individuals with whom certain institutions have become far too incestuously associated, who not only have the power to hand out tenures but also to send their followers abroad through several new fellowships' – the size of the crumbs by which the 'followers' could be deflected to toe the line itself shows their inner worth. But to continue with her account:

> 'Academic feudalism,' says a lecturer at JNU,[3] 'is so acute in History because there are so many opportunities now.' Academic feudalism – that is, the relations that develop between an influential professor and his protégés – takes many forms. Sometimes protégés are used by the feudal lord of the department as domestic help, to take charge of the cooking if the lord's wife is ill. Sometimes, protégés function as research assistants, helping to craft the trendy tome that will catapult the patron to a trans-Atlantic hall of fame. Sometimes, the

[1] Paulo Freire, *Pedagogy of the Oppressed*, Penguin, Harmondsworth, 1973.

[2] The description of the Soviet Union by the Indian communists to explain their about-turn – from opposing the British when the Ribbentrop-Molotov Pact was signed between Hitler's Germany and Stalin's Russia, to sabotaging the Quit India Movement because by then Hitler had attacked the Soviet Union: as the Soviet Union is our Only Fatherland, they declared in their party documents, our policy must be the one that serves its interests: c.f., my '*The Only Fatherland*,' op. cit.

[3] The Jawaharlal Nehru University.

feudal lord treats his followers as ideological allies to further the cause of liberalism or Marxism-Leninism on committees and in the university generally. And sometimes academic feudalism manifests itself as a power-sharing arrangement between a particular teacher and his students to keep 'outsiders' out of the staff room.

'A chief characteristic of academic feudalism,' says a JNU lecturer, 'is that the protégé must not be too good. If he is bright enough to overthrow the master, he cannot ever be anyone's protégé.'

In JNU, an eminent nationalist historian,[4] Professor Bipan Chandra, was so well known for placing his students in departmental posts that others did not even bother to apply if they did not have his support. Tripta Wahi, convenor of the Delhi University Teachers' Association (DUTA) and lecturer at Hindu College, DU,[5] says that the appointments made by the senior historian could not be challenged by anyone because of his reputation. 'Yet the people he has placed in my college are totally mediocre. In fact they are third divisioners whose only claim to fame is that they do not teach any school of History which is at variance with their teacher.'

...Academic feudalism is often the result of doctrinal strife which sometimes spills over into bitter personal animosities ... [The journalist described the divergence between the traditional progressives and the new ones, influenced by Foucault!]

Consequently, a student of DU complains, 'We have to be very careful. If a post-modernist tutor thinks our work is too traditional he may not recommend us for a scholarship abroad. But if we happen to fall under the supervision of an old-fashioned Leftist who thinks us too post-modernist, he may give us a bad mark...'[6]

[4] 'Nationalist' in the sense that the historian was looking at 'history from above' rather than from the point of view of the 'subalterns' – he is otherwise as 'progressive' as can be.

[5] Delhi University.

[6] Sagarika Ghose, 'The politics of history,' *Outlook*, 6 December, 1996, http://www.outlookindia.com/article.aspx?200318#.UhSPLg-icF8.email

The consequences were inevitable. As new central universities were set up – fifteen in the last few years – the protégés of these eminences are the ones who have been appointed to key posts. They have continued teaching the same stuff. They have perpetuated the same patron-protégé relationships. They have used the same techniques of networking, mutual promotion, blackballing and the rest to keep scholars of other hues out. But what is it that they have been perpetuating? More than the line, which is much enfeebled by now in any case, they have been perpetuating mediocrity all round – no one must be brighter than the patron, remember; the touchstone is not academic excellence but personal fidelity to and personal service for the patron, remember.

That these eminences were in control of journals, of history congresses, and university departments, had another immediate consequence: no one dared question their work. They hadn't to explain their 'theses', they could serve up any concoction as 'evidence'. In regurgitating the same assertions, they convinced themselves that they were being consistent; in arriving at the same reductionist explanations for diverse phenomena, phenomena millennia apart, they convinced themselves that they were fortifying the theory. In fact, all they were doing was repeating themselves. There was nothing new to be learnt as it had all been explained before! In a word, unquestioned, above being challenged, they slipped into shoddiness, and thus stagnation – Jha's Address is an illustration of the kind of drivel that came to pass as scholarship.

This conquest and control of institutions was rationalized as the new line. The Congress has been an instrument of the ruling classes, went the thesis. Indeed, the Independence that it has brought about is a mirage – India continues to be a lackey of imperialism, the Communist Party and its intellectuals declared. As the masses did not flock to the party, nor to the much-trumpeted 'struggles' it launched, progressives opted for bringing about 'Revolution from within'. This became the great rationalization for associating with, for allying with, for penetrating the ruling groups – in particular, the Congress. From the beginning, this device had its limitations: so long as India did not become a fully Marxist state, how revolutionary could the measures they goaded and shamed the Congress into taking be? Yes, the Soviet-lobby, as it came to be known, successfully nudged the Congress to adopt a series of 'progressive' measures. But these measures turned out to be disasters – the nationalization of the wholesale trade in wheat exemplified their fate, as did the inefficiencies that marred the functioning of public sector units. As a result, there was, as there was bound to be a recoil from within the Congress.

It wasn't long before the ones whom these progressives controlled began losing control. The Congress lost ground in several states. The communists hung on – but not by their record, they kept office through intimidation, through toughies, through cultivating Muslims as a vote bank. But the waning was writ large. The first to feel the impact was the 'solar system of front organizations and smaller committees around the Communist Party' that had been set up – the solar system on the planets of which many of these eminences shone as stars: the front organizations gave them platforms; in turn, they leant intellectual pretensions to what were no more than fronts. These organizations lost energy. Where are those organizations today, the formidable armada of agitprop? The All-India Friends of the Soviet Union? The Peace Committees and the Peace Movement, headed by the All India Peace Committee that was rallying people around the cry that the Soviet Union was the principal force for peace in the world? The India-China Friendship Organization? The All India Progressive Writers Organization? The Indian People's Theatre Association? The All India Association of Democratic Lawyers?[7] How prominent they were even in the 1950s and '60s!

[7] For the list and place of this 'solar system', Gene D. Overstreet and Marshall Windmiller, *Communism in India*, The Perennial Press, Bombay, 1960, pp. 406–65.

What attention the clichés uttered by intellectuals speaking at these fora commanded! And today? Getting published in their publications – *Mainstream, EPW, Patriot, New Age* – was such distinction in those days. Today, the circulation of many of these journals and papers is limited to the 'diehard faithful' – so many of them aged, the rest aging. They controlled such publications, and others, that of the ICHR, say: but the abysmal quality of articles in them ensured that the control amounted to little. They controlled bodies like the ICHR; but with such being the theses propounded by their presidents as we have seen in Jha's Address, what purchase could that control fetch?

Structural changes put paid to many of the causes fulminating about which the eminences had built their reputations, and thence their little jagirs. For instance, even till the 1980s, every strike was a 'struggle', every trade union leader was, ex officio, a paragon of virtue. But as the economy modernized, it became more and more integrated. Disruptions by smaller and smaller numbers, inconvenienced larger and larger numbers – 2,000 electricians of the UP Electricity Board could shut off the entire northern grid. People turned against militant trade unionism, and with that the rationalizers of such unionism lost the people's hearing. Similarly, the young who had been potential recruits for 'struggles' and for those fronts, turned to lucrative professions – IT and the rest. And so many just flew off: I was hardly surprised the other day to hear one of these progressives lament that the 'best and brightest' had but to get their degrees from JNU, and they rushed to universities abroad, and then just stayed on there – the very fact that the JNU had a 'good reputation' in those foreign universities, chiefly because of its emissaries who had got positions earlier in those foreign universities, made it that much easier for these 'best and brightest' to get positions abroad.

Similarly, the fact that India remained a free society, that it became an ever-looser society, while disabling in many ways, also didn't help their cause: it loosened their teeth! When you shout and charge a state that is so weak and loose with being an oppressor and exploiter, you are boxing air. Moreover, the people tire of being told of their problems – they don't need to be reminded of the problems, they are living them every single moment. They want to know what should be done, what *you* will do about those problems. And here, the progressives had little to offer. They had a long list of things that were wrong – in the past, of course, but also in the present. But they had little to say about the future, about what should be done, short of 'Expropriate the expropriators'. The measures they proposed short of that final expropriation – nationalization, ever more extensive and intricate controls, more and more PSUs, Soviet-style planning – as we have noticed above, just didn't work. Most of all, they didn't work in the states in which the progressives were themselves in power – West Bengal, Kerala.

Their forte had been polemical discourse. But that was swamped by the trivialization of all discourse. The first stage was 'balanced journalism', the 'Left, Right, Centre' phase – that is, all sides got equal time to shout at each other: the progressives, who had been the sole campaigners on the podia, were now just one of three. Soon, the controllers of the fora – the anchors on TV shows, say – wanted no details at all, just the sound byte: so the progressives' ability to conjure up details, true or not, correct or exaggerated, was brought to naught. Finally, discourse came to be so driven by one's official position or the strength of the party or group that, as the communist and Congress parties lost ground, the space these scholars got at the hands of the media, dwindled. So, their felicity in spinning out complicated sentences came to count for less and less.

As it became increasingly difficult to go on asserting the line – what with its manifest failure both in theory and practice – and their psychological inability to acknowledge that it was wrong, the eminent intellectuals branched out. They took up new causes: that of oppressed women, of Dalits, of tribals, of peasants, of pavement dwellers, of those displaced by irrigation projects, of the environment. Some began to follow new Schools: we soon began hearing of 'schools' that had become the talk among academic circles abroad – Post-Marxian; Structuralist, Post-Structuralist; Gramscian; Deconstructionist; Modernists; Post-Modernists; Post-Colonialists; and several more. A few founded a new school: Subaltern Studies.

But this escape – of dodging the failure of the line by diversification – has had several inherent difficulties.

The mission of the collective was indeed laudable – to bring into hearing the voices of those who had been subsumed in the sweeping categories in which history had been written: 'classes', for instance; to endow agency to those who had been obscured – by colonial and other forces, and who had been lost from view in the way history had been excavated and written. They set out to bring to light the methods, language, means, structures the oppressed and neglected had devised to resist 'colonization', to preserve their voice and autonomy. As recollections and archives that had not been explored were brought to light by members of the collective, there was justifiable excitement. The collective was noticed and applauded. There were legitimate questions, of course. The collective seemed to attach overweening importance to the nature of colonial discourse as an explanatory variable. By attributing such power to colonial discourse, were the new historians not doing exactly what they had charged others with doing, that is, robbing the subalterns of agency? If everything was the result of how the colonials – and in the case that the new historians were considering, that of India, that meant the British – how were the myriad changes in pre-British India to be accounted for? In any case, was the new determinant, colonial discourse, altogether new and original? Had it not taken over some of the categories and characterizations that existed before colonization by the British? If so, should the causality not be shifted back farther? The new historians were portraying the subalterns as having agency, but did the subalterns themselves believe that they were acting autonomously? Were our historians detecting resistance and autonomy or were they inventing it, much as anthropologists were said decades ago to have been inventing tribes through unwarranted differentiation?[8]

But these were just the sorts of controversies that fuel academic advance. By themselves, they would have led the historians to more robust analyses and research. In actual fact, the school took the trajectory that was typical of others, and soon, within just a few years of its founding, it lost sheen.

Several factors contributed to the denouement – and these are the ones that hold general lessons. First, the familiar split! Within three-four years of the formation of the collective, a disagreement arose. Should the search continue to be for, or be confined to archives and other material that directly embodied the voices of the subalterns? Were these voices themselves not so influenced by colonial discourse that one should focus on the latter? In the event, those advocating the latter viewpoint prevailed. Members of the collective reverted to 'deconstructing' the familiar texts and records. They insisted that they were studying the material from a new angle – the viewpoint of the marginalized. One of the founding members declared that they had taken the subaltern out of 'subaltern studies' – he was nudged aside. Their reversal to focusing on texts of the elite and the rulers was dubbed as '*bhadralok* studies'. These historians have gone back to 'desk history', the charge went.[9] The familiar course.

[8] For representative critiques, see, Richard M. Eaton, '(Re)imag(in)ing Otherness: A Postmortem for the Postmodern in India,' *Journal of World History*, Volume 11, No. 1, Spring 2000, pp. 57–78; Vinay Lal, *The History of History, Politics and Scholarship in Modern India,* Oxford University Press, New Delhi, 2003, in particular, pp. 186-230.

[9] See, for instance, Ramachandra Guha, 'Subaltern studies and *Bhadralok* studies,' *Economic and Political Weekly*, 19 August 1995, pp. 2056–58.

The second difficulty had been inherent in this, as in the other 'schools' – 'materialist', 'structuralist', 'post-structuralist', and the rest. Like the others, the subaltern school was, in a sense, just the domestic application of 'textbooks written abroad,' to recall Mao. Marx, Hegel, Heidegger, Gramsci – Gramsci, above all! – Michel Foucault, E.P. Thompson, Eric Hobsbawm, Edward Said – these were the inspirations, indeed they were the ones whose methods and propositions these historians sought to apply. But the ones – the 'subalterns' – they were writing about were universes away from these personages and their ways of looking at things, including their own condition. They lived the Mahabharata, the Ramayana, truths and conundrums from the Upanishads, Puranic legends. They put their faith in much pre-colonial stuff – astrologers, wisdom embodied in our aphorisms… For the historian, the touchstone was the fidelity with which his peer had applied or, better still, extended some phrase of Foucault, or enlarged his lense. For the subject about whom he was writing, the touchstone was so far removed from Foucault and the rest that the conclusions arrived at through Foucault's lens were an irrelevance.

Moreover, there was an inherent difficulty to their search for and discovery of subalterns. The problem with taking up causes of specific groups is that there are always other groups that equally merit attention, there are always finer divisions of groups that could yield even finer insights. After all, if you take up the cause of 'oppressed women', aren't you aggregating too much? Manifestly, the oppression that you will detect in the case of rural women is very different from that of urban women. And is 'rural women' also not too gross a category? The oppression that widows among them will face is very different from what married women are having to contend with. What about 'widows'? Clearly, too wide a category: widows who remain in the village, or in the family and widows who get sent to Vrindavan face very different futures. And isn't 'married women' also too gross a category? After all, girls who were married off when they were still children will face a life very different from what those who were married when they were in their teens will face. The subaltern school rebelled against the traditional Marxist way of looking at history. One of their points of difference was the emphasis of the Marxists on 'classes' as the categories for study and analysis. The subaltern historians set out to deconstruct 'class' and give voice to finer groups. But who could not find even finer groupings whose voice was distinct from the category into which they had been fit? In writing about the subaltern school, Vinay Lal, whom we have encountered earlier, delivers a typical reproach: 'Until very recently, subaltern history showed itself as entirely impervious to contemporary urban India, as if the slum-dwellers, urban proletariat, small-town tricksters, the countless number of street vendors, and even the lower middle-class Indians suffocating in dingy office buildings do not constitute the class of clearly subordinate people that Guha[10] designated as the "subalterns"...'[11] But what about the disabled? What about beggars? Certainly distinct, certainly subaltern. But '*disabled*'? '*Beggars*'? Spastics have lives, and therefore voices, often no more than silence, that are very different from those of the hearing impaired. Doesn't the category 'disabled' cry out for deconstruction? Similarly, the beggars who are on their own will have a past, they will have experiences, they are liable to have a future very different from those who are sent out on the daily round by an 'owner'. So, 'beggars' must be deconstructed. And what about beggars in Mumbai as distinct from those in Guwahati? That holds for each of the categories that Lal listed – 'slum-dwellers, urban proletariat, small-town tricksters, the countless number of street vendors, and even the lower middle-class Indians suffocating in dingy office buildings' – in *each* of these categories, wouldn't the homosexuals, say, or the transvestites, or those with broken homes, or those who, in

[10] Ranajit Guha, the 'founder' of the school.
[11] Vinay Lal, op. cit., p. 221.

spite of the odds, are making it as against those who, in spite of initial success, are losing grip of things – wouldn't each of these sub-categories be distinct? Wouldn't they have experiences that are entirely distinct from and, therefore, a voice that is entirely different from the general category of 'slum dwellers', 'urban proletariat', 'small town tricksters', 'street vendors' into which they might fall? So, deconstruct right down to the individual. But an *'individual'*? The individual when she is well is very different from when she is in an ICU. Ad infinitum.

More significant from the point of view of public discourse, each school has followed the trajectory that is typical of niche specializations: the language has become more and more opaque; the controversies have become more and more arcane, of interest only to that narrow circle of specialists in *that* specialization; academics within each school have been talking to narrower and narrower circles; the preoccupations have become the comment of some member of that narrow group on one's paper, the conference to which one has been invited or not. In a word, as the schools have multiplied, each has become more and more removed from life, from the groups on whose behalf its members are declaiming, in whose name its leading lights have set up shop. Moreover, just as there is no end to the sub-groups into which a group may legitimately be split for further studies, the number of schools also is not subject to closure – all the more so in our academia. As the very nomenclatures of these schools suggest, the new schools originated from, they drew their inspiration from, they were the domestic versions of schools that had sprung up abroad. But there, ever-new ones keep emerging.

In any event, these intellectuals, specializing in ever-narrower fields, could never exercise the influence on the general climate of opinion that the earlier generation had exercised: the earlier generation had forged spectacles through which the literati, through which those engaged in public discourse and public life looked at *everything*. These specialists have been dealing in splinters of glass – with bits and pieces of lenses of those spectacles.

Ideological commitment, or at least a predisposition towards the Left having become a necessary qualification for appointments, for prominence, the entire discipline came to shut its eyes to a pile of evidence on a whole range of issues. It was de riguer to declaim about 'Hindu communalism', but one just had to shut one's eyes to the way large swathes of Sikhs came to admire, if not appropriate Bhindranwale and his men – 'One thing you have to accept,' many would say in 1982, 'they are idealists;' 'One thing you have to concede. They may be wrong in the way they are going about their demands, but they do have a point...' Given their larger presence among the voters in West Bengal and Kerala, in a number of the constituencies that the progressives targeted, eyes had to be shut even tighter lest they spot communalism among Muslims: that had always to be portrayed as a reaction to Hindu communalism; it must never be talked of as something germane to the teachings or teachers of Islam. Even in regard to 'Hindu communalism', one had to make out that the 'communalism' among Hindus was the doing of one party, of one organization – the RSS – at the most of a few figures: it was not a characteristic of the mass of Hindus: one must shut one's eyes to the way the Hindus appropriated the 1984 violence against the Sikhs in Delhi. Similarly, one may, indeed one must declaim about the inequities from which women suffer, but one must shut one's eyes to what the Shariah provides in regard to women. How is it that while our feminists were so vigorous in denouncing the condition of women in Western societies, in India, they did not produce even a few worthwhile studies to explain the curious anomaly, one to which Maulana Wahiduddin Khan once called attention – that while Islam is said to give such high status to women, in every single Islamic society and country, women are in a pitiable condition? Yes, it was absolutely mandatory to denounce what was happening to the environment. But one must not see the incongruity of pouring scorn on the worship of trees, and rivers, on the veneration of nature in general, of such beliefs having been pilloried as 'animism' and superstition, and then lamenting the consequences when people began to look upon nature as others had been taught by their religions to do, that is, as something that had been created by God for the 'enjoyment' of man.

Another difficulty arose. The ones they had been denouncing learnt their skills: of intimidation; of attacking as a pack; of using strong words, even abuse. Indeed, if the denouncers are to be believed, their targets leaped ahead, at least in one regard – they came to master the new means of communication much faster than the eminences and their protégés. The historian works a scare: 'Hindutva or openly militant Hindu histories flourish on the Internet,' he writes, 'and they have cornered the market in Indian history…' 'More than any other organized religion, Hinduism is a decentered and deregulated faith,' he writes, 'and in this it appears akin to cyberspace.' And Hindus have flocked to Silicon Valley. 'The importance attached to cyberspace communication and politics and the Non-Resident Hindu Factor is, incidentally, nowhere better illustrated than in the fact that the BJP, which used to shout itself hoarse over *swadeshi* (self-reliance) and is nauseatingly jingoistic,' he writes, 'locates its website in the United States, as does the paramilitary organization, the Rashtriya Swayamsevak Sangh (RSS).' '… Whether cyberspace is "Republican" is a matter on which we can defer judgement,' he writes concluding his book, 'but it is poised, alarmingly, to become a Hindutva domain, considering that there are scarcely any web sites which offer competitive narratives.' He is filled with foreboding: '*Dhramakshetre, kurukshetre* (on the field of dharma, righteousness; on the field of the Kurus, the clan that is said to have given birth to Bharat or India), says the Bhagvad Gita in its opening line, but today this might well be: *dharmakshetre, cyberkshetre*. If the computer scientist-historian types who inhabit Silicon Valley, and their diasporic brethren, have it their way, Hinduism will become that very "world historical religion", they have craved to see, and Hindutva history will be the most tangible product of the wave of globalization over which they preside from their diasporic vantagepoint.'[12]

Control had another, in a sense a final consequence. That they controlled journals, university departments, history congresses placed them in the controlling elite. They became parts, and very conspicuous parts of the very establishment that they had been traducing. They could not sustain the pose of martyrdom – they were not the ones who were defying censors and persecution. They were now the censors. They were the ones who were derailing and blocking the careers of others, they were the ones who were blackballing others, destroying their reputations. Everything about them and their positions spoke to their being part of the ruling establishment: the intertwining webs of connections with those in office; the manifest fact that they owed their positions and prominence to those connections; their membership of governmental committees and delegations; the schools and universities to which they sent their children; their perks and salaries. A professor at the Jawaharlal Nehru University today gets around Rs 1,30,000 a month as salary with a dearness allowance. And there is the rent allowance (around 30 per cent of the salary if the person is not living on campus), and then the conveyance allowance. In a country where the poverty line is officially drawn at Rs 12 a day or Rs 360 a month, to get Rs 1,50,000 or thereabouts a month and write fiery essays on the immiserization of the poor comes across as a theatrical performance, the indignation is a bit too obviously worked up. Not the martyrs they would want us to take them to be, rather top dogs revelling in what Northcote Parkinson had called 'underdoggery'![13]

[12] Vinay Lal, op. cit., pp. 21, 252, 262–63.

[13] C. Northcote Parkinson, *Left Luggage, A caustic history of British Socialism from Marx to Wilson*, Houghton Mifflin Co., Boston, 1967.

Being part of the establishment also means that you are better able to fly off! I requested a young historian to see where the ten were now whose names seemed to figure prominently among those in the early years of the subaltern collective. One is in Austria; one is a professor at the University of Chicago; one is teaching at Columbia University; one is at the Emory University in Atlanta; one is a professor at Princeton University; one is teaching at the University of Minnesota; another has been at Columbia University for long. We could locate only three in India – one is a feminist writer and columnist; one is the director of a centre in Kolkata; a third has retired but is professor emeritus at the Delhi University – he had been cast out of the collective much earlier.[14]

Apart from the fact that, given the privileges and pelf that the conspicuous Leftist had garnered, there was another consequence, an intra-Left consequence, so to say. The ones who saw through the radical cry the soonest, and with the greatest bitterness, were the fellow-radicals who had *not* been

[14] Vinay Lal is eloquent on the subject: 'Of the core members of the collective, the greater majority of them are now placed in some of the leading universities in the United States and Britain, and of those who are settled in India, they have sinecures and arrangements for leave that are the envy of Indian academics. Some among the former sometimes represent themselves, usually informally, as unwilling exiles, as receiving a more sympathetic hearing in the Western academy than in Indian universities, as speaking in a language that places them at odds with their Indian colleagues. There are other ambivalent narratives woven into this tale as well, since educated Indians, who are sworn to the motto that "there is no honour in one's own country", like to believe that recognition in the West is a precondition for success in India.

'The criticism that seems to deserve a more sympathetic hearing, and which is a corollary to the suggestion that the subaltern historians have rendered themselves into exiles, pertains to the manner in which subaltern historiography has itself been rendered into exilic history...' Vinay Lal, op. cit., p. 219. He signs off his book, 'Vinay Lal, Los Angeles, 30 January 2005'!

able to rake in those privileges and perches. The latter had lived the lie as faithfully. They had participated in 'struggles' 'for the teacher and the toiler' even more earnestly. That their comrade had secured those privileges and positions and they had not, was proof manifest that he had 'sold out'. While to the 'practical revolutionary', the fact that he was muting his message was a regrettable tactical necessity – continuing on that perch was so vital for the larger cause, after all – to the comrade who had been left behind, the fact that their colleague was now muffling the trumpet was conclusive proof of the fact that he had crossed the barricades, that he was now part of the system that they had together set out to overthrow.

A Few Lessons

In a word, the influence of these eminences is on the wane. But their trajectory holds important lessons for those who lament what they have done over the decades to our self-perception and our discourse.

First, they believed in reflection, in reading and writing. True, as we have noticed, many of the icons of the Left poured scorn on 'intellectuals'. But many on the Right are not just anti-intellectual, they give the impression of being anti-intellect. Traditions cannot be rejuvenated, however, nations cannot be built, certainly ever-changing challenges cannot be met without ideas – without ideas worked out in detail.

Second, several of them were hardworking. That cannot always be said of those who would supplant them. No more proof of this is required than the fact that the fabrications of these historians, the kind we saw Jha deliver himself of, have gone unexamined for so long.

Third, several of them were skilled in polemics. Many of those who would displace them have been talking only to the converted.

Fourth, one must at all costs, adhere to the truth. The

falsehoods and fabrications of the Left have blown their case. Falsehood will fall apart just as certainly in the case of the Right, and invite the same consequence. Vinay Lal's survey, heavily tilted though it is, provides a telling example. Even as he compliments them for their 'courage' in speaking out on the Babri Masjid issue, he chastizes the Left historians for engaging in the negotiations and the dispute – their premise that such matters could be solved by recourse to history was wrong, he says. His bias is evident in the fact that he totally blacks out the absolutely disgraceful concoctions that the Marxist historians put together for the All Indian Babri Masjid Action Committee – that Ram was actually a Pharaoh of Egypt, that in fact Sita was Ram's sister whom he had married ... the shameful way they dodged the archaeological evidence, pretending that they had not examined it, that they had not met the archaeologists concerned – when in fact they had met the principal one just the day before, and how, when it became evident to all that the 'documentary evidence' which they had complied for the Babri Action Committee just did not match what was submitted on behalf of the Vishwa Hindu Parishad, they just failed to turn up at the final meetings. It was *this* failure to turn up for the meetings that led to the breakdown of negotiations, and killed all prospects of a negotiated settlement. Lal has not a word on any of this. But I am on another point. He *does* give a telling example, one that holds a lesson for those who would supplant the Marxists. He cites an article that Gandhiji was alleged to have written, and which was circulated at the time in support of the VHP's point of view. He points out that Gandhiji never wrote the alleged article.[15] I asked a diligent scholar who warmly endorses the Ram Mandir project about the article. He confirmed that no such article was ever written by Gandhiji, and, even though he, the scholar, was actively involved in collating the evidence and thus in the know of what was happening at the time, he just

[15] Vinay Lal, op. cit., pp. 156–57.

had not been able to find out how the fabrication had been put into circulation and by whom. This is just the kind of untruth that those who lament what the Left has wrought must avoid at all cost. One fabrication, one bit of exaggeration undermines the entire case.

Fifth, facts – not abuse. Adept at hurling abuse himself, Lenin had a good phrase for one who had used strong words against him: he is trying to 'hide inconvenient facts under a shroud of angry words,' Lenin wrote. That doesn't work. The shroud shreds in no time. Examining facts, dissecting arguments, exposing their double standards, nailing their fabrications – these, rather than denunciation. In the case of those who are out to do down our traditions and religion and history, who would deny and scatter our identity, in their case too, sunlight will prove the best disinfectant.

What holds for abuse, holds all the more for intimidation. The answer to a book is a better book, not working up a rage and demanding that it be banned or taken out of circulation. The book will not be available in bookstores in India, but the ideas – let us concede that they are the *wrong* ideas, that the 'evidence' is manufactured – will be all over. Indeed, by the attention that the protestors would have attracted to the book, the ideas and 'evidence' will reach an even larger number than they would normally have. So, even if one's sole consideration is to 'protect' our religion or tradition, intimidation and the demand for bans run against common sense. They also run counter to the law, and to principle.

After all, every plea for reform offends. Were we to write against sati, I am sure that the 'deep religious feelings' of someone or the other will be offended. When we write that the inequities against women that are built into the fabric of the Shariah should be purged, surely the 'deep religious feelings' of many are offended. Swami Dayanand's efforts to rid us of ostentatious religiosity trigger anger to this day. Gandhiji's reinterpretation of the Gita, his campaigns to rid us of the curse of untouchability – these offended the deeply held beliefs of many. Every Muslim who has pleaded for change – from Iqbal's *The Reconstruction of Religious Thought in Islam*; to Dr Zakir Hussain's innocent act of printing under the imprint of the Jamia Millia the translation of Joseph Hell's German book; to Maulana Azad's *Tarjuman al-Quran*; down to the work of A.A.A. Fyzee and Asghar Ali Engineer – has been set upon by ones who set themselves up as the guardians of religion and honour. In a word, *all* reform offends, every plea for reform offends. Should the case for reform not be advanced for that reason? Should those pleas not be made?

And, as I said, these demands for banning, etc. go against the law.[16] It would take us too far afield to recount the numerous judgements on this question. In any case, the main point is simplicity itself and has been well put by the Supreme Court in S. Rangarajan vs P. Jagjivan Ram. A film was produced, *Ore Oru Garmathile.* It was cleared by the censor board. Looking for an issue, some commenced agitations, charging that the film was against reservations. They threatened to burn down theatres that exhibited it. Citing the threat of violence and disorder, the Government of Tamil Nadu banned it. The Madras High Court upheld the ban. The Supreme Court reversed the High Court's judgment in ringing terms.

In doing so, the Supreme Court declared,

[16] As we used to be regularly set upon in *The Indian Express*, I have had several occasions to review the judgements – both in response to the banning of books that the new 'protectors' of our religion and history would approve of, and those which they wouldn't: 'Fomenting reaction' and 'The point we always evade' [reprinted in Sita Ram Goel, *Freedom of Expression*, Voice of India, Delhi, 1998, pp. 63–78] were written in response to the ban on Ram Swarup's *Understanding Islam Through Hadis*; 'A few extracts from the book' and 'The ban and the law' [reprinted in my *We Must Have No Price, and Everyone Must Know We Have No Price*, The Express Group and RUPA, New Delhi, 2010] were written in response to the ban on Jaswant Singh's *Jinnah, India-Partition-Independence.*

> It is our firm belief, nay, a conviction which constitutes one of the basic values of a free society to which we are wedded under our Constitution that there must be freedom not only for the thought that we cherish, but also for the thought that we hate.

And this is not to be an abstract commitment. The court held that the danger which is alleged to be liable to follow the dissemination of an idea must not be remote, conjectural or far-fetched; it must be proximate and it must have a direct nexus with what is being said or exhibited. To warrant restriction by the state:

> The expression of thought should be intrinsically dangerous to the public interests. In other words, the expression should be inseparably locked up with the action contemplated like the equivalent of a 'spark in a powder keg'.

Second, while the Tamil Nadu government and others had been pleading that the exhibition of the film would create very serious law and order problems in the state, while they had been citing as evidence for their apprehensions the threats that had been held out by several groups and their warnings that they would proceed to damage theatres screening the film, the court observed:

> We are amused yet troubled by the stand taken by the state Government with regard to the film which has received the National Award. *We want to put the anguished question, what good is the protection of freedom of expression if the state does not take care to protect it?* If the film is unobjectionable and cannot constitutionally be restricted under Article 19(2), freedom of expression cannot be suppressed on account of threat of demonstrations and processions or threats of violence. *That would tantamount to negation of the rule of law and a surrender to blackmail and intimidation. It is the duty of the state to protect the freedom of expression since it is a liberty guaranteed against the state. The state cannot plead the inability to handle the hostile*

audience problem. It is its obligatory duty to prevent it and protect the freedom of expression.

The court concluded its judgment with words which apply in particular to the sort of writing which we are considering. It said:

Freedom of expression which is legitimate and constitutionally protected, cannot be held to ransom by an intolerant group of people. The fundamental freedom under Article 19(1)(a) can be reasonably restricted only for the purposes mentioned in Article 19(2) and the restriction must be justified on the anvil of necessity and not the quicksand of convenience or expediency. Open criticism of government policies and operations is not a ground for restricting expression. We must practice tolerance to the views of others. Intolerance is as much dangerous to democracy as to the person himself.

Words that we should all bear in mind – if for no other reason then for a pragmatic one: freedom is indivisible.

In a word, not abuse or intimidation but facts. And in regard to facts, there is no need to be prickly. What if someone says that beliefs and practices between Hindus in different parts of India vary; or that beliefs and practices of Hindus belonging to different sects, differ; or that they have evolved and changed? Well, they *have.* So? How does that make Hinduism less of a religion? How does it dilute our identity in the slightest? Which is the religion or tradition or culture that has not evolved and changed? Which is the religion in which beliefs and practices do not vary? Hinayana and Mahayana Buddhism? Shwetambara and Digambara Jainism? Not just Catholic and Protestant Christianity but the sects among Protestants? Not just Shia and Sunni Islam but the seventy-three sects of Islam that the Prophet had prophesied? And *every* religion claims that it is the original, pristine one. Every variant of every religion claims that *it* embodies the true teaching of the religion. Why get worked up when some Western scholar says that our beliefs vary among groups, that they have changed over time? OK, so they have. So?

What if someone says that, though cows are held sacred today, beef was eaten thousands of years ago? One way to answer the argument is to examine in minutest detail the texts and evidence he proffers – that, of course, must be done, thoroughly – especially as he happens to be the very same D.N. Jha whose fabrications and outright falsehoods we have just seen. The other is to tell him, 'OK, our beliefs *have* changed. Today, the Hindus – from Sri Ramana, from Gandhiji down to us specks – hold the cow to be sacred. Which is the religion that has not changed? Today a riot will break out if someone so much as bruises a brick of the mausoleum of a Muslim pir. But the Prophet had strictly forbidden worship at the graves of or of the remains of anyone howsoever pious the person might have been in life, including himself. He had forbidden it on what was for him the decisive ground, namely that this is what Jews and Christians do. But beliefs have changed. Muslims worship at graves of these personages. They revere the hair of the Prophet himself at Hazratbal in Kashmir. And *that* is what matters, does it not? Why not in the case of our reverence for the gentle, blameless and kind cow, then?'

Nor is it necessary to defend every syllable in every scripture. So much in our scriptures is priceless, so much embodies insights which are as profound as they are unique, so much reflects such deep insights into the mind, into nature, into life itself that in sum the scriptures are a sublime heritage. Equally, some of what is contained in them is bound to be dated – it naturally reflects the knowledge that was available at the time when the texts were written. Surely, clinging to every word in every text as if it were a matter of honour is unnecessary. The example we would do well to keep in front of us is that of the Dalai Lama. He was giving a discourse on a Tibetan text about meditation. He read out a sentence, laughed and remarked, 'Buddhist theories of creation, a disgrace! Must throw them out!' He advises that we should keep a wastepaper basket nearby – whatever doesn't accord with what we know now, we should cast into that basket. 'Buddhism must face facts,' that is what he teaches. Accordingly, he has opened Buddhist texts to minute examination. He has instituted collaborations between Tibetan meditation masters and neuroscientists the world over. He is the moving spirit behind the Mind-Life Institute – a gathering of scientists and Buddhist masters who examine the teachings contained in Buddhist texts in the light of the findings of modern sciences, from physics to neurology. *That* reflects confidence in one's tradition. *That* is true service to the tradition. *That* is the way to preserve for the future 'the pearl of great price' in it.

Sixth, we have seen that one of the main reasons on account of which Marxism ossified, one of the main reasons on account of which nonsense pedalled by these eminent historians held the ground so long among the Leftists themselves was that no one in the Left dared question what those who had come to control the organizations and journals put out. But organizations of the Left are not the only ones that are hierarchical and disciplined, that are, in a word, oligarchies. Those of the Right are no less so. Unless they become open, unless they encourage questioning, unless they inculcate in their members the habit of examining and exhuming 'truths that are self-evident' just because some authority revered in the organization had stated them, the consequences cannot be different. The organizations will ossify. The teachings will be set aside by reality.

The final lesson goes to the heart of the matter—it concerns the relationship of individuals and organizations to the State. As we have seen, the Leftists acquired influence because, through offices and personnel of the State, they were able to establish control over journals and institutions. That control itself had debilitating consequences for the standard of their work. That control itself triggered intra-Left resentments and feuds. That control itself vaulted them into the establishment to vanquish and demolish which had been their raison d'être. It did more. The state had become their perch. As the ground shifted from beneath their props – the communist and Congress governments – they were left levitating in the air. But the sudden rush of seminars and colloquia being organized by governments of the Right; the swift rush of the mediocre to the new centres of power; the type of persons who were put into positions of control in academic institutions when the opportunity arose; the lawyers' defence being advanced to explain away blemishes of their governments – all this bodes ill for the Right. Unless such temptations are resisted, unless academic excellence is the sole criterion in choosing persons for positions of academic influence, the nemesis cannot be long in coming.

The same goes for the wider functions of the state. The easy way is to do something demonstrably 'nationalist', manifestly 'Hindu' – naming a scheme after some icon of the Right, commencing it on some day regarded as holy or auspicious by the Hindus. But look at it the other way. What would have made a difference for the line of the Left – that the scheme had been named after Marx or Lenin, or that it had been well-conceived and well-implemented? Surely, the same will hold for schemes of governments of the Right.

Doing things that are stereoscopically nationalist or 'Hindu' is not the way to banish pseudo-secularism, to establish true secularism, to ensure that the nationalist Line prevails. The way is for persons with these values to provide good governments – efficient, responsive, just, clean, dedicated solely to the country's interests.

Provide such governments for twenty to thirty years, ensure that every person holding public office is an exemplar of integrity, and the scourge that has plagued our public discourse for sixty years will automatically be erased.

Index

Acknowledgements

I am most grateful to the Program for Asian Projects, which is administered by the Magsaysay Foundation and endowed by the Rockefeller Brothers Fund, for their help in my work.

To Sita Ram Goel for numerous suggestions, for many corrections, and most of all for his steadfast encouragement over the years.

To teachers in West Bengal and Kerala for directing me to textbooks in use in those states.

To staff members of the Indian Council of Historical Research for information about the goings-on in the Council.